RITUAL IRONY

RITUAL IRONY

POETRY AND SACRIFICE
IN EURIPIDES

Helene P. Foley

Cornell University Press

ITHACA AND LONDON

Cornell University Press gratefully acknowledges a grant from the Andrew W. Mellon Foundation that aided in bringing this book to publication.

First published 1985 by Cornell University Press.

International Standard Book Number 0-8014-1692-2
Library of Congress Catalog Card Number 84-17470
Printed in the United States of America
*Librarians: Library of Congress cataloging information
appears on the last page of the book.*

*The paper in this book is acid-free and meets the guidelines
for permanence and durability of the Committee on Production
Guidelines for Book Longevity of the Council on Library Resources.*

To R. M. P. and D. K. F.

Contents

Preface

Euripides, last of the three great Attic tragedians, captured for the sophisticated audience of his late plays the demise of a great empire and of an extraordinary genre. Although tragedy survived into the fourth century, Athens' enjoyment of self-criticism and iconoclasm in its theatrical festivals did not. Philosophy soon challenged the intellectual role of drama in the city. Comedy, inspired by Euripides, survived by adapting itself to a growing taste for bourgeois realism and the drama of private life. Tragedy limped on, often in the form of revivals of Euripides. The poet's art ambiguously reflects the complexities of a long transitional period.

Clearly, then, the critic of tragedy, and especially of Euripides, cannot afford to read that poet's texts out of their social, political, and religious context or the circumstances of their dramatic production. These circumstances are hard to recapture. Euripides' characters speak the language of Thucydides or the Sophists, and the plays' metaphors and plot patterns reflect actual ritual performance. Yet attempts to specify the political implications of drama have rarely remained true to a reading of the plays as a whole. In this book I undertake the equally slippery task of exploring the representation of ritual in Euripides' tragedy. I hope the result will not only be valuable to scholars and students of tragedy but also contribute to the expanding dialogue between classics and anthropology.

In order to make the text accessible to those who do not read

Preface

Greek, I have translated all quotations and have transliterated the Greek wherever possible, indicating omega (long *o*) and eta (long *e*) with a macron (*ō* and *ē*). In transliterating Greek names I have used the most familiar version. All translations aim to be as literal as possible and are my own except where noted otherwise. I have confined consideration of technical problems to the notes and appendixes, aiming only to make the reader aware of their existence and nature and to summarize current critical opinion. The Greek text is cited from the Oxford Classical Text of Gilbert Murray, *Euripides Fabulae,* 3 vols. 2d ed. (Oxford 1913), with deviations indicated in the notes.

This book is a remote descendant of my dissertation (Harvard 1975), and I remain grateful to my advisers, J. H. Finley, Jr., and Cedric Whitman, for their sense of style and their generous support of a dissertation topic distant in certain respects from their own preoccupations. Christian Wolff, whose work and teaching on Euripides shaped my interest in this topic, offered pertinent criticism of the dissertation and of early drafts of this book. Michelle and Renato Rosaldo and Bridget O'Laughlin helped me to venture beyond my training as a classicist into anthropology, and Carolyn Dewald served as a stimulating listener during the initial stages of the book. Ann Bergren, Rachel Kitzinger, Piero Pucci, Froma Zeitlin, and my colleagues Helen Bacon and Lydia Lenaghan provided challenging and incisive commentary on earlier versions. Leonard Muellner and an anonymous referee gave me invaluable readings for Cornell University Press, and Ann Hawthorne served as a thoughtful copyeditor. Rick Griffiths demonstrated stamina as a critic through all stages of the book. I am also grateful for opportunities to test this material on discerning audiences at Princeton, Stanford, the University of Victoria, B.C., the University of Southern California, Cornell, Dartmouth, and Haverford. Through Stanford University and Barnard College I received two Mellon grants that aided in the completion of this manuscript. Chapters 2 and 5 incorporate in revised form material published in *Arethusa* 15 (1982): 159–80 and *Transactions and Proceedings of the American Philological Association* 110 (1980): 107–33, respectively. I thank these journals for their kind permission to use

Preface

this material. Most of all, I am indebted to the inspiration of my
father, Robert M. Peet, and to my husband, Duncan Foley, for
everything from insightful readings and emotional and logistical
support to assistance in using a word processor.

HELENE P. FOLEY

New York City

Abbreviations

ABV	J. D. Beazley, *Attic Black-figure Vase-painters*, Oxford 1956
AC	*L'Antiquité Classique*
AJA	*American Journal of Archaeology*
AJP	*American Journal of Philology*
ARV2	J. D. Beazley, *Attic Red-figure Vase-painters*, 2d ed., Oxford 1963
CJ	*Classical Journal*
CP	*Classical Philology*
CQ	*Classical Quarterly*
CR	*Classical Review*
CSCA	*California Studies in Classical Antiquity*
CW	*Classical World*
Daremberg-Saglio	C. V. Daremberg and E. Saglio, *Dictionnaire des antiquités grecques et romaines d'après les textes et les monuments*, 10 vols., Paris 1877–1919
DK	H. Diels and W. Kranz, eds., *Die Fragmente der Vorsokratiker*, 3 vols., 6th ed., Berlin 1952
Frisk	H. Frisk, *Griechische etymologische Wörterbuch*, 3 vols., Heidelberg 1960–72
GRBS	*Greek, Roman, and Byzantine Studies*
HSCP	*Harvard Studies in Classical Philology*
ICS	*Illinois Classical Studies*
IG	*Inscriptiones Graecae*, Berlin
JHS	*Journal of Hellenic Studies*
K	T. Kock, ed., *Comicorum Atticorum Fragmenta*, 3 vols., Utrecht 1976

[13]

Abbreviations

Kinkel	G. Kinkel, ed., *Epicorum Graecorum Fragmenta*, Leipzig 1877
LEC	*Les Etudes Classiques*
LP	E. Lobel and D. Page, eds., *Poetarum Lesbiorum Fragmenta*, Oxford 1955
LSJ	Liddell, Scott, Jones, and McKenzie, eds., *A Greek-English Lexicon*, 9th ed., Oxford 1940 and supp. 1968
MB	*Musée Belge. Revue de philologie classique*
Mette	H. J. Mette, ed., *Die Fragmente den Tragödien des Aischylos*, Berlin 1959
MH	*Museum Helveticum*
MLN	*Modern Language Notes*
N	A. Nauck, ed., *Tragicorum Graecorum Fragmenta*, 2d ed., Leipzig 1889; supp. ed. B. Snell, Hildesheim 1964
NJbb	*Neue Jahrbücher für Philologie und Paedagogik*, 1831–97; *Neue Jahrbücher für klassische Altertum, Geschichte und deutsche Literatur und für Paedagogik*, 1897–1924
PCPhS	*Proceedings of the Cambridge Philological Society*
PMLA	*Publications of the Modern Language Association*
POxy	B. P. Grenfell et al., eds., *The Oxyrynchus Papyri*, London 1898–1981
R	Stefan S. Radt, ed., *Tragicorum Graecorum Fragmenta*, vol. 4, Göttingen 1977
REA	*Revue des Etudes Anciennes*
REG	*Revue des Etudes Grecques*
RSC	*Rivista di Studi Classici*
S	B. Snell, ed., *Pindarus*, 2 vols., Leipzig 1964
SBAW	*Sitzungsberichte der Bayerischen Akademie der Wissenschaften, Philosophie-Historie Klasse*, Munich
SMSR	*Studi e Materiali di Storia delle Religioni*
TAPA	*Transactions of the American Philological Association*
W	M. L. West, *Iambi et Elegi Graeci*, 2 vols., Oxford 1971–72
Wehrli	F. Wehrli, ed., *Die Schule des Aristoteles*, 10 vols., Basel 1944–49
WS	*Wiener Studien*
YCS	*Yale Classical Studies*

RITUAL IRONY

] 1 [

Drama and Sacrifice

Euripidean scholarship has been grappling for centuries with the supposed structural imperfections of his dramas, the supposed irrelevance of his choral odes, and the supposed rationality, not to say irreverence, of Euripides himself. Aristotle complains that Euripides' inadequate plots ignore the necessary and the probable and require the intervention of a deus ex machina to straighten them out. He hints that Euripides' choruses had begun to approach the decorative interludes that they became in later tragedy. The poet's characters are inconsistent, changing their minds for no apparent reason, and his stylized debates seem more rhetorical than true to character. Sophocles reportedly said that he made men as they ought to be, Euripides as they are. Aristophanes implies that Euripides undermined the dignity of tragedy and contributed to the moral decline of Athens. The poet's sophistic and iconoclastic attacks on the anthropomorphic gods of Homer and his soul-destroying irony won him few first prizes even in his own time. According to the philosopher Nietzsche, Euripides destroyed tragedy.

The plot of the *Heracles,* for example, veers so abruptly and unexpectedly that the initial scenes seem to lose organic relation to what follows. Similarly, the mad Heracles of the peripety little resembles the pious father who rescues his family from the tyrant Lycus and a corrupt Thebes in the opening suppliant action. Neither Heracles matches the superhuman culture hero celebrated in the choral odes. In the final scenes the hero's rejection of suicidal despair implicitly denies the repellent and vengeful anthropomorphic Olympians that the audience has just witnessed onstage in the peripety. The play thus concludes by turning directly against its own mythical tradition.

Yet the puzzling discontinuities that characterize Euripidean tragedy should be seen not as the result of inconsistency or as mere polemics, but as a serious and thoughtful response to poetic, social, and intellectual tensions within Attic culture. On the one hand, the poet confronts the corrupting effects of continual war between Athens and Sparta, the excesses of contemporary democracy, and the collapse of traditional social and religious values. On the other hand, he faces the disparity between the myths on which he bases his plots and the values of the society to which he adapts them.[1] A poetic tradition peopled by self-assertive and often explosive kings, queens, and aristocratic warriors hardly suits the ideology of an egalitarian democracy in which the state circumscribes and subordinates the interests of the family and the extraordinary individual. The apparent opposition between "rational" prose argument and the "irrationalities" of myth, poetry, and ritual posed difficulties for all Attic tragedians. Yet the gap is wider for Euripides than it was for Aeschylus, and he brings the dialectic between the unpredictability of events and the pattern asserted by myth and ritual closer to the surface of his work. At the same time, Euripides presents drama at a religious festival honoring the god Dionysus, and he is sharply conscious that the performance of tragedy is itself a kind of ritual. Hence he must in some sense remain true to this ritual setting for his own art in the face of the sophistic reaction to myth and to the arbitrary, vengeful, petty, and even comic Olympians inherited from the epic tradition.

This book will explore the questions raised by Athens and Dionysus for Euripides' poetics and theater through a critical study of four problematic late plays: the *Iphigenia in Aulis*, the *Phoenissae*, the *Heracles*, and the *Bacchae*. By concentrating largely on the overt theology of the plays, critics of Euripides have often made a sim-

---

[1]My approach to the complex dialogue between past myths and the Attic democracy in tragedy has been influenced by Vernant 1970 and Vernant in Vernant and Vidal-Naquet 1981: 1–27.

plistic equation between the religious views of Euripides and those of the contemporary Sophists. As a result, current interpretations of Euripides' plays tend to the bleakly ironic. By emphasizing the ways in which the plays are built on or around ritual and confirm religious practice (if not traditional Olympian theology), the book offers a modified view of Euripidean irony. Furthermore, the lyric and ritual aspects of Euripides' late dramas operate in close harmony and more strategically than earlier interpreters have thought. The odes of each of these plays, far from being merely decorative and nonfunctional, form a continuous song cycle that gains significance precisely from its studied contrast with or disconcerting relation to the action. Ritual, by serving in these plays to link odes and action, the mythical and the secular, past and present, ultimately enables the poet to claim for drama and its archaic poetic tradition a continuing relevance to a democratic society.

Typically, Euripides' characters and the world of the action of his plays seem resistant to the higher realities and irrationalities of myth and ritual. Euripidean prologues, for example, are apt to include the protagonist's questioning of his own myths. Helen doubts that she was born from an egg (*Helen* 17–21). In such plays as the *Orestes* the plot threatens to depart its myth altogether, requiring the intervention of a god on the machine to reassert tradition. The Euripidean chorus persists in drawing on tradition, celebrating gods and myths in a manner reminiscent of the poet's epic and lyric predecessors. Yet these typical remarks made by the chorus of the *Electra* succinctly express their difficulty in upholding this role; myths, they argue, even if mere fictions, are nevertheless necessary for men (737–46):

> So it is said. But I have little belief in the tale that the golden sun left its hot quarter and, to chastise mortals, changed its course for a man's misfortune. Terrible myths are a gain for men and for the worship of the gods. Forgetting these things, you, the sister of noble brothers, kill your husband.

Some characters, such as Iphigenia in the *Iphigenia in Aulis* or Menoeceus in the *Phoenissae,* make a voluntary choice to act in conformity with divine oracles and a poetic ideal expressed in the choral odes and thus to return a wavering action to its myth. Such actions are invariably undertaken through ritual and through sacrifice.

From Xenophanes to Aristotle, Greeks began to see their view of the gods, at least as expressed in epic, as a projection of their own human forms and social needs:

> For this reason all men say that the gods are governed by a king, for men themselves are either still ruled by a king, or were so in ancient times. And just as men represent the appearance of the gods as similar to their own, so also they imagine that the lives of the gods are like their own. (*Politics* 1252b)

Does man, then, disguise in his worship of the gods a worship of himself and his own need for order? So the poets seem to imply in many dramas in which the city itself becomes a source of salvation alternative to the gods (see, for example, Euripides' *Suppliants, Heracleidae,* or *Heracles*). Danaus in Aeschylus' *Suppliants* says to his daughters (980–83):

> My children, we must pray to the Argives, sacrifice and pour libations to them as to gods Olympian, since they unhesitatingly preserved us.

Although Euripides never fully dismisses the Olympians, he apparently comes to see them in his later plays as beings indifferent to men or representative of a force equivalent to *tuchē* (chance; sign of divine intervention in human affairs) that may on occasion, especially when human effort plays an important subsidiary role, produce beneficial results, as in the *Iphigenia in Tauris* and the *Helen*. More frequently, however, these remote and impersonal divine forces create what appears from the human perspective to be inexplicable disorder:

> Which mortal could say that, after searching to the farthest limit known to man, he has discovered what is god, what is not god, and what is in between—when he observes the dispensations of the gods rapidly leaping hither and thither and back again in ambivalent and incalculable incidents? (*Helen* 1137–43)

In the *Helen,* the prophetess and priestess Theonoe, avoiding the dilemmas posed by an unpredictable or amoral divinity, burns purifying sulphur to commune with a *pneuma* (breath of air) from the heavens, a supra–Olympian realm of purity that informs her decidedly human wisdom and piety (*Helen* 865–72). She relies for moral judgment on her own *gnōmē* (wisdom and judgment) and on a shrine of justice in her nature (1002–3).

Yet in the very plays in which Euripides' characters reject the fickle and immoral Olympians, religious rituals (prayer, suppliancy, ritual offerings, and festival) and especially sacrifice continue to play a central and often surprisingly positive role. In contrast to earlier choral lyric, deaths in Attic tragedy are frequently undertaken or metaphorized as sacrifice:[2] that is, they occur in a sacrificial setting and/or are described in the text as a form of *thusia* or *sphagia.*[3] The action of several of Euripides' plays turns on a sacrificial death: the *Alcestis,* the *Medea,* the *Heracles,* the *Electra,* the *Iphigenia in Tauris,* the *Phoenissae,* the *Bacchae,* the *Iphigenia in Aulis,* and the fragmentary *Erechtheus.* Other plays include a sacrificial death as an important element in a more complex plot: the *Heracleidae,* the *Hecuba,* the *Andromache,* and the fragmentary *Phrixus* and *Cresphontes.* The perverted human sacrifices of the *Heracles* and the *Bacchae* serve to define a larger social and religious crisis and ultimately to reflect the poet's ability to reconstruct through violence a new if fragile link between myth and society. But in the *Iphigenia in Aulis* and the *Phoenissae,* in which an idealistic youth sacrifices herself or himself to resolve a cultural crisis, Euripides allows the gesture to resolve the plot and to offer a putative cure for an otherwise hopeless politics of self-interest and desire.

The poet also habitually closes his dramas with the establishment of new rituals for which the plays themselves become an aetiology.[4] The *Iphigenia in Tauris,* for example, concludes with

---

[2]On this point, see Burkert 1966a: 116. On possible sacrificial elements in epic deaths, see, for example, Lowenstam 1981 on the death of Patroclus.

[3]This definition excludes the death of Evadne in the *Suppliants.*

[4]On these cult references at the close of Euripides' plays, see esp. Kamerbeek 1958 and Whitman 1974, esp. 118–19. In contrast to Whitman, I view these aetiological conclusions as central to the structure and meaning of the play, not as a last-minute act of desperation.

[21]

the establishment of a cult of Artemis at Halae, now purified of the human sacrifice that tainted it among the Taurians. Once again Euripides seems to find in ritual processes a transcendent though ironized value. The hero cult and sacrifices offered to Heracles at the close of the *Heracles* and the cult offered to Hippolytus at the close of the *Hippolytus* hardly succeed in assuaging the suffering of the heroes. Yet the offer of a cult to Heracles gives him an opportunity to choose survival despite unbearable disaster and to become a hero meaningful to a modern *polis* (see Chapter 4). Hippolytus' tragic resistance to sexuality and Phaedra's near adultery, permanently commemorated in a ritual special to unmarried girls, will, however ironically for Euripides' characters, come to assist brides in their complex and potentially painful transition to marriage and womanhood. Medea's violent "sacrifice" of her sons becomes rationalized in the harmless repetition of the children's cult at Corinth. Ritual may be used to recall the past for the purpose of reordering and even predetermining the future. In the sacrificial deaths of tragedy Euripides seems to be drawing on ritual largely as metaphor and symbol while his own ambiguous art liberates itself from subordination to actual practice. But in these closing references to cult Euripides seems to wish to establish links for his art with ritual as an effective and precisely repeated performance enacted by the community rather than observed by it as audience to a tragic performance.

As the intellectual revolution transformed Greek theology, popular and deeply rooted ritual practices apparently remained relatively unchanged. And Euripides is not alone in insisting on the preservation of ritual performance while debunking theological superstructure. Plato, too, although his views of the Greek gods are both elusive and clearly not traditional, in the *Laws* expresses no doubt about the need for ritual and for specific ritual practices. Euripides apparently ignores possible contradictions between the maintenance of ritual and a modified view of Olympian deities. And in practice, if not in literary tradition, Greek gods may often have come close to embodying "the incalculable non-human element in phenomena" that they seem repeatedly to represent in late Euripides.[5] Ritual practice does not seem to have depended on

[5]On this point see esp. Nock 1972: 260. Kirk 1981, esp. 78–80, has recently argued that a similar deincarnation of the Olympians was occurring during the

certain knowledge of who the divine recipient would be; Greeks often sacrificed, especially in times of crisis, to unnamed or vaguely named gods (*theos, theoi*).[6] In his understanding of men's motives for making ritual offerings to the gods, Euripides seems to approach the views expressed by early sociologists of religion such as Durkheim (here interpreted by Beidelman):

> . . . gods are manifested through things which in themselves are subject to flux. Men then make offerings because of the instability of the external world, both physical and social (for society too manifests itself physically through persons and things). The gods then are as unstable as men. The stability of either realm is reasserted through symbolic acts, and because this is an illusion, an existential act not really inherent to the nature of things, it must be repeated again and again. . . . Religious rites become the repeated efforts by social men to reassert an illusion by endowing it with the palpability of a physical and group experience.[7]

The repeated celebration of cult and festival in which Athens continually came to terms through song, ritual, and drama with its own complex social crises, its everyday transitions, and its violent mythical and theological traditions seems to embody for Euripides that same effort "by social men to reassert an illusion by endowing it with the palpability of a physical and group experience."

Modern readers, of course, have particular difficulty with the sacrificial deaths of tragedy since blood sacrifice figures little in our own religious practice. Furthermore, the relation between Greek theology and Greek ritual practice is mysterious at best, for a shifting and contradictory theological speculation was the province of poets and philosophers, not of priests and a religious hierarchy. Ritual practices, on the other hand, though performed under the

---

Homeric period but was arrested by the later development of the fine arts, which emphasized the anthropomorphic aspects of Greek deities.

[6]See the discussion of sacrifice to unknown gods in the recent study of voluntary human sacrifice by Versnel 1981: 171–79.

[7]Beidelman 1974: 60. Beidelman is here discussing Durkheim's reaction to Robertson Smith. Unlike Smith, Durkheim insists on the fundamental importance of oblation in sacrifice. While turning to his own ends Smith's view that ritual and sacrifice reinforce community, Durkheim argues that mortals, in offering gods food and, even more important, *thought,* keep gods alive (1965: 388).

influence of certain beliefs (usually unknown to us), are difficult to comprehend and, in most cases, to reconstruct in detail. Of these religious practices, which include many forms of prayer, festival, and ritual, the central and primary religious activity in the fifth-century Greek *polis* was sacrifice, the offering of fruits and vegetables or the killing of domestic animals in honor of an enormous pantheon of gods, demigods, heroes, and dead spirits. Although we cannot recreate fully the nature, function, and meaning of this ritual in ancient culture, we can clarify Euripides' experience of and possible assumptions about sacrifice.

Despite major obstacles to interpretation, anthropologists and scholars of Greek religion have made some progress in reconstructing and analyzing sacrifice both cross-culturally and in ancient Greek society, and literary critics have begun to use these insights to offer new interpretations of the sacrificial metaphor in drama.[8] Since this book is concerned primarily with the literary rather than historical representation of ritual, and especially of *human* sacrifice, the discussion here focuses on conclusions that articulate with and illuminate the role of sacrifice in drama. The discussion begins with a summary of relevant views of ancient writers on the function of sacrifice and with a reconstruction of a typical classical *thusia*. The next section summarizes sociological and specifically structuralist definitions of the place and significance of sacrifice and sacrificial procedures in the Greek religious system and in the Greek culture of the classical period. From this perspective sacrifice is a symbolic system, like a language, whose gestures must be decoded both in relation to each other and in the overall social context of classical Athens. This part of the discussion draws heavily on the work of Rudhardt, Vernant, Detienne, and Durand.[9] The third section examines evolutionist interpretations of sacrifice, which stress the origins and historical development of sacrificial ritual and its possible relation to the emergence of tragedy. Scholars adopting this approach have usually been par-

[8]For important works that treat the sacrificial motif in Greek tragedy, see Zeitlin 1965, 1966, 1970a, 1970b; Lebeck 1971; Vidal-Naquet 1981a; Wolff 1963; Vickers 1973; Pucci 1980; and Girard 1977. For a general critical article on ritual and literature, see Hardin 1983.

[9]See esp. Rudhardt 1958; Vernant 1976, 1979, 1980, 1981; Detienne 1979a, 1979b; and Durand 1973, 1979.

ticularly concerned with the nature of sacrificial violence and its psychological effects on the participants in the ritual. In this group the work of Meuli, Bataille, Burkert, Girard, and Guépin are the most directly relevant for Greek drama.[10] The second and third sections close by presenting examples of the relevance of each of these two major analytical approaches for the interpretation of tragic texts. The reader thoroughly familiar with past scholarship in this area may wish to turn directly to the final section of the chapter ("Poetry and Sacrifice"), which clarifies the relation between earlier work and the approach to ritual adopted in the rest of this book.

The nineteenth- and early twentieth-century theorists on sacrifice tended to combine, in ways that at times seem confusing and contradictory, evolutionist, psychological, sociological, or functionalist approaches in cross-cultural theories of ritual.[11] The structuralists reject the cross-cultural approach in favor of culture-specific analysis and respectfully take issue with a range of earlier views, including those of their closest predecessors in the *Année Sociologique* school. The evolutionists, acknowledging their debt to a wide range of sources, including Durkheim, Freud, and ethologists such as Lorenz, draw more directly and sometimes less critically on earlier theories of ritual and base their conclusions on cross-cultural material. This theoretical eclecticism has been the source of considerable controversy with the structuralists.[12] Considerations of space, suitability for literary analysis, and methodological clarity made it necessary to restrict discussion to the most recent and fully drawn theories of Greek sacrifice and to avoid attempting to resolve major controversies. Indeed, despite the many acknowledged differences in the emphasis, methodology, and conclusions of the two approaches considered here, they can be used in a complementary fashion in the study of the

[10]See esp. Meuli 1946; Burkert 1966a, 1972, 1981; Bataille 1962; Guépin 1968; and Girard 1977, 1978a.

[11]For useful methodological discussions on theories of sacrifice, see esp. Evans-Pritchard 1965; Vernant 1976, 1981; Detienne 1979b; Burkert 1981; and Kirk 1981.

[12]While subscribing to many of the reservations of the structuralists about cross-cultural theories of sacrifice, I have found the cross-cultural analyses of, for example, Douglas 1966 and Turner 1969 to be compatible with the views of the structuralists and valuable for a study of Greek tragedy.

highly eclectic and sometimes contradictory treatment of ritual in drama. Finally, because this book is concerned with the role of ritual in drama, the summaries of various theoretical points are confined as much as possible to literary examples.

Greek Evidence for Greek Sacrifice

The relation between Greek gods and men was predicated on sacrifice, which established communication between divine and human realms through offerings from men to gods. The tragic "sacrifices" with which we are concerned are blood sacrifices; hence this discussion examines only the ritual killing of animals (and, by extension, humans). The etymology of the word *thuein*, "to burn so as to provide smoke,"[13] is to some extent misleading for the classical period. Certainly fire transformed the offering of an animal into the fatty smoke that the gods preferred from man and turned its meat into edible food for men. But by the classical period *thusia* and *thuein* referred primarily to blood sacrifice, in which the victim was eaten, in opposition to *sphagia, sphazein,* and *enagizein,* in which the victim was not consumed.[14]

Archaeological and literary evidence establishes that sacrifice served a wide variety of purposes, and ancient testimony about contemporary sacrificial practices gives various explanations for the ritual. First, sacrifice was a form of *timē* (honor) or *dōron* (gift) presented to the gods on the analogy of gift-giving practices within the hierarchies of human society. (For sacrifice as *timē, charis,* and *chreia tōn agathōn,* see Porphyry *De abstinentia* 2.24; for sacrifice as an exchange of gifts between god and men—*do ut des*—see Hesiod *Works and Days* 336–41.) The vestiges of this sacrificial function persisted, for example, in the details of the distribution of sacrificial meat. Epic gods and heroes insisted on their prescribed due, and into the classical period the cuts of sacrificial meat continued to confirm hierarchy for priests and other officials. In *Odys-*

---

[13]See Schol. A *Il.* 9.219; Schol. *Od.* 14.446; Eustathius p. 641.61; Frisk I, 699.
[14]See Casabona 1966: 84. The term is most frequently used in this way, although *thusia* can refer to a wide range of offerings other than animal victims and is not always consumed.

sey 5.101–2 Hermes remarks deprecatingly that Calypso's island is remote from the source of sacrifices: "Nor is there nearby any city of mortals who offer to the gods sacrifices and choice hecatombs." Similarly, Demeter's angry destruction of the crops in the Homeric *Hymn to Demeter* must be stopped because she is depriving the gods of their expected sacrifices (310–13):

> And now she would have utterly destroyed the race of men with cruel famine and have deprived those who dwell on Olympus of their glorious honor [*timē*] of gifts and sacrifices, had not Zeus taken note and pondered it in his mind.

In Argonautic legend Hera's wrath at Pelias derived from his having slighted her at sacrifice; in Hesiod's *Works and Days* the gods destroyed the men of the Silver Age for their failure to sacrifice (135–39). On the human level, Oedipus cursed his sons, Eteocles and Polyneices, because, in one version of the myth, they gave him an inappropriate share of the sacrificial meat (*Thebaid* frag. 3 Kinkel; Schol. Sophocles *Oedipus at Colonus* 1375).

This gift to the gods created a limited reciprocity between gods and men (based loosely on the model of human *xenia* or hospitality) and served various functions: to provide thanks and recognition to divinities (*charis*), often for benefits already received; to request future benefits, fertility, or good fortune (*chreia tōn agathōn*); to propitiate deities whose anger can be deduced from a social crisis; or to prevent divine jealousy of or hostility to enterprises about to be undertaken. In these last two areas the sacrificial gift can be understood as a form of compensation.[15] Nestor at *Odyssey* 3.178–79 thanks Poseidon for his safe return to Pylos; at *Odyssey* 3.159–60 the Greeks offer a prayer for a favorable voyage, and at *Odyssey* 3.143–47 a sacrifice is offered to appease the wrath of Athena. Aristophanes' plays mark the recovery of fertility and peace with a celebratory sacrifice (although the irony of sacrificing an animal to Peace is not lost on the poet; see *Peace* 1019–25 and also 924–34). The *Oedipus Rex* opens with a group of suppliants performing sacrifices to propitiate the gods and cure the plague that has gripped

---

[15]For sacrifice as compensation, see the recent argument of Versnel 1981.

the city. The chorus and characters in Aeschylus' *Libation Bearers* supplicate Agamemnon's ghost with a promise of gifts in exchange for his aid to Orestes in the performance of his matricide (483–85). The king of Argos in Aeschylus' *Suppliants* hopes to avoid the bloodshed of kin by sacrifices (449–51):

> In order that consanguine blood remain unshed, we must sacrifice many cattle to many gods, a cure for grief.

By interpreting various signs during the ritual and by examining the inner parts of the victim, men might receive messages from gods concerning divine acceptance of a sacrificial plea and the chances for the success of an enterprise. As Theseus in Euripides' *Suppliants* optimistically asserts (211–13):

> What we cannot know, the seers disclose for us as they scrutinize sacrificial flames, the flight of birds, and the convoluted entrails of victims.

These major explicit functions of sacrifice are often summarized as acts of supplication, thanks, divination, and propitiation (apotropaic ritual, the attempt to turn aside evil, is a subset of this last function).[16] As Plato says, sacrifice is primarily a gift of man to god for man's own benefit: *to thuein dōreisthai esti tois theois* (*Euthyphro* 14c). It is a gift man makes to recognize past services of the gods to himself, to request future ones, or to avoid divine disfavor toward human enterprises. But these openly acknowledged functions for sacrifice only begin to explain its complex place in Greek religion and culture. For sacrifice is an act of ritual *killing* by men and for gods preliminary to a *meal*. Ancient writers had their own views concerning sacrifice as a form of killing and as a kind of

---

[16]See Rudhardt 1958: 249ff., for a good summary of the purposes of sacrifice and the contradictions between or blurring of the lines between the various functions (e.g., gift and thanks) and recipients of sacrifice (gods, heroes, the dead). He stresses the impossibility of giving one explanation for all parts of the ritual from the preliminary rites to distribution of the meat (see esp. 250ff.) and emphasizes the middle value of *thuesthai* except in rituals of thanks (267).

shared meal. We shall return to some of these after a summary of the procedures involved in a typical classical *thusia*.[17]

The ritual normally consisted of three important stages: the consecration and killing of the victim, the extraction and ritual use of certain parts, and the separate butchery and distribution of the remaining parts.[18] The celebrants had to be pure (not criminals, women who had just given birth, adulterers, or the like) and clean, and the victim (a domestic animal) had to have special qualities suitable to the occasion. In animal sacrifice the celebrants and the victim were garlanded for the sacrificial procession; sometimes the horns of the animal were gilded. A vessel containing water and a covered basket containing whole grain brought by a virgin were carried around the altar. The participants began by purifying themselves (washing their hands) and sprinkling the victim with water. A torch was plunged into water. The victim was made to nod its head in consent to its sacrifice. The sacrificial knife, hidden beneath the barley in the basket, was then uncovered. The participants threw whole grain (or occasionally leaves or stones) at the victim and the altar. Following a moment of silence and a prayer, the priest cut a few hairs from the victim's forehead and threw them into the fire. The animal, now fully dedicated to death, had its throat cut with its neck turned toward the sky; the women screamed (*ololuzein*), marking the moment of religious intensity at which the animal's life departed its body (*Odyssey* 3.449–55). The *aulos* (Greek pipe) was played and the blood was caught in a vessel and poured on the altar. Chosen participants flayed the animal, cut out the thighbones, wrapped them in fat, and burned them with incense on the altar for the gods. Sometimes the tail, gall bladder, or small pieces of meat from the entire animal were included. Wine was poured over the flames. All full participants toasted on spits

[17]The version of *thusia* given here is a synthesis drawn from literary and archaeological sources that accounts neither for the variation in actual practice nor for our uncertainty concerning the order of the procedures. For excellent recent summaries of sacrificial procedure, see esp. Burkert 1972: 10–14 and 1966a: 106–8 or Rudhardt 1958: 258ff. Stengel 1910 is a classic earlier work. For further bibliography, see Burkert 1972: 9 n. 2.

[18]The emphasis on three stages is that of Rudhardt 1958: 290.

and immediately ate the *splangchna* (heart, lungs, liver, kidneys, or the parts containing the blood and vital principle of the animal). The rest of the animal was butchered in accordance with precise procedures and distributed in different ways determined by the context. The meat was either boiled on the premises or carried elsewhere to be eaten. The skulls of bulls and rams and the horns of goats could be preserved in a sacred place, and the skin sold for the benefit of the cult.

In contrast to *sphazein* and *enagizein, thuein* tends to be used for sacrifices made on a high altar in which the victim is consumed. The term *sphazein* refers specifically to the cutting of a victim's throat to produce a libation of blood, not a burnt offering or a meal. It is often made in extraordinary circumstances requiring a form of propitiation: at the beginning of a battle, at the crossing of a body of water, to appease the winds. *Enagizein* generally refers to a sacrifice made on a low altar to heroes and the dead. The application of these three terms for sacrifice (there are a number of other terms and variant procedures) and the distinctions among them do not hold consistently in every case. *Thuein* and related words can be used for almost any kind of sacrificial offering, including vegetable offerings. The following discussion concentrates on the form of *thusia* outlined above, both for the sake of clarity and because, as Casabona has argued,[19] *thuein* always retains its technical ritual meaning in classical literature, whereas *sphazein,* for example, is used both outside and within ritual contexts.

The Sociology of Greek Sacrifice: The Structuralist Approach

Structuralist analysis stresses the way sacrificial procedures turn the killing of an animal into a legitimate act that renders the meat of domestic animals acceptable for men and defines in specific ways the relation between god and man and among men in a Greek *polis.* Greek sacrificial procedures deny, neutralize, and ex-

[19]Casabona 1966 has the most comprehensive discussion of Greek sacrificial terminology.

clude the violence involved in the killing of the victim. As the Hesiodic myth of the first sacrifice emphasizes, sacrifice concerns principally the distribution of sacrificial meat. The Promethean myth passes over in silence the question of animal slaughter. Men kill to *eat,* and the participants in sacrifice must not experience their act as a crime.[20] The preliminary rites insist on the purity of all participants.[21] Up to a certain point sacrificers and victim are identified with each other, since both are garlanded and purified. The mass pelting of the victim implicates all participants in the killing and perhaps, since human scapegoats (often actual criminals) were similarly pelted, symbolically condemns or partially separates the victim from the community. The animal, liberated from its domestic subservience, moves freely to the altar. The beast's shiver, when sprinkled, indicates its purity (Plutarch *De defectu oraculorum* 437b), and its nod of consent denies the potential illegitimacy of the killing. (See especially Plutarch *Quaestiones convivales* 729F or Prophyry *De abstinentia* 2.9. Similarly, in the law courts the victim of a crime and/or his relatives could voluntarily free the criminal from prosecution.[22]) The actual killing is sudden and surprising, as if to contain a potential spread of violence. The sacrificial knife is concealed in the basket of grain, and other weaponry is excluded from the sacrificial precinct.

Attic myths about the origin of civic sacrifices also repeatedly legitimize the killing of sacrificial animals, although they occasionally hint at other, darker motives, such as famine, anger, or fear. The first swine was unintentionally slaughtered by a woman named Clymene. Her terrified husband consulted the Delphic oracle; since the god did not condemn the practice, swine were routinely sacrificed thereafter. An oracle permitted an inspector of sacred rites to sacrifice a sheep if he washed his hands and allowed the sheep to die a voluntary death. A goat was first sacrificed in Icarus, a mountain district of Attica, because it had cropped a vine. (For all three stories see Porphyry *De abst.* 2.9–10.) The Attic Bouphonia apparently symbolically reenacts a "history" of the first sacrifice of a plow ox. In this ritual, which takes place at the

[20]See esp. Vernant 1981: 6ff. and Detienne 1979b, esp. 18–20.
[21]See Rudhardt 1958: 258 and 299.
[22]MacDowell 1963: 8 and 148–49.

opening of the threshing season, the slayer of a sacrificial bullock, abandoning his ax, takes flight after killing a bull that has previously been let loose to eat offerings at the altar of Zeus Polieus. The remaining participants, called into the Prytaneion, throw blame on each other. A knife is finally condemned and thrown into the sea, the sacrificer purified, and the bull flayed, stuffed with straw, and harnessed to the plough in an act of resurrection. In Theophrastus' account of the myth in explanation of the ritual (Porphyry *De abst.* 2.10, 29–30), the plow ox, the domestic animal closest to man (and highest on the scale of what were to become sacrificial victims), fell victim to human anger because it ate and trampled on some vegetable offerings. The setting is prepolitical, and the slayer a foreigner. Since at this time the killing of domestic animals was criminal, the ox was buried as if it were a human being, and its slayer departed for exile. Subsequent oracular instructions promised benefits to all if the exile expiated his crime, the murderer was punished, and an effigy of the slain animal was raised where it fell. The exile returned and responded to the oracle by inventing what was to become the familiar sacrificial rite. To make himself a member of the community and deflect blame from himself, he involved the entire citizen body in the killing of another ox. Women brought water, one man struck the ox with the knife, another cut its throat with a knife. The stuffing and harnessing of the ox to the plow and the judicial process followed. Civic sacrifice and the tribunal of justice thus emerge together from the first murder of an ox and establish a new set of boundaries between the human and animal realms. The ox no longer eats food set out for the gods but is filled with its own appropriate nurture, fodder; men can eat meat.[23]

The butchery and consumption of the animal occurred in two stages. First, the gods received their share of the victim and showed divine signs of favor or disfavor to the participants. In Greek sacrifice, in contrast to practice in the Near East, the group, not a priest, made the offering to the gods. The sharing of the

---

[23]For a recent discussion of the Bouphonia, including sources and a summary of controversies surrounding the rite, see Parke 1977: 162–67 and nn. 211–17. For a structuralist interpretation, see Durand 1973 and Vernant 1981.

roasted innards (the most sacred and vital parts) by all full participants in the rite (usually male citizens) marked the egalitarian and
symbolically more primitive essence of the rite. The Greeks treated
roasting as a more primitive method of cooking, since the dried
and burnt meat might still be partially raw.[24] This phase of the
ritual completed the communication between god and man.

The butchery that followed was of a more varied and secular
nature. At this point the distribution of the meat could reflect the
hierarchies of the community or reemphasize the equality of the
participants.[25] Male citizens, for example, always received a larger
share than their wives and children, who were not full members of
the political community. Women were thus generally auxiliary
rather than full participants in the ritual.

Unlike the sacrificial procedures of other cultures, Greek sacrifice apparently had no rites of exit to reestablish a boundary between the sacred and the profane.[26] Even the preliminary procedures concentrated special powers in the victim without setting
it apart from the secular world; garlands, worn in both political
and religious contexts, established a link between sacrificial and
secular contexts.[27] The participants, because of the mediating role
of the animal victim, symbolically never departed the profane
realm; the ritual made the victim edible for man and incorporated
the benefits of the sacrifice directly into the community as a whole.
As evidenced in the mantic signs offered by gods to men through
the beast, communication with the divine was established in sacrifice through the immolation of the victim, through prayer, and
through the sacrificial smoke created by the burning of the portions set aside for the gods.[28]

[24]See Detienne 1979a: 76–78.
[25]On the details of sacrificial butchery, see esp. Durand 1979, Detienne 1979b:
20–24, and the bibliography in Detienne and Vernant 1979. On the role of women
in sacrifice, see Detienne 1979c.
[26]Rudhardt 1958, esp. 296, arguing against Hubert and Mauss 1964 (1898), esp.
19–51 and 95. Rudhardt's views have been adopted by Vernant, Kirk, and others,
whereas Burkert 1972 continues to accept Hubert and Mauss.
[27]Rudhardt 1958: 258, 292–94, 299.
[28]Here the structuralists take issue with earlier cross-cultural theories of sacrifice. Hubert and Mauss 1964 (1898): 11, 52, 55, and 97–99 emphasize rites of
entrance and exit and argue that these rites permit a safe approach to the dangerous

As Rudhardt in particular has argued, sacrificial procedures thus mark the incorporation of the individual into a particular social group.[29] Virtually no political activity was performed without sacrifice.[30] *Only* members of a particular social group could share in a particular sacrifice or receive its benefits. Through sacrifice man gave up something for a gain, but in so doing he submitted himself to the group and to the religious rules of the group. The individual never fully controlled the benefits of his sacrifice. When he performed sacrifice for divination, for example, the gods offered positive mantic signs only if his planned action accorded in some mysterious way with the religious order. No amount of pious ritual activity could assuage or persuade an unfavorable divinity. Hence sacrifice benefited the individual, yet it always remained a collective act in that it was performed according to certain procedures determined by the group and was effective only if the larger context was propitious. At the same time, Greek authors often failed to mention to which gods a sacrifice was made; hence emphasis fell on the human side, as sacrifice reaffirmed the continuity of family or civic life.[31] The Greek gods were powers that, through ritual, served to integrate man into the social order and social hierarchies, into nature, and into a sacred order.[32] They justified human culture yet kept it within strict limits, so that the power that men received through sacrifice was precisely the power that gave cohesion to the community.[33] For this reason, perhaps, sacrifice could be used to enforce oaths or remove pollution from a criminal and permit his reentry to society.

---

divine realm through the death of the victim and a substitution of the victim for the sacrificer. For a comparable ancient view, see *Sallustius: Concerning the Gods and the Universe* (ed. Nock 1926: lxxxxiii–iv), secs. 15–16. Arguing that sacrifice serves the interest of mortals only (the gods need nothing from them), Sallustius sees the victim as an intermediary who brings god and human together in the offering of a third life.

[29]Rudhardt 1958, esp. 257ff. and 294ff.

[30]See Detienne 1979b: 10–11. Vernant 1976, esp. 30–31, and 1980: 100–101 stresses the relation between the structure of Greek social life and the sacrificial ritual.

[31]Rudhardt 1958: 289, 294, 297.

[32]Vernant 1980: 109. Vernant 1976: 37 emphasizes that individualism is regularly expressed in Greek culture and religion through the group.

[33]Rudhardt 1958: 293.

Those who chose to dissent from the community regularly formulated deviant patterns of eating and sacrificing, as Detienne and Sabbatucci have argued.[34] Whereas sacrificial procedures normally served to legitimate the killing and eating of animals and incorporated the individual into the *polis,* Pythagoreans and Orphics withdrew in various ways from the community and refused meat and sacrificial killing, or, in the case of Pythagoreans who were not vegetarians, refused certain meats (oxen, as opposed to pigs or goats). This group was implicitly refusing the violence inflicted on a member of the community (the domestic animal) on which sacrifice was predicated and was treating it as murder or cannibalism. Dionysiac cult (in myth if not in reality; within the *polis* Dionysus was worshiped with the same sacrifices as other gods) and the Cynics, on the other hand, resisted traditional culture by a symbolic return to savagery and the eating of raw meat. The Pythagoreans and Orphics denied the cultural delineation made between men and gods and, by returning to the imagined practices of a Golden Age, sought direct communion with the gods. The second group of deviants denied the separation between man and nature by a return to the ways of beasts.

Structuralist analysis draws several important general conclusions from its examination of sacrificial procedure and the literary treatment of sacrifice.[35] First, along with marriage and agriculture, sacrifice comes to be understood in the symbolic system of Greek thought as a way of marking out the special precinct of the human, of setting men apart both from the immortal gods with their imperishable food (nectar and ambrosia) and from beasts who eat raw food. Whereas beasts kill each other with impunity, man imposes taboos on the killing of fellow humans and eats no meat of domestic animals without previously sacrificing and cooking it. By delineating sharply the boundaries and differences between god and man, sacrifice, like Greek popular wisdom, serves to keep its participants strictly within the limits of the human.

[34]Detienne 1979a and Sabbatucci 1965. These deviant attitudes and procedures indirectly confirm the structuralist view that normal sacrifice legitimized sacrificial killing and served to separate mortals, gods, and beasts.

[35]For a good summary of these views, see Vernant 1976: 31–32 and 1980: 134–38.

Structuralist analysis shows that sacrifice operates in analogous ways to other ritual performances in the community, and that the religious system of the *polis* functions with a remarkable consistency. Sacrifice, marriage, and funeral rites, for example, share similar procedures: purification with water, garlanding, the cutting and dedication of hair, music, and a feast.[36] In marriage rites the couple is pelted with flowers and other objects, and perfume rather than incense plays a central role. All three rites help to effect a transition for the central participants, from domestic animal to edible meat, from unmarried (and wild) status to married (and cultured), from life to death. Marriage, like sacrifice, serves to distinguish man from beasts (promiscuous) and gods (incestuous) and incorporates individuals into a (new) social group. Marriage rites include sacrifice as part of the proceedings. Sacrifice, which could be performed both publicly and in the household, provides a link between public rituals, which are aimed at creating social unity on a large scale, and rituals oriented toward individuals such as marriage, funerals, and initiation rites, which emphasize social transition and learning, often through a confrontation with pain or death.

In the public rather than the private realm, sacrifice, *agōn* (contest), and festival, the most important civic rites in Greek life, ritualize potential violence within a community and delineate the relations between gods and men.[37] Thus athletic *agōnes* such as those in Patroclus' funeral games in *Iliad* 23 represent in a controlled and peaceful form the destructive antagonism of war. The games contrast with Hector's terrible race for life on the battlefield at 22.159–61. Such contests are the only form of physical violence acceptable within a society. In the *Odyssey* the Phaeacians, a society without war and foreign policy, still have games to bring the aggressive competition of their young men into equilibrium.

---

[36]Initiation rites also include some similar procedures. On initiation rites for women see Chapter 2, and for men Chapters 4 and 5. On marriage and funeral ritual see Chapter 2. See Burkert 1972: 68 on the overlap between rites and myths of sacrifice, funeral, and initiation.

[37]Rudhardt 1958 analyzes festival, dance, *agōn,* and burial in terms comparable to those he applies to sacrifice. See Chapters 4 and 5 for further discussion and bibliography.

Sophocles (*Oedipus Rex* 879–81) emphasizes the positive force of good competition in a *polis,* whereas Demosthenes (20.108) stresses the centrality of the agonistic spirit in a democracy. The victor in an athletic contest may momentarily reach a godlike status, but epinician poetry reminds him that he must compete in submission to the rules of his society and for its benefit and glory as well as for his own.

Festivals in honor of the gods included both sacrifice and many kinds of *agōnes* (musical and theatrical among them).[38] Frequently the whole society, not just male citizens, participated. These festivals also served, in ways discussed in more detail in the chapter on the *Bacchae,* to incorporate the whole community into the social system and to define its relation to the gods.

The testimony from tragic and epic passages cited earlier shows that sacrifice creates a reciprocal relation between god and community through gift and a shared meal. The Pythagoreans were not alone in their critical response to this practice. Comic writers mock the divine "need" for sacrifice. In Aristophanes' *Birds,* for example, the characters plot to dethrone Zeus and the Olympians by depriving them of the smoke from their sacrificial meat. Pindar (*Olympian* 1.46–53) responds to the awkward implications of divine cannibalism in the Tantalus myth by offering a different, whitewashed version. On a more abstract level, Euripides' characters, adapting the views of pre-Socratic thinkers such as Xenophanes (frags. 1, 11, 12, 23, and 24 DK), often seem repelled by the notion of a divinity who needs or is directly involved with men (see especially *Heracles* 1345–46 or *Hecuba* 799–801) and suggest that divine anthropomorphism is an invention of men.

Unlike Near Eastern myths, Greek myths do not baldly acknowledge that man was created to feed and labor for the gods. But Greek poets do note the apparent disparity between divine and human portions in the sacrifice. How can one rationalize human sacrifice, when men receive and use the edible parts of this gift whereas the gods receive only the smoke from the unusable parts such as the thighbones, fat, gall bladder, and tail? Hesiod's story of Prometheus raises the issue of sacrificial distribution. In a series of

[38]See Chapter 5 for further discussion and bibliography on festival.

articles Vernant has clearly shown the important, if implicit, point about this story of the first sacrifice.[39] The introduction of sacrifice is a deceptive advantage for men, who previously shared meals with the gods but are now condemned to a separation from divinity and to mortality. The immortals eat imperishable food, symbolized by the smoke, incense, and spices they receive from men, whereas mortals eat food made only marginally less perishable by cooking. Sacrifice thus becomes a part of the definition of the human in Greek culture.

Sacrifice denies by its procedures its own violence, and legitimizes the killing and eating of domestic animals. Greek vases and literary texts reflect this denial in their refusal to depict the animal's moment of death. Human sacrifice, however, is depicted on vases.[40] Similarly, tragedy, though it is reticent about displaying sacrificial death onstage, can dwell on the moment of slaughter in verbal descriptions. Human sacrifice in tragedy, however, perverts actual sacrificial practice, which normally prohibits the slaughter of men, and thus logically becomes a part of the social disruption and crisis typical of the tragic plot.

While ancient historians offer putative examples of either actual human sacrifice or the threat of it before military expeditions, such victims were rare and probably nonexistent.[41] Themistocles, for example, was advised to sacrifice three captured Persians to Dionysus before the battle of Salamis (Phainias of Eresus, frag. 25 Wehrli = Plut. *Them.* 13.2). Pelopidas was warned to sacrifice a virgin at Aulis before the battle of Leuctra (Plut. *Pelop.* 21). Phylarchus makes the unlikely claim that it was common for Greeks to slaughter human victims before battle (Phylarchus ad Porphyry *De abst.* 2.56). Although archaeological evidence now suggests that human sacrifice may have been practiced in Minoan and dark-age Greece, all later examples of human sacrifice in Greece are generally agreed to be modeled on myth. Nevertheless, Greek mythical

[39]See esp. Vernant 1979 and 1980: 168–85.
[40]Durand 1979: 138.
[41]For an important discussion, see Henrichs 1981 and Burkert 1966a: 112–13. For discussion of the actual practices involved in sacrifice before battle, see esp. Lonis 1979: 95–116 and Pritchett 1971: 109–115 and 1979: 83–90. See also Pritchett 1979: 1–10 on the ritualized nature of Greek battle.

tradition offers many examples of festivals and cults that preserved the uncomfortable "memory" of human sacrifice at their origins. In the *Iphigenia in Tauris,* for example, Euripides presents the substitution of an animal for a human victim in the cult of Artemis as a historical transformation of the ritual from barbarian to Greek. But, as a drop of blood is taken from a human throat, the origin of the Greek rite is recalled each time an animal victim is sacrificed (1458–61).

In sum, sacrificial procedure offers to the poet a kind of grammar of procedural terms by which to articulate in a compressed and symbolic form the nature of the relations of men in the community and of men to the larger world of animals and gods around them. Participation in sacrifice binds the worshiper to his community, organizes his place in that community, and implicitly obtains his consent to the violence upon which this organization is in part predicated. Through ritual a kind of equilibrium or justice is reached between man and his larger environment. Douglas, in discussing the range of ritual as metaphor in *Purity and Danger,* makes an amusing but apt comparison between money and ritual as two varieties of social currency:

> The metaphor of money admirably sums up what we want to assert of ritual. Money provides a fixed, external, recognizable sign for what would be confused, contradictable operations: ritual makes visible external signs of internal states. Money mediates transactions; ritual mediates experience, including social experience. Money provides a standard for measuring worth; ritual standardizes situations, and so helps to evaluate them. Money makes a link between present and future, so does ritual. The more we reflect on the richness of the metaphor, the more it becomes clear that this is no metaphor. Money is only an extreme and specialized type of ritual.[42]

A correctly performed ritual, then, offers a standard by which to measure the health of a community. The healthy community, as in sacrifice, formally expels violence from within itself, distributes its goods in an orderly and just manner, eats according to specific rules, makes social transitions in a ritualized manner, and limits

[42]Douglas 1966: 85–86.

itself to what its religious and social practices define as human. The proper performance of sacrifice thus becomes a sign of civilization, of a recognition that life cannot be led without a communal order and shared standards of behavior. The voluntary sacrifices of virgins in tragedy mimic proper sacrificial procedures. The victim is pure and goes willingly to death in propitious silence. By substituting themselves for the community, these heroic victims can, at a drastic cost, symbolically unite and rescue a fragmented society.

Ritual can suffer a number of improprieties with regard to its phases and their order, the choice of victim, the role of the sacrificer, the purity of the participants, the method of killing and butchery, and the suppression of the victim's consent. These improprieties can become a sign of uncontrolled violence and social disorder, psychological and social alienation from the community, or a collapse of communication between the divine and human realms. Hence Thucydides saw the breakdown of ritual, especially burial ritual, during the plague at Athens as symptomatic of a more general social disintegration (2.51–53). Corrupt sacrifices in tragedy are murders thinly disguised as sacrifice and symptomatic of a social environment in which violence is proliferating uncontrollably and cultural distinctions are collapsing. Proper procedures are violated, animal sacrifices become human, man aspires to become god, sacrificial gifts become unjust bribes, men eat their children.

The central role of sacrifice in society thus makes it a useful and multidimensional symbol for the exploration of social crisis that forms the basis of so many tragic plots. The sacrificial metaphor in Aeschylus' *Oresteia* is a much-studied example. The crime that opens the trilogy, the slaying of Iphigenia, is a ritual tainted by the victim's lack of consent to her death. In contrast, her Euripidean counterpart willingly submits to sacrifice for Greece. The death of Iphigenia resonates through the language of sacrifice with the "preliminary sacrifices" made by the Greek army at Troy, with Agamemnon's desecration of the temples of the gods at Troy, and with the "sacrificial" deaths of himself and Cassandra (*Ag.* 65, 1118, 1293, 1310; see also Homer *Od.* 4.535 and 11.411, which compares the death of Agamemnon to that of an ox in his stall).

[40]

Clytemnestra calls her murder of Agamemnon in retribution for her daughter a sacrifice and blasphemously pours out his blood, instead of wine, as a third libation to Zeus, savior of the dead (*Ag.* 1385–87). Here she perverts the propitious libation poured to Zeus Soter at banquets. Clytemnestra sacrifices Agamemnon as he bathes in a *lebēs,* a word normally used to describe a kettle or container for water at a sacrifice, and never elsewhere for a bath-tub.[43] In the *Agamemnon* the series of sacrificial victims, connected by a chain of revenge or "justice," is human, and the feasting on the flesh of the victims becomes cannibalism (Thyestes' children and Orestes, whose blood the Erinyes threaten to suck in the *Eumenides*). The imagery, as in the omen of the eagles (*Ag.* 109–20), suggests a confusion of boundaries between sacrificer and victim, man and beast. As Zeitlin has argued, the characters who make these sacrifices deceive themselves as to the justice and correctness of their acts by calling their crimes performed with tainted motives "sacrifices."[44] The result is a collapse of the political order into a tyranny dominated by a woman, and a sense of theological crisis, in which the divine order seems to become increasingly remote and unreadable for man, while the line between the "violent grace" of Zeus and secular violence becomes indistinguishable.

Order and piety begin to be restored only when Orestes refuses to deceive himself as to the nature of his matricide and correct ritual procedure begins to reemerge (although it still serves to promote murder) in the tomb ritual of the *Libation Bearers.* Now the gods not only send their oracles to man but in the end literally appear onstage in the *Eumenides* to reestablish ritual and the control of internal social violence through rites of purification, cult, and a system of secular justice. The Eumenides close the triology by accepting a cult in Athens and marriage sacrifices. The *ololugmos,* the ritual cry of women at the sacrifice, regains its proper function, and Zeus once more receives his proper epithet "Savior."[45] The

[43]On the *lebēs,* see Lebeck 1971: 62 and Guépin 1968: 52–53.
[44]Zeitlin 1965 and 1966. Lebeck 1971, Vickers 1973, Vidal-Naquet 1981a, and Burkert 1966a: 119–20 also treat aspects of the sacrificial imagery in this play.
[45]Zeitlin 1965: 507.

restoration of ritual marks and confirms the restoration of the
social order.

Structuralist analysis of ritual illuminates what the sacrificial
metaphor expresses about the larger social context. This approach
makes it clear why the destruction of Helen's marriage to Menelaus is logically connected to the "preliminary sacrifices" made by
the Greek army at Troy, how the failed marriage of Clytemnestra
results in her "sacrifice" of Agamemnon, and why marriage, sacrifice, and agriculture are simultaneously restored in the cult of the
Eumenides that closes the triology. Such analysis explains why the
violation of sacrificial procedure in the death of Iphigenia can express simultaneously both psychological corruption in the individual and an inversion of the entire social order; for in Greek
thought, as in Plato's *Republic* 8, the structure of the individual
psyche and of society often reflect each other. As in the myth
about the Attic Bouphonia, sacrifice and the problem of justice are
related, since sacrifice is organized to control the relation of men
and beasts and of citizens to each other and to bring benefit out of
violence. Hence the ability to understand divine justice, lost in the
corrupt world of the *Agamemnon* and regained in the *Eumenides,*
can be expressed through the performance of the ritual act by
which communication takes place between the two spheres, and
by which god and man are both united and divided. Structural
analysis provides a way of reading the language with which sacrifice speaks to the audience, and a method of decoding the function
of the sacrificial metaphor in the whole world of a play. In short,
to call murder sacrifice is to put an act of human violence into a
social and religious context whose larger implications the spectator
can begin to understand.

Furthermore, the sacrificial ritual, as an institution that retains its
form throughout the historical period represented in the triology
(the society formed at the close of the triology is basically that of
Aeschylus' audience), provides a crucial symbolic link between
past and present, between myth and contemporary life, and between Athens and other cities (Argos). Whereas political systems
and the relations between the sexes shift through time, ritual remains to bridge the gap between the sexes and between public and
private life. For, like the Erinyes, women remain public actors for

the society in cult even when they are barred (unlike Clytemnestra) from the political arena in democratic Athens.

In the *Electra* of Euripides the characters actually perform the murders of Aegisthus and Clytemnestra on ritual occasions, the first at a festival of the nymphs, the second at a ritual for the birth of Electra's fictional child by the farmer to whom she has been unwillingly married. The play as a whole is set on the day of the Argive festival of Hera, to which the chorus are en route in festal dress. As Zeitlin has shown, the festival of Hera stands in the play as an "examplar of ritual regularity" or normal cult activity against which we can measure the life and actions of the house of Atreus.[46] Electra is strongly characterized by her social alienation: neither married nor unmarried, neither princess nor farmer's wife, she preserves a perpetual mourning for her father that will not allow her to join the women of the chorus in the festivities. She lives banned from the palace in an isolated rural setting. Orestes, too, has lived so separately from the land of his birth and his noble position that he can achieve a full recognition with his sister only at great length (the Aeschylean recognition scene between brother and sister is parodied as impossible in this play) and through the mediation of others; he laments in a long speech the impossibility of distinguishing true nobility (367–400). The chorus (743–46) defends the value of mythical stories as *paradeigmata* that, whether they are true or false, lead men to refrain from evil; but the message of the heroic past is lost on the protagonists. Electra romanticizes her solitude and her lost brother to the point that she, too, has great difficulty discovering the presence of the savior for whom she has longed. She also fails to recognize the messenger who returns with the news of Orestes' success (765–66).

In contrast to Aeschylus' version, the hurried appeal of the siblings to their father's ghost is abruptly cut off (684) and initiates a series of ritual distortions in which Electra imagines the return of Orestes with Aegisthus' head as the triumphal entrance of an athletic or military victor.[47] Orestes participates in the sacrifice for the

---

[46]Zeitlin 1970b: 669; my discussion of the role of ritual in the *Electra* combines my own views with insights from Zeitlin's article.

[47]See lines 590–91, 614, 686, 694–95, 751, 761–62, 776, 824–25, 864–65, 872, 880, 888–89, 954–56, 987, 1174 for agonistic imagery in the play. For brief discus-

nymphs falsely, pretending that he has already performed the proper ablutions (793–94) and accepting Aegisthus' invitation to show his skills as a foreign expert at butchery. He then kills Aegisthus from behind with an ax as Aegisthus concentrates on the unfavorable entrails. The murder becomes an extension of this sacrificial butchery, which is described in horrifying clinical detail. The vague and terrifying sacrificial deaths of Aeschylus' triology are replaced by gross specificity, as the agent of Apollo's will turns butchery—the division of a legitimately killed animal according to rules that reflect the structure of authority in the community—into murder and a claim for his lost throne.

Electra, too, turns a ritual for birth into a murder, destroying her mother and turning her back on Hera, goddess of marriage; the command by the Dioscuri that Electra marry Pylades can hardly transform this "unmarried one," as her name specifies, into a promising bride. In the *Electra* ritual fails to become, as it does in Aeschylus, a source of form or integration. The characters are too alienated by their distorted fantasies and unheroic lives to find a place in the normal processes of religious life and society. If Apollo's command to Orestes was appropriate, it cannot be interpreted as such when performed by the protagonists of this play, as the Dioscuri apparently imply at 1244: "She [Clytemnestra] has met with justice, but you have not done justly." In the final scenes Orestes and Electra seem to be aware of the true nature of their crime and the hollowness of the future promised them by the gods, but the play deserts them at the threshold of exile.

In this play Euripides, like Aeschylus, uses ritual (sacrifice, *agōn*, rituals for birth, and festival) as a method of measuring and exploring the problems of justice and the social control of violence. But the world created by the two poets is radically different. In Euripides' play the secular world is not reformed or apparently reformable. The political context in Argos remains obscure; secular justice is provided offstage and in a remote context (1258–75). The gods speak cryptically, and doubt is cast on their words and ac-

---

sion, see also Adams 1935 and O'Brien 1964. Armed soldiers discovered at Olympia were impounded and held for ransom, a policy that confirmed the separation of war and athletic *agōnes*.

tions (1245–46, 1302). The patterns of ritual and myth are held up
before the protagonists like maps that they are able only to misread
as they turn sacrifice into butchery, butchery into glorious victory,
Apollo's oracle into a travesty of justice, and marriage and birth
into an occasion for falsehood and death. Electra's fictions seek
authority in ritual but reflect instead her own alienation and self-
delusion. The world of Euripides almost never provides the uplifting convergence of political and religious life, of domestic and
public interests, to be found in Aeschylus. Yet ritual and the patterns it offers for alleviating suffering, for integrating the individual into social life, for coping with violence, do not always, as
in the *Electra,* fall on deaf ears. As we shall see in the plays examined in the following chapters, because sacrifice contains in itself an
implicit definition of a civilized community, the ritual often provides Euripides with a solution of the last resort in a world in
which public life, political corruption, and social alienation remain
the dominant aspects of a disintegrating environment.

Nevertheless, Greek tragedy goes beyond using ritual and sacrifice as a complex standard by which to measure social unity or
disorder and as a means of defining the cultural system in terms of
relations among gods, humans, and beasts. Myths, ritual procedures, and divine authority all render the killing of domestic
animals legitimate. At the same time there is something intrin-
sically repellent about a divine/human relationship in which communication so often occurs in terms of violence, whether through
sacrifice, rape, plague, or revenge. Whereas epinician poets such as
Pindar were at pains to explain away illegitimate divine violence
and to transform myths that denigrated the gods, Greek tragic
poets deliberately exploited the violence that lay at the heart of the
sacrificial ritual, of communication between gods and humans, and
of the myths upon which they based their plays. As we have seen,
Greek poets and philosophers had begun self-consciously to examine and question their religion as a collective system of ideas,
symbols, and ritual practices that reflected and reinforced social
structures. Thus, in Aeschylus' *Oresteia* divine justice becomes
comprehensible only through the establishment of a human institution, trial by jury, in the context of Athenian society. The
triology assumes that theology depends on and changes with polit-

ical systems: monarchy, tyranny, or democracy. The emerging recognition that social relations form a model for religious conceptions articulated with a growing concern about the origins and psychological effects of religion and ritual. Although Hesiod's cosmology presented an original divine violence as ultimately rationalized by the rule of Zeus, eventually the anthropomorphic gods came to seem false and inadequate projections of the human spirit, perhaps invented especially to justify human vices or to control an unruly human society with fear of divine retribution. Euripides' sophistic characters often explain their surrender to violence and immorality by alluding to divine precedents. In their aetiological explanations of ritual and cults, poets frequently assumed an origin in human sacrifice for the tamer practices of their own day. Since, however, this uneasy search for origins and concern with divine and human violence is so often made in Greek literature through myth and allusion to ritual practices about which little is known, the speculations of modern theorists can again be helpful in illuminating the assumptions implicit in such complex poetic representations.

Sacrificial Violence and the Question of Origins

Whereas structuralist analysis concerns itself with the way that sacrifice functioned both as a system and within the cultural context of classical Greece, evolutionist theories are specifically concerned with the emergence and survival in human culture of sacrifice as a mode of ritualized *killing*.[48] Meuli and Burkert, who expanded upon Meuli's work, argue that prehistoric sacrificial ritual was organized primarily as an atonement for the destruction of life, an appeasement of violence. Meuli, developing the work of earlier scholars, saw the origin of sacrifice in the rites of Paleolithic hunters. The hunter, closely identified with the animal he killed, regretted killing it and feared its vengeance. Wishing to save the animal from complete destruction and to regenerate symbolically

---

[48]See note 10 above. I have selected from a large body of evolutionist theory the representative ideas of three historians of religion, Meuli, Burkert and Guépin, and of two nonclassical philosophers of culture, Bataille and Girard.

his future source of food, the hunter removed and treated its internal organs in special ways and buried or preserved certain of its bones, often reconstituting them in a particular pattern that, supplemented by the addition of small pieces of meat from other limbs, suggested the regeneration of the whole beast. Neolithic pastoral and agricultural peoples transformed this procedure, wrapping animal thighbones (which contain, as it were, the marrow of existence) in fat for the gods.[49] These hunting rituals also explain the special treatment of the *splangchna* or internal organs in Greek sacrifice, and the Homeric practice of *ōmothetein*, the placement of small pieces of meat from other parts of the animal on the bones. (Primitive hunting practices also suggest origins for the *chernibes*, the sprinkling of the animal with water, and possibly for the *ololugmos*). The Greek sacrificial ritual was, then, a kind of "comedy of innocence" or "drama of escape from guilt" (*Unschuldskomödie*). The ritual retained its essential elements from Paleolithic times because man, the only being that needed ritual to come to terms with his own death, continued to want to assuage the guilt incurred from killing animals for his own benefit.

Burkert, building on the work of Freud and ethologists such as Lorenz, departs from Meuli's emphasis on the "comedy of innocence," which obscured sacrificial violence, and argues that ritual, and sacrifice in particular, works also to control impulses of human aggression. Whereas powerful animals control their competitive impulse to kill, man has no such instinctive control of his competitive drives. Man's deeply aggressive nature and his attempts to control it through ritual are reflected in myths of early man such as the biblical tale of Cain and Abel, which combines intrafamilial murder and sacrifice.[50] For Burkert the threat of regression to human sacrifice stands behind every performance of the ritual, and it is precisely the ability of the ritual to dramatize the moment of killing that ensures and perpetuates its success as a form of collective therapy.[51] Hence sacrifice is structured as "prep-

[49]Guépin 1968: 100 argues against Meuli 1946: 231–32 that the dedication of the thighbones is a *pars pro toto* offering, not an attempt to regenerate the animal symbolically, and thereby assuage guilt.

[50]See Burkert 1966a: 111 and 1972: 8.

[51]Burkert 1966a: 109 and 111–12 and 1972: 45–60.

aration, terrorizing center, and restitution."[52] The *ololugmos,* the ritual cry of the women, dramatizes the emotions evoked at the moment of the animal's death. The shock and guilt precipitated by sacrifice united agricultural peoples even more powerfully than the earlier hunters and gatherers to the extent that killing had become less familiar in the procurement of food.[53] Hence sacrifices and related rituals, the expulsion of members of a community in scapegoat rituals or human sacrifices, could be used to overcome social crises.[54]

Bataille, who also locates the origin of animal sacrifice among the early hunters, sees sacrifice as one part of an important system of taboos created to protect and organize the world of work and social reproduction and to set this world apart from the world of nature, which operates on a different basis. Man wished to deny his own violence and death and to control sexuality, thereby preventing the recognition that only death guarantees life. This denial was, of course, impossible. Hence his social life was built around ritualized transgressions of taboos against intracommunal violence and promiscuity, transgressions that organized violence and sexuality for the benefit of the community: war, sacrifice, and marriage. Through his relation to the sacred world in ritual, man effected a controlled confrontation with the persistence of nature insofar as it could not be ordered by the world of work. For the early hunter, animals were beings like himself, but beings not subject to the taboos concerning intestine violence and promiscuity, and therefore more sacred and godlike (early gods were frequently represented in animal form); hence the killing of animals appeared a sacrilege. For the early hunter "animal nature formed a cathedral, as it were, within which human violence could be centered and condensed."[55] Through animal sacrifice man came

[52]See Burkert 1972: 97. For ancient evidence on sacrifice as primarily a ritual killing see, e.g., Sallustius 16.1, *zoēs de dia thusiōn aparchometha* or the assumption in *De abst.* 2.27 that sacrifice arose out of cannibalism. Meuli follows Hubert and Mauss 1964 (1898), esp. 33, 58, in emphasizing that sacrifice is in essence a crime.
[53]Burkert 1972: 53–58.
[54]Burkert 1966a: 111.
[55]Bataille 1962: 85. For the other arguments by Bataille presented here, see esp. 42–59, 63–64, 67–68, 73–74, 81–84.

face to face with the limitless continuity of nature and its insistence on reproduction through death, a continuity denied by the organized world of work. Whereas Burkert views sacrifice as man's way of confronting his own aggression, Bataille views it as a way for man to confront his own nature as if it were something separate from human culture, and hence to some extent separate from himself; the ritual system serves simultaneously to obscure and yet to confirm man's part in the uncontrollable world of nature. This notion that sacrifice both confronts and conceals human nature and the possibility of an uncontrolled proliferation of human violence is shared in a different form by Girard.

Girard's theory, upon which the work of Bataille had some influence, grows out of the work of the French sociologists of religion who, following Durkheim, locate the origin and reality of religious phenomena within the social process. Such analysts of religion try to strip away the symbolic forms of religious representations to find the ultimate social referents beneath: to discover, for example, how sacrifice engenders god.[56] For Girard the earliest social life is characterized by a dangerous lack of cultural distinctions. Reciprocal violence between men originates in a process of ever-escalating "mimetic desire" in which each self desires what another desires simply because the other desires it, and as a result comes into violent competition for a series of desired objects. This process is without limit unless the aggressions released in mimetic rivalry can be deflected onto an arbitrarily selected victim who is defined as marginal to the group, a cause of ills and a repository of violence. The community unites and transforms itself by a collective act of unanimous violence against this scapegoat or "surrogate victim." This original (and historical) act of violence founds religion and human culture. The violence of the community, expelled by this original act of unanimity, is now defined as sacred and beneficial, a power outside itself.[57] In short, god is the massive violence expelled by this original act of unanimity. Once this violence is mystified as deity, it becomes a source of order and control

[56]On this point see also Hubert and Mauss 1964 (1898): 77 and 91. Girard 1977: 89–92 differs from Hubert and Mauss in that he posits a real historical moment for the origin of sacrifice.

[57]See esp. Girard 1977: 30 and 266. On mimetic rivalry, see esp. ibid., 145–59.

of reciprocal violence within the community, which fears to confront it. The ambivalence of the sacred as a source of both danger and benefit arises from its origins in a violence that becomes a source of cultural order and remains a source of order as long as these origins remain concealed.[58]

In Girard's theory, the community prohibits strife by reenacting the experiences that originally brought an end to it. "Ritual is nothing more than the regular exercise of 'good' violence."[59] Religious rituals and festivals and scapegoat myths refer to and commemorate the generative act of victimage and mimetic competition, while simultaneously effacing or distorting the true nature of the act and thus perpetuating the delusion that sacred violence resides outside the boundaries of the human. The sacrificial victim must be as similar to the surrogate victim as possible, yet it cannot be, like the original victim, a full member of the community, whose death would promote violence and demand revenge, but a domesticated animal or, in the case of human sacrifice, a marginal person—a criminal, king, or virgin.[60] The abritrary selection of the original victim is preserved only in the element of chance that may accompany the sacrifice.[61]

These theories of the origin of sacrifice share the view that sacrifice is structured to allow its participants to confront violence. In contrast to the structuralists, who de-emphasize the moment of death, the ritual killing of the animal is the centerpiece and essence of the rite. But Burkert, Bataille, and Girard differ in their emphasis on what truth about human nature or human social existence man receives at the moment of the animal's death. Burkert posits that man effects a dramatic and therapeutic confrontation with his own fundamental aggressiveness; Bataille stresses that sacrifice is part of man's attempt to define culture against nature and its uncontrolled violence. Girard sees human violence as a product of social conflict; sacrifice becomes part of a system of religious mystification that controls social violence by projecting it away from man and onto a divinity. Although no one would deny the impor-

[58]See esp. ibid., 24, 258–73, and 310.
[59]Ibid., 37.
[60]See esp. ibid., 13, 101, 269–73.
[61]See ibid., 311 and 314.

tance of violence to ritual and in human culture generally, recent studies have questioned the fundamentally aggressive nature of man and his ape ancestors, and ethological theories that generalize about human culture on the basis of animal behavior have in any case won only limited support.[62] Some consider Girard's work to be distorted by an eagerness to link primitive religious practice with the sacrifice of Christ in a gigantic theory of culture that defies the boundaries of time and place.[63] And indeed, just as it is difficult to say precisely what sexual drive means in a universal sense, given the enormous variety of mating and marriage patterns that exist in various cultures, it is equally difficult to generalize about what aggression or violence means outside a specific cultural context. The structuralists stress that religious phenomena cannot be studied separately from social and material life; sacrificial violence may mean something fundamentally different to a classical Greek than to a Paleolithic hunter or a Neolithic farmer.[64]

Unlike the structuralists' theories, the views of the evolutionists have not been and probably cannot be sufficiently documented by a study of Greek theory and practice. Archaeological evidence confirms Meuli's views on the practices of prehistoric hunters. But there is no such historical evidence either for the origin or evolution of sacrificial ritual. Indeed, in a recent examination of Homeric practices Kirk argues that epic sacrifice in fact placed less emphasis on the moment of death than did the classical ritual: there is no mention of the victim's nod of assent, the arrangement of bones in specific patterns, or the concealing of the knife in a basket. In addition, archaeological evidence from the Bronze Age suggests that most sacrifices from this early period were vegetable rather than animal.[65] The historicity of the evolu-

[62]As Burkert himself is aware (1972: 8 n. 1), many recent studies have questioned both the innate aggression of primates and the application of animal studies to human behavior.

[63]For critical discussions of Girard, see esp. Detienne 1979b: 35 n. 1; Nelson 1976; and the whole of *Berkshire Review* 14 (1979) or *Diacritics* 8 (March 1978). Detienne 1979b: 25–35 discusses the biases produced by the Christian sacrifice of god and Christian communion on all discussions of sacrifice from Robertson Smith and Durkheim to Cassirer and finally Girard.

[64]On this point see Vernant 1976: 29 and Rudhardt 1958: 295 and passim.

[65]Kirk 1981: 68–77.

tionists' views on sacrificial ritual and its origins is essentially irrelevant to the present study, however. Here we are exclusively concerned with the value of their theoretical constructs for a reading of Greek tragedy. Do Greek tragedians use sacrifice and the sacrificial metaphor to describe the purging of guilt, or to confront directly and dramatize human aggression and the moment of death? Do they use the ritual to confront but simultaneously mystify and transform sacrificial violence by making it something foreign (bestial or divine) to men? Does the Greek poet, like Bataille, fundamentally associate *erōs* with violence in the ritual context? We shall return to these and similar important questions after discussing Burkert's, Guépin's, and Girard's theories about the relation between sacrifice and tragedy.

For Burkert, tragedy in essence reproduces the sacrificial scenario in dramatic form by bringing its audience into a therapeutic confrontation with a sacrificial death. Translating *tragōidia* as "a song at the sacrifice of a goat," Burkert finds the origins of tragedy in a group of masked, and therefore anonymous and guiltless, men who form a chorus to confront and lament death at a sacrifice. Just as the killing of the sacrificial animal included the *ololugmos* and the accompanying music of the *aulos,* so the tragic chorus went on to lament the tragic hero to the music of the *aulos.*[66] Although "*tragōidia* emancipated itself from the *tragos* . . . the essense of the sacrifice still pervades tragedy even in its maturity."[67] The *Agamemnon;* the *Trachiniae* of Sophocles, in which Heracles concludes the play by sacrificing himself on a pyre on Mount Oeta; and the *Medea* of Euripides, in which Medea "sacrifices" her children and then establishes for them a cult at Corinth in which restitution is made for their deaths, preserve prominent traces of the origins of the genre in song at a sacrifice.

Guépin's study, which owes a good deal to the earlier speculations of Harrison, Murray, and the Cambridge school,[68] asserts that the tragedies performed in honor of Dionysus grew out of

[66]Burkert 1966a: 114.

[67]Burkert 1966a: 116. Burkert's subsequently influential discussion of the sacrificial metaphor in tragedy wisely divorces itself from too specific a relationship to his theory of origins, which is far more speculative and controversial.

[68]See esp. Murray 1927.

Dionysiac myth and cult.[69] The sacrificial deaths of tragedy were intimately connected with the sacrifice of the bull at the altar of Dionysus, an altar located at the center of the theatrical orchestra, and with myths about a god who was sacrificed and reborn. The tragic hero repeatedly dies like a sacrificial animal, a victim of crime, amid choral dances around an altar.[70] For Guépin, tragedy *is* a sacrifical ritual, and the tragic hero is in essence a sacrificial victim or scapegoat, both criminal and holy, who is killed or banished to produce benefit out of crime and a chain of proliferating guilt and social violence (as in the case of Oedipus). He argues further that tragic plots frequently assimilate earlier myths to a Dionysiac pattern. The deaths reenact an original preharvest sacrifice performed at the harvest of grapes or grain (threshing was done on a circular floor like that of the orchestra).[71] Orphic theology had made the sacrificial rending of Dionysus a crime, thereby preparing for the assimilation of Dionysiac myth into tragedy. Tragic plots often include the motif of resistance to the divine typical of Dionysiac myth.[72] Similarly, Dionysiac madness, like the fear created by tragic plots or the tragic protagonist's own criminal delusions, takes the participant out of himself.[73]

For Girard drama, like almost all culture, originates in violence: "All religious rituals spring from the surrogate victim, and all the great institutions of mankind, both secular and religious, spring from ritual."[74] Order in ritual cultures depends on social differentiation and distinction. In a period of "sacrificial crisis" mimetic rivalry proliferates, hierarchy collapses, and the distinction between sacred and secular violence dissolves. The crisis can be re-

[69]For Guépin's general thesis, see esp. xi–xiii, 1–5, 12–23, and 120ff. For Guépin a sacrificial death in tragedy typically follows the model set in the *aitia* for sacrifice given by Pausanias. A crime is followed by a plague. After an oracle is consulted, the murderer is punished and a sacrifice is instituted to commemorate the event. *Oedipus Rex* follows this pattern precisely except for the failure to institute a cult at the end (see ibid., 10–11).

[70]See ibid., 1, 16–17, and 24. In fact the sacrificial death takes place offstage.

[71]See ibid., xiii and 19. Another basic tragic plot connected with agricultural ritual includes the disappearance and return of a woman, who is often linked to Korē or Persephone (ibid., 120–33).

[72]See ibid., 32–39.

[73]See ibid., 19.

[74]Girard 1977: 306.

Ritual Irony

solved only by a repetition of the original act of violence against a
scapegoat and by a remystification of divinity. For Girard, the
classical period during which tragedy reached its height is poised
on the edge of a dissolution of ritual culture. Tragedy stands in a
transitional position between actual ritual performance and the
original spontaneous model that ritual and myth attempt to re-
produce or reflect.[75] The verbal *agōnes* (contests) of tragedy recapture much of the danger of mimetic violence and loss of hierarchical distinction characteristic of a "sacrificial crisis," as it sets
members of a family and by analogy a whole community into
uncontrollable conflict. Tragic *katharsis,* like ritual, restores health
to the community through the dramatic "sacrifice" or expulsion of
a scapegoat who takes upon himself or herself the violence of the
community and transfigures it into the sacred. Members of the
audience identify with a hero who is neither altogether like (because of his *hamartia*) nor unlike themselves. The audience resolves
its ambivalence when it finally abandons the hero to a destiny that
removes him from the community.[76] Like ritual, tragedy advances
to the very brink of revealing the origin of culture and then withdraws and effaces these hints with a return to myth and a restoration of cultural and aesthetic differences.[77] Tragedy reflects and
uses ritual; yet it is also competitive with ritual in that it performs
similar functions.[78] Whereas ritual celebrates lack of differentiation, tragedies can represent a reaction against an excess of com-
munality by asserting the claims to heroism of a suffering individual destroyed by necessity.

Girard offers Sophocles' *Oedipus Rex* and Euripides' *Bacchae* as
primary examples of tragic myths that simultaneously commemorate and efface the original crisis. The sacrificial crisis of the
Oedipus emerges in the mysterious and contagious plague that has
gripped the city of Thebes, a plague that has arisen from the collapse of differences between the generations of the royal family and
between king and city. Tiresias and Creon are drawn against their

[75]See ibid., 131. On "sacrificial crisis" generally, see esp. ibid., 49, and below,
Chapter 5 on Dionysus in the *Bacchae.*
[76]See Girard 1977: 290–91.
[77]See esp. ibid., 64–65, 129, 135–38, 292, 318.
[78]See ibid., 168.

will into a destructive mimetic rivalry with their king. Oedipus finally takes the collective violence upon himself, accepts the guilt for the plague, and offers to expel himself from the community as a scapegoat. His discovery of the truth vindicates Apollo's oracles and thus restores divine authority and divine responsibility for the violence to the community. The pattern recurs in the following generation in the mimetic rivalry of Eteocles and Polyneices, and resolves itself by their deaths and the final extinction of the house of Oedipus. And, as Girard might have added, the death of the brothers, as Euripides makes clear in the *Phoenissae,* repeats the original disastrous internecine violence of the "sown men" or Spartoi who became the first citizens of Thebes.

The *Bacchae,* in Girard's interpretation, opens in a similar state of cultural crisis and loss of hierarchy and distinction. The maddened women have left the city and its culture to behave like men. In the course of the drama distinctions of rank disappear as everyone adopts the dress and worship of the god; the collapse of the royal palace is symbolic of a larger collapse of the political order. The Dionysiac festival, like sacrifice, commemorates the precultural and undifferentiated state of humanity and takes it back to its violent beginnings, to its origins in reciprocal violence and a mimetic rivalry enacted here by the doubles Dionysus and Pentheus. The *sparagmos* (tearing apart) of Pentheus reenacts the original unanimous and spontaneous killing of the surrogate victim, as well as restoring order to the community and recreating religion in the form of the cult of Dionysus. Dionysus will now be as beneficial from afar as he was dangerous and violent in proximity. This play presents both the generation of religion from spontaneous collective violence against a single victim and the god as the origin of this violence.

The *Bacchae,* as Girard interprets it, "demystifies the double illusion of a violent divinity and an innocent community."[79] But instead of allowing human violence to create order, peace, and divinity, Euripides distorts the historical process by blurring from the start the distinction between good and bad violence and between divine and human causes for action.[80] The poet alternately

[79]Ibid., 136.
[80]See ibid., 137–38, also 37.

[55]

defends and denounces Dionysiac religion. He comes to the brink of revealing the truth about religion, and simultaneously withdraws from and mystifies the truth by attributing the final origin of violence to the god.

Classical scholars such as Rubino and Griffiths have gone on to argue that Aeschylus' *Oresteia* is the most extensive example of a Girardian sacrificial crisis in tragedy.[81] In the *Agamemnon* the action unfolds by reference to a series of sacrificial deaths. The cycle of reciprocal violence has plagued the house of Atreus in an endless series of intragenerational rivalries resulting in adultery, cannibalism, and murder presented as sacrifice. Iphigenia's social marginality fails to make her a neutral victim, for her mother Clytemnestra claims a right to avenge her daughter, a right not ordinarily considered legitimate for a woman. Among the many rival doubles of this play—Agamemnon and Aegisthus, Clytemnestra and Cassandra—man and wife also compete in a world where the divisions between public and private life have disintegrated. For the chorus, Zeus should be a source of beneficial violence. Yet the ambivalence of the chorus toward Iphigenia's sacrifice is one of many symptoms of an accelerating breakdown of ritual control in the world of the play. In the *Libation Bearers* the united forces of Electra, Orestes, and the chorus attempt with the help of Apollo's command to reestablish ritual control and divine responsibility for human violence; the rituals at the tomb of Agamemnon recreate a spirit of unanimous violence toward Clytemnestra. It is a sign of this process of remystification that her death is no longer termed a sacrifice. Yet Apollo fails to purify Orestes by ritual alone, and the sacrificial crisis invades the divine world itself. The Erinyes insist on a return to uncontrolled vengeance. The resolution of the *Eumenides* gives ritual a subsidiary role as a source of justice, and civil justice replaces sacrifice as the primary mechanism for controlling intestine violence in human society.

---

[81]Rubino 1972 and Griffiths 1979. The argument summarized here is primarily that of Griffiths. Griffiths uses Girard's theory to make interesting distinctions among the three poets in their use of ritual.

Poetry and Sacrifice

The evolutionists cannot, of course, document the transition from prehistoric cult and myth to tragedy. Indeed, classical scholars such as Else have attempted to deny that tragedy had originally any connection with the cult of Dionysus.[82] Leaving aside the questions of origins, Burkert and Guépin essentially go no further in their literary interpretation of ritual in tragedy than to assert the importance of the audience's cathartic confrontation with sacrificial death. Girard's substantial discussions of tragedy are problematic for the critic precisely because he is not offering a literary interpretation of the texts as they stand. Instead, as in his treatment of the *Bacchae,* he unmasks the play's mystification and transformation of the truths that actually dominate it. The *Oedipus Rex* does not in fact reach a Girardian resolution, since Oedipus himself, not the community, violently discovers and attempts to make himself a scapegoat; in the concluding scenes he has not left Thebes, and it remains unclear whether or when he will.[83] In the *Bacchae* the destruction of Pentheus is neither spontaneous (it is directed by the god) nor unanimous (only the women of the city perform the act). At the close of the play Thebes will not enjoy peace and order as a result of the establishing of the god's divinity but will continue to face additional dangerous external Dionysiac invasions. Indeed, owing to the presence of a foreign chorus that departs at the conclusion of the drama and to the infrequent appearance of Thebans other than Pentheus onstage, the city itself establishes little more than an illusory presence in the play. Hence the pity evoked for the house of Cadmus that so dominates these final scenes makes Dionysus' establishment of his divinity seem little short of disastrous.[84] In short, even if we were to agree that the Girardian scenario forms the implicit background to Greek myth and ritual, uncovering its traces in tragic

[82]Else 1967 weakens his case by de-emphasizing the role of the chorus and avoiding the ritual material in tragedy itself.

[83]On the failure of the *Oedipus Rex* to conform to the typical scapegoat pattern, see Howe 1962.

[84]On this point see Pucci 1977: 193–94 n. 15.

texts is a complex process and does not explain how and why a tragic poet, working within the limits of his genre and a particular cultural context, has chosen to present mythic and religious truth in specific tragic texts.

Yet the literary critic does not need confirmation of a historical connection between tragedy and sacrificial ritual (should such a thing be possible). Critics of Girard who complain that his texts derive not from history but from literature indirectly confirm the importance of his work for a study of tragedy. Indeed, the texts of the plays themselves offer the best, and perhaps the only solid, evidence that the concerns of the evolutionists are relevant to an understanding of Greek ritual in the classical period. Tragedy continually affirms a relation between ritual and drama and demonstrates a concern both with the often violent origins of cults and with the social and psychological effects of sacrificial violence. The notion among the Greeks that the gods are an ambivalent source of violence and order was, for example, pervasive and even axiomatic. For Heraclitus as well as for the poets, "violence [or war] is the father and king of all" (frag. 53 DK). For Aeschylus god made himself known through *charis biaios* (*Ag.* 182, violent grace, if the emended text is correct) and through learning by suffering, although the older poet has more respect for this divine violence than Euripides, who was apt to question it in the most shocking manner. A fragment of the tragic poet Critias (*Sisyphus* frag. 1 N) suggests that a wise man invented the gods to deter men from evil (*hopōs eie ti deima toisi kakoisi*). Euripides (unless, as some have thought, this fragment actually belongs to his own *Sisyphus,* not to that of Critias) does not, at least explicitly, go quite so far. In the *Iphigenia in Tauris,* for example, barbarians, not Greeks, attribute their own violence to the gods. As Iphigenia says of the Taurians' practice of sacrificing foreigners to Artemis (389–91):

> I think these people here, being murderers themselves, displace their own vice onto the goddess. I will not believe evil of the gods.

Yet Euripides also undercuts this patriotic view by reminding us that Iphigenia was herself nearly sacrificed to Artemis by Greeks, and the Greek cult of Artemis established in the final scene recalls for its participants the specter of human sacrifice underlying the more benign rite. The *Bacchae,* as Girard points out, does come close to presenting the establishment of god through mass violence. And in the *Heracles,* as we shall see, Euripides hints that Hera's transcendent spite masks Lycus' corrupt human politics, while the real nature of the gods transcends altogether such human limitations.

Greek poets consistently create the kind of social crisis that Girard describes before a sacrificial death and sometimes use a heroic sacrifice to resolve this crisis,[85] if not precisely in the manner that Girard might lead us to expect. Euripides' *Iphigenia in Aulis* and *Phoenissae* are cases in point. Thucydides, too, analyzed the Athenian plague and the Corcyrean revolt in terms that suit Girard's "sacrificial crisis." He linked the plague to the breakdown of the social and religious order, found the origin of revolution in mimetic rivalry and the ensuing lust for revenge, and identified the source of democratic instability in its lack of social differentiation and its willingness to make scapegoats of outstanding men.

In short, despite the well-documented claims by the structuralists that the procedures in the Greek sacrificial rite aim to efface violence, Greek poets use the sacrificial metaphor to confront and explore divine and human violence. Although the extant tragedies are hardly the Dionysiac drama that Guépin proposed for the origins of tragedy, Euripides does allow his plots to be structured by or around sacrifices. The conclusions of Euripides' plays in particular insistently link myth and actual cult practice, often stressing the origins of cult in sacrificial deaths and demanding that the audience make connections between tragic violence and daily experiences of sacrifice. The poets may, as Girard suggests, have been unwilling to pursue the implications of their views of gods and ritual to the ultimate possible conclusion: to declare the gods a fiction created by human violence and to give to all sacrifice an origin in human slaughter. Indeed, they had a stake in preserving a religious system in which their own drama played a central part. Yet of the three tragic poets, Euripides consistently comes closest to such dismantling of the divine superstructure, while simultaneously insisting on a restoration of ritual to a central place in the politically and socially unstable worlds he creates.

---

[85]See also Henrichs 1981, esp. 224, where he emphasizes the parallels between tragic and "historical" human sacrifices.

Evolutionist theories, by stressing the potential emotive effects on the observer of sacrifice as a ritual killing, and by considering what questions the rite might raise for such highly intellectual observers and participants in ritual as the Greek poets, also draw attention to the therapeutic effect of tragic violence on the audience. Tragedy indeed strives to understand or justify the deaths of its characters by provoking terror finally balanced by an ensuing release. In its preoccupation with social crises and disasters tragedy calls attention to its own violence and allows it to spill over into the community in a way that violates normal sacrificial procedure. Even the uplifting voluntary sacrifices of Euripidean youth are made to seem deceptive and wasteful in the shabby world in which they are performed. In the inverted world of tragedy, sacrificial deaths can produce *katharsis* through pity and fear for its victims even if an actual sacrificial ritual might produce an indifferent reaction to the animal victim. Indeed, the stress of the evolutionists on the cathartic experience of violence provoked by sacrificial death seems more apt for the deliberately aberrant human sacrifices of tragedy than for ritual practice in the classical period. At the same time, however, tragedy "ritualizes" and distances its sacrificial deaths by having them occur offstage and reported by messengers who mute or transform the violence of the murder by their own attitudes of pity, admiration, or anger.[86] Even Medea imbues her murder of the children with the aura of sacrifice before it occurs (1054). The literary critic must in fact recognize, first, that tragic sacrifices, although they drew originally and continued in part to draw on an external model, may operate in ways that are not precisely comparable to the real event to which they refer; and second, that the sacrificial metaphor had a complex independent development in tragic texts from Aeschylus to Euripides.[87] As we shall see, this independent literary development of the sacrificial metaphor leads Euripides to imply, especially in the *Heracles* and the *Bacchae,* that his tragedies function in a manner analogous to actual sacrifice. The remedies produced by a real sacrifice and the

[86]On this point see Pucci 1977, esp. 179–80.

[87]The development of the sacrificial metaphor from Aeschylus to Euripides is beyond the scope of this book. For the complex and unstable relation between tragic sacrifice and real sacrifice, see Pucci 1977 and 1980.

remedies generated by a poetic discourse that reenacts a sacrificial death have similar therapeutic effects.[88]

For the literary critic considering the use of the sacrificial metaphor in tragedy, important considerations remain. Structuralist and evolutionist theories of sacrifice can be said to complement each other only on the most general level. Both establish the importance of sacrifice and related rituals to Greek culture, and hence the potential importance of the sacrificial metaphor to tragedy. Both approaches assert that the ritual recognizes, uses, yet also serves to control in specific ways the killing of domestic animals, although for Burkert and Girard sacrificial violence immunizes the community against its own intestine aggression, whereas for the structuralists sacrifice serves to define what must be shut out from the civilized *polis*. Yet we have also seen that these theorists disagree strongly with one another on a wide range of issues, extending from the possibility of universal or cross-cultural descriptions of sacrifice to the difference between social and individual/psychological explanations of ritual. It is not useful for the literary critic of tragedy to attempt to resolve these differences or to side polemically with one viewpoint or the other. We cannot expect tragedy to reflect theoretical consistency on ritual, and in fact we shall see that it does not. In their use of the sacrificial metaphor, Euripides' plays often deliberately hint at several incompatible views of human society and divinity and close without definitely affirming any of them. Whereas theories about sacrifice can never by themselves successfully compel arguments about literary texts, we have already seen that both modes of analysis of ritual have helped to generate important questions about ritual in tragedy, although the critic must be more wary in applying the insights of the evolutionists. Furthermore, our concern with tragic *representation* of *human* sacrifice, rather than with actual ritual, necessitates the eclectic use of modern theory adopted in the remaining chapters.

The major questions addressed in the following chapters concern the relation between Euripides' use of ritual and his larger poetic strategies. Despite references to a large number of sacrificial deaths in the Euripidean corpus, there is no attempt to be compre-

[88]Pucci 1977, esp. 165 and 169.

hensive. Instead, each of the remaining chapters confines itself to close examination of one of the poet's four late plays for the issues each raises concerning ritual and drama in its larger social and intellectual context.[89] All four plays present sacrificial deaths in a ritual setting as the central moment in the drama. The *Iphigenia in Aulis* and the *Phoenissae* are the most important examples of sacrificial actions involving a youth's voluntary self-sacrifice for a society in crisis. Euripides apparently favored this folktale plot, which is not found in the extant works of other Greek dramatists, to exploit its potential ironies. Here the ritual experience of women and children, who are excluded from political participation, offers an apparent cure for the political crises produced by men and forges unexpected links between public and private worlds. The plays stress the disparity between a political world riven by strife and a ritual world (characterized especially by sacrificial performance, marriage, and lament and reflected in the poetry of the choral odes) that offers an alternative vision of social unity and order. Each play also emphasizes that its current "sacrificial crisis" has a long and consistent history that threatens repetition in the present: youth will destroy itself to appease the curse of civilization. Ritual here mediates in complex and often ironic ways between the divine and human realms, opens moments of communication between political reality and the mythic tradition presented in a connected cycle of choral songs, makes ritual a temporary model for action, and to some degree incorporates the benefits of poetry and the sacred into the profane world.

The *Bacchae* and the *Heracles* serve as examples of plots in which divine vengeance demands an involuntary sacrificial death. Here the sacrificial death(s) also become, as in the *Electra,* a perverted song, *agōn,* and festival. The entire public system of ritual in the *polis,* the function of the tragic chorus, and the poetic tradition

[89]Leaving aside the fragmentary plays, of the plays that focus on a central sacrificial death, the motif in the *Electra* was discussed earlier in this chapter; *Medea* has been well discussed by Pucci 1980; Alcestis' sacrificial death (74–76) has no sacrificial setting; and some aspects of the *Iphigenia in Tauris,* in which the sacrificial death never occurs, are treated in Chapter 2; see Wolff 1963, Sansone 1975, and Strachan 1976 on the sacrificial motif in the *IT.* The happy resolution of these last two plays, which nevertheless need further analysis, puts them in a different category.

upon which Euripides drew to create his plays stand in jeopardy. These two plays create a fundamental social and poetic crisis and close with the emergence of a new order which makes survival possible, but at a cost so unbearable that their endings have been read as simply ironic or self-deluding. Here the "sacrificial crisis" also entails an explosive confrontation between men and god in which the normal limits between the divine and human worlds collapse simultaneously with the whole political environment, as the poet hints at the kind of identity Girard draws between divine and human violence. Both plays conclude ambiguously with a redefinition of the divine and its relation to men, marked by a restoration of ritual or the establishment of a new cult. Finally, both plays draw a new kind of attention to an overlap between ritual and tragic theater. Ritual, like tragic theater, involves staging, symbolic gestures, dressing up, and role-playing. Both ritual and drama may offer an experience of liminality that establishes or confirms links between past and present, individual and society, as well as among man, god, and nature.[90] Ritual performance may incorporate myth into everyday life, whereas tragic performances implicitly bring mythical tradition into a vital and often restorative confrontation with the politics of democracy. Euripides tries to link his plays with the special ability of ritual to be repetitious and effective in the real world. Yet tragedy ultimately transcends ritual in its capacity to confront ambiguously and with historical consciousness both the fictions upon which the social order is based, and individual identity and suffering.

In each of the four plays, then, ritual does, as it logically should, become the point at which communication occurs between the divine and human realms, between public and private worlds, between past and present, and between myth or choral lyric and a more secular interpretation of events given in the iambic scenes. The model of social relations implicit in sacrifice—timeless, authoritative, efficacious, expressive, and self-contained—is placed in ironic juxtaposition with a historical disorder in the political realm. Finally, both ritual and myth offer similar kinds of fictions and deceptions that aid man in ordering his life, in coming to terms

[90]See Turner 1969 on liminal states of ritual.

[63]

with suffering, and in learning to make difficult and irreversible transitions such as those involved in birth, initiation, marriage, and death.[91] Whereas Electra's fictive rituals and Iphigenia's choice for sacrifice in the *Iphigenia in Aulis* may be self-deceptive, Helen in the *Helen* and Iphigenia in the *Iphigenia in Tauris,* for example, invent rituals that aim both at the fulfillment of a divine plan and at a constructive escape from the disaster of a crippling past. The references to cult that close Euripides' tragedies offer the audience the opportunity to reenact and to reconsider perpetually both the remedies offered by myth and the disasters heroically faced by the tragic protagonists. Tragedy and ritual are linked by a common claim to offer therapy and immortality, despite a reality that may be incommensurable with them.[92] Whatever the costs to the characters in the dramas, citizens can bring the heroism of Heracles or Alcestis into their lives through festival and hero cult. The remaining chapters examine the ways in which Euripides, in his involvement with ritual, is simultaneously ironic, theologically iconoclastic, and intensely religious. Even more important, Euripides' poetic imagination is formed by his experience of and response to a ritual culture. Above all, then, our concerns here are to understand how the sacrificial metaphor shapes and becomes an intrinsic part of Euripides' dramaturgy as a whole.

[91]On sacrifice as an irreversible transformation, see Burkert 1972: 50. On ritual as a source of learning and necessary deception, see esp. Wolff 1963 and 1965.
[92]Discussions of tragedy's claim to therapeutic effect have been popular since Aristotle. For recent treatments see esp. Pucci 1977 and Simon 1978: 122–54.

]2[

The *Iphigenia in Aulis*

The voluntary sacrifice of young people to save family or city or nation in a situation of social crisis (usually war) is a common theme in Euripides.[1] Besides Iphigenia in the *Iphigenia in Aulis,* other examples are Polyxena in the *Hecuba,* Macaria in the *Heracleidae,* Menoeceus in the *Phoenissae,* and, in the lost plays, the daughter (ultimately daughters) of Erechtheus and Praxithea in the *Erechtheus* and Phrixus in the *Phrixus.* These voluntary sacrificial deaths share several features. The victim is always a virgin, usually a young woman. The sacrifice is made as an act of piety in response to a supernatural command or pronouncement voiced by an oracle, prophet, or ghost. Generally the kin of the victim attempt to dissuade the young person from obeying the supernatural

A shorter and somewhat different version of this chapter was published as Foley 1982b.

[1]On voluntary sacrificial action in Euripides, see Schmitt 1921, Roussel 1922, Strohm 1957: 50–63, Burnett 1971: 22–26, and Vellacott 1975: 178–204. I refer here exclusively to voluntary sacrificial actions that involve the ritual slaying of virgins in times of social crisis, and not to the voluntary acceptance of death or suicide by adults, as in the case of Megara in the *Heracles,* Evadne in the *Suppliants,* or Pylades in the *IT.* Human sacrifice at times of social crisis was threatened and reported actually to have occurred at rare moments in Greek history. On this question, including a discussion of the Iphigenia myth, see Henrichs 1981. Accordingly, the voluntary sacrifices of tragedy must be understood as primarily fictional, an opportunity for the victims to express an active choice for *aretē* and *eukleia* despite the resistance of their near relations (on these aspects of voluntary sacrifice, see especially Strohm). On animal sacrifices before battle, see the discussion of Pritchett 1971: 109–115 and 1979: 83–90 with further bibliography.

command, thereby sharpening for the audience the conflict between the interests of family and city. Frequently, the assertion of the victim's determination to die is followed by farewells, departure, and a messenger's account of the heroic death. In each case, however, the dramatic context in which the sacrifice occurs creates special problems for the interpretation of this ultimate act of heroic resignation and/or piety and devotion to family or community. The focus on the innocent victim intensifies sympathy for his or her noble death, but the cause for which the victim dies is frequently dubious and the consequences of the ritual death are often ambiguous.

In the *Iphigenia in Aulis,* performed posthumously with his *Alcmaion* and *Bacchae* in 405, Euripides expands the motif of the voluntary sacrifice of an innocent youth to form the basis for and climax of an entire dramatic action. This expansion of the motif is only one of the apparently unique features of the voluntary sacrificial action in the play. Iphigenia dies not to save a threatened city or family, but for a Panhellenic war that has not yet begun and apparently does not have to be undertaken. In Calchas' prophecy Artemis demands the sacrifice of Iphigenia only *if* the expedition is to be undertaken. The sacrifice closes the play and clearly achieves its purpose: the Greek army can now depart for Troy. The plot develops without any obvious divine interference, and Iphigenia's heroic decision returns the myth to its traditional course and thus serves the function of the typical deus ex machina.[2] Yet the text makes clear that the cause for which the sacrifice is made, Helen and the Trojan war, is a dubious one. It is uncertain whether the play closed with the substitution of a deer for Iphigenia and an apparent translation of the girl to divine status, reported by a messenger; with the appearance of Artemis on the machine to make a similar point; or only with Iphigenia's assertion that she should not be mourned in the fashion traditional to other such sacrificial victims. In all three cases the play affirms a divine status for its heroine markedly different from her known predecessors.[3]

[2]For a recent discussion of Iphigenia's role as a deus ex machina, see Schreiber 1963: 57–60. See Chapter 3 on Menoeceus' similar role.
[3]A fragment of Euripides' *Erechtheus* promises divine honors to the king's sacrificed daughter and her sisters, but this promise occurs after their deaths, whereas

The major difficulty for interpreters of the play is how to evaluate Iphigenia's final idealistic conversion to self-sacrifice.[4] On the one hand are the dubious cause for which the war is fought and the rhetoric and tone of the action before the final scenes: the ever-increasing lust (*erōs*) for violence (*eris*) in the Greek army, the vacillations and self-serving motives of Agamemnon and Menelaus as leaders of the expedition, the pomposity of the future war hero Achilles, and the fiercely personal outlook of Clytemnestra. The heroine barely manages to escape the terrible involuntary sacrifice described as her lot in Aeschylus' *Agamemnon* and a virtual lynching by an enraged mob. On the other hand are the beautiful meditations on love and war, marriage and sacrifice, presented in the choral odes. Scholars have generally considered that these odes have little relation to the action or relevance to an interpretation of the play. Yet Iphigenia, as she explains and justifies her idealistic change of mind and accepts her sacrifice, appears to bridge the gap between the action and the lyrics. Is the ending, then, either ironic or a burst of pure and cleansing heroism, or both? Problems in the text compound the difficulties of interpretation since the exact contents of the prologue, exodus, and several intervening passages are dubious at best. Of necessity, then, any reading of the text remains speculative.

The structure of the *Iphigenia* hangs on the performance of a sacrificial ritual that is disguised for a large part of the action as a

---

Iphigenia hints at this possibility before her sacrifice. See Austin 1968: frag. 65 = Papyrus de la Sorbonne 2328.

[4]Positive readings of the *IA* tend to celebrate Iphigenia's exercise of free will and acquisition of knowledge; ironic readings tend to emphasize the corrupt world of the play. As with many late Euripidean plays, the ambiguity is almost certainly deliberate. For a summary of older views, see the judicious discussion of Conacher 1967a, esp. 264. Among relatively recent views, those of Garzya 1962, Snell 1968, Strohm 1957: 50–63 passim and 137–46, and Arrowsmith (introduction to Merwin and Dimock 1978) make the strongest case for a positive reading of the sacrifice. Arrowsmith and Strohm emphasize Iphigenia's heroic exercise of free will, and Garzya her isolated moral superiority to the world of the play. Snell stresses the philosophical tone of Euripides' late plays and the movement from moral disorientation to a new idealism and determined action. Cavander 1973, Dimock in Merwin and Dimock 1978, and Vellacott 1975 focus on the overwhelming effect of the atmosphere of uncontrolled violence and political corruption in the play.

fictitious marriage rite. As is increasingly the case in Euripides' later tragedies, ritual and action become one; the sacrificial ritual becomes the organizing principle of the plot. Why does Euripides expand the two motifs of the sacrifice of Iphigenia and her ficti- tious marriage with Achilles, both mere footnotes in the previous tradition, until they dominate the play? Why does he emphasize continually the homologies between the two rites? A close exam- ination of this neglected aspect of the text offers a useful starting point for an analysis of the complex counterpoint between the choral lyrics and the action culminating in the sacrificial death of Iphigenia. The discussion will proceed in four stages. The first section analyzes the intertwining of sacrifice and marriage in the action of the play; the second considers the treatment of these same themes in the odes. The third section examines the intersection of marriage and sacrifice in Greek society and literature to clarify the social, religious, and literary background of Iphigenia's self-sacri- fice. The final section briefly considers the ritual and poetic syn- thesis of marriage and sacrifice in its ironic political context. As a whole the discussion shows how Iphigenia's sacrifice is first dis- guised as marriage, then unmasked and actually transformed into a real marriage, only to be undertaken finally as a combined mar- riage/self-sacrifice meant to redress Helen's perversion of her mar- riage to Menelaus. From this perspective, Iphigenia's sacrifice is not, as many critics have argued, a sudden, inexplicable fluke, but a well-motivated resolution of the play's social and political con- flicts by way of confirmed analogies in ritual and myth between marriage and sacrifice.

The Intertwining of Rituals:
Marriage and Sacrifice

The ruse of marriage to Achilles that Agamemnon uses to lure Iphigenia to Aulis was known to Euripides from the epic tradition. The poet, however, may well have invented the presence of Cly- temnestra and the deception of Achilles to elaborate on and com- plicate a traditional motif.[5] But what is even more striking in

[5]For a summary of treatments of the myth before Euripides, see Conacher 1967a: 250–53, Schreiber 1963: 66–71, and Henrichs 1981: 198–203.

Euripides' version is that the false marriage motif is expanded until it shares a nearly equal place with that of the sacrifice. Both the marriage and the war require a preliminary sacrifice (*proteleia*) to Artemis. In the early scenes of the play, while Iphigenia and Clytemnestra are still deceived as to the real purpose of Iphigenia's summons to Aulis, Euripides plays on the common details of these two rites, which have, at least superficially, a mutually exclusive aim: marriage is the happy prelude to a new life and procreation, whereas sacrifice ends in death. But by the end of the play Iphigenia against all expectation unites the two rituals. She becomes a sacrifice to Artemis and a bride, not of Hades, but of all Greece. As Cavander has suggested, "The whole play, in fact, is a grotesque wedding celebration, with the Chorus as attendants."[6] The constant repetition of ritual detail in the context of deception apparently undermines the meaning and purpose of both rites. Yet it is this very emphasis on the shared aspects of the rituals that ultimately uncovers an intrinsic harmony in the structure and purpose of marriage and sacrifice and makes possible the final transformation. In the closing scenes Iphigenia ecstatically repeats this same ritual detail in an attempt, by her acceptance of her marriage/sacrifice, to restore positive significance to Greece's political adventures and its social and religious life.

Because Clytemnestra says that she put the marriage wreath on her daughter's head (905), we know that from the moment of Iphigenia's entrance the ambiguities of her situation are plainly visible: the victim of a sacrifice, as well as a bride, is wreathed before the beginning of the ritual. If the text is correct, a messenger precedes her arrival and immediately announces to Agamemnon, the leader of all the Greeks (414), that the "ceremony" can begin: "Begin bringing round the baskets, wreathe your head . . . make ready the marriage hymn . . . let the flute play in the house and let the beat of feet in dance begin. For this day comes as blessed to the virgin" (435–39). All these procedures except the joyous song and dance are common to both sacrifice and the initial rites of marriage. Linguistic factors and the heavy irony of the messenger's

[6]Cavander 1973: 13–14; see also 82. Schmitt 1921: 82–83 emphasizes the intertwining of marriage and sacrifice in the first scene between Agamemnon and Iphigenia.

request have caused commentators to excise this passage.[7] Yet a transitional scene is necessary to motivate Agamemnon's decision to sacrifice Iphigenia rather than to abandon the expedition to save her, and the ironic use of ritual language is consistent with the rest of the action. The use of the otherwise later Greek verb *protelizō*, meaning to initiate or consecrate by a ceremony, including sacrifice, preliminary to a marriage (*Artemidi protelizousi tēn neanida, / Aulidos anassēi*, 433–34), is not merely technically precise. It also anticipates the use of the noun *proteleia* in later scenes and effectively recalls the repeated and ironic use of the same term in Aeschylus' *Agamemnon*,[8] where Iphigenia's *proteleia* is linked to the first deaths at Troy and to the corruption of the marriage ritual by Helen and Paris (see *Ag.* 65, 227, 720). Iphigenia is to become a "preliminary sacrifice." The crucial question raised in both plays is: preliminary to what other ritual or action? Yet the *IA* expands this preliminary moment until it gains a completeness and a surprising independent significance of its own.

The messenger goes on to evoke a lyrical picture of the women waiting in a meadow just outside the camp. Iphigenia's sacrifice also occurs in a meadow sacred to Artemis (1463). In the literary tradition the image of the meadow is particularly associated with a virgin just before a rape or marriage.[9] And in the archetypal case of Persephone, her rape by Hades, god of the impenetrable underworld, leads also to a form of symbolic death. The arrival of Iphigenia in a chariot may simultaneously evoke the ominous arrivals for a sacrificial death of Agamemnon and Cassandra at Argos in Aeschylus' *Agamemnon,* or of Clytemnestra in Euripides' own *Electra;* but it also suggests the image, popular in the fine arts, of the wreathed bride departing in a chariot for her husband's home, accompanied by a *numphagōgos* (escort of the bride to the

---

[7]On the case for treating the messenger scene at 414–39 as an interpolation, see esp. England 1891 ad loc. and Page 1934: 152–54. On the other hand, most commentators agree that a scene similar to this must have occurred here for the reasons given in my text. For the importance of a scene similar if not identical to this, see esp. Cavander 1973: 99.

[8]On the use of the term *proteleia* in the *Agamemnon,* see esp. Lebeck 1971: 10, 48, and 68–73 and Zeitlin 1965: 465–67.

[9]On the complex and multifaceted image of the meadow in ancient Greek literature, see Motte 1973.

groom's house, 610) and greeted on arrival by female contemporaries.[10] (The word *numphagōgos* normally describes a man, but in the unusual circumstances of this play it is used to refer to Clytemnestra.[11]) In all three plays the occupants of the chariot are prepared to celebrate a festive occasion and are deceived as to the sacrificial death awaiting them. In each case they are greeted emphatically as royal, and much is made over the process of disembarkation.[12] But in the *IA* the occupants are pure of guilt, and the scene becomes a domesticated and more pitiful version of its predecessors.

In the moving first scene between Iphigenia and her father the text (despite its uncertainties) calls attention to the deceptively similar preliminaries to marriage and war by stressing the detail of the sacrifice common to both. The scene emphasizes the motif, popular in both poetry and vase paintings, of marriage as a rite of passage, a transition from a blissful girlhood presided over by loving parents to an unknown life with a man she has not met.[13] Iphigenia's playful pretense of ignorance as to the purpose for which she was brought to Troy reinforces our sense of her anxiety at the coming separation from her family; Agamemnon plays the role of a fond father suffering over the coming departure of a favorite daughter in marriage (668–80):

Iph. Shall I sail on this voyage with mother or alone?

Ag. Alone. Separated from father and mother.

Iph. You won't have me live in the homes of others, father?

Ag. Let this alone. It is not right for young girls to know such things.

[10]For general treatments of the procedures in Greek wedding ritual, see esp. Collignon 1904, Erdmann 1934: 250–66, Magnien 1936, Sutton 1981, and Redfield 1982. Sutton's chapter on marriage contains an up-to-date summary of the artistic evidence for Athens insofar as the vase paintings depict both men and women.

[11]On the use of the term *numphagōgos*, which normally refers to a male but may have had a more general application, see Erdmann 1934: 257, esp. n. 91. The bride's mother often accompanied the marriage cart on foot on its journey to the new household.

[12]Textual problems make the exact nature of this greeting scene in the *IA* uncertain.

[13]See van Gennep 1960 (1909); Sutton 1981, esp. 146–48, 151–52, and 158; and my discussion later in this chapter.

Iph. Hurry back from Troy to me, having put right things there, father.
Ag. First I must sacrifice a certain sacrifice here.
Iph. With holy rites [or victims] one must revere the holy.
Ag. You will see it. For you will stand near the holy water.
Iph. Then shall we start the dances around the altar, father?
Ag. I envy you for the ignorance I do not have. Go inside—young girls should not be seen—and give me a kiss and your hand, since you are about to live apart for so long from your father.

The ironic play on ritual continues in the dialogue immediately afterward between Clytemnestra and Agamemnon (718–21):

Κλ. προτέλεια δ' ἤδη παιδὸς ἔσφαξας θεᾷ;
Αγ. μέλλω 'πὶ ταύτῃ καὶ καθέσταμεν τύχῃ.
Κλ. κἄπειτα δαίσεις τοὺς γάμους ἐς ὕστερον;
Αγ. θύσας γε θύμαθ' ἃ ἐμὲ χρὴ θῦσαι θεοῖς.

Clyt. And the *proteleia*, have you already sacrificed for our child to Artemis?
Ag. I am about to. We are just on the point of doing so.
Clyt. And then shall you hold the marriage feast later?
Ag. When I have sacrificed the sacrifice I should sacrifice to the gods.

The ironic disparity between the perspectives of the two characters is underlined by the alliteration of 721 (also 722) and the word order of 718, which ominously juxtaposes *paidos* and *esphaxas*. Clytemnestra then domesticizes the scene further by insisting, almost to the point of comedy, on her role as the bride's mother. She worries about the performance of the *proteleia* (718), the wedding banquet (722), her role as torchbearer in the ceremony (732), and the lineage of the groom (695–96). She is horrified that Agamemnon intends to deprive her of her traditional role as torchbearer (734–36) and that the wedding banquet for the women must take place by the ships (722–24).[14] Agamemnon responds to this domestic tone by turning Peleus' traditional capture of his bride

[14]On the woman's role as torchbearer, see Sutton 1981: 192–93, Erdmann 1934: 258, and the scholiasts on Euripides' *Phoenissae* 344 and *Troades* 315.

Thetis into a proper marriage with *enguēsis* or engagement (*Zeus ēnguēse kai didōs' ho kurios*, 703). Clytemnestra's daughter will marry a very well-brought-up young man (709–10).

The deception and the light tone continue briefly in the ensuing scene between Clytemnestra and Achilles. Clytemnestra at first takes her future son-in-law's negative reaction to her warm greeting as an extreme form of the *aidōs* appropriate to a well-educated young man in the presence of women. She is deprived of her illusions about the marriage by the old man, whose loyalty to her is pointedly based on his having been a *sunnumphokomos* (48), a part of her dowry from Tyndareus (860). Yet she still tries to appeal to Achilles for help for herself and Iphigenia on the basis of the fictional engagement. Though the engagement was fictional—Achilles' name alone was committed—he is nevertheless compromised. As Roussel has argued, Achilles in this scene essentially accepts his role as Iphigenia's bridegroom and as the future *kurios* of the bride.[15] In Greek marriage the *enguēsis*, the agreement over the marriage between the groom and the father of the bride, was tantamount to marriage and a binding agreement even without the marriage ceremony. When Achilles says at 940, *hagnon d' ouket' esti sōm' emon*, "my body in no longer pure," he almost certainly means that the false marriage has compromised his status as an unmarried man. This point is important for two reasons. Achilles, by agreeing to act as Iphigenia's bridegroom, has complicated the sacrifice plan and undertaken a binding role in conflict with his myth, that is, with his fate at Troy. Second, the audience may be reminded here that sacrificial victims should be pure, that is, unmarried. In the *Phoenissae* Haimon could not be sacrificed for the city because of his engagement to Antigone (*Phoen.* 944–46). Roussel also invokes the "historical" example of Aristodemus (Pausanias 4.9.2–10), whose sacrifice of a daughter is blocked by a Messenian who claims an *enguēsis* to her. The audience might also presume, given Iphigenia's entrance as a wreathed bride, that she had already performed part of the marriage ritual, such as the dedication of her childhood toys to the gods and the farewell to the gods of her father's hearth. As the fictional marriage between Achilles and Iphigenia takes on an ever-

[15]Roussel 1915, esp. 240–44.

increasing reality, Agamemnon's determination to sacrifice her becomes even more dubious, for Iphigenia's status as an appropriately
virginal victim is by implication technically compromised along
with the traditional plot.

In the second scene between husband and wife, Agamemnon
continues with this fiction of the *proteleia* for marriage (1111–13):

> The lustral waters are prepared and the barley for throwing on the
> purifying fire and the victims, which must fall before marriage to the
> goddess.

With a typically Euripidean wordplay on *onoma* (speech) and *ergon*
(reality), Clytemnestra challenges his fiction (1115–16) and rup-
tures the deceptive coherence between the fictional marriage and
the sacrifice (1146–47):

> ἄκουε δή νυν˙ ἀνακαλύψω γὰρ λόγους,
> κοὐκέτι παρῳδοῖς χρησόμεσθ᾽ αἰνίγμασιν.

> Hear me now. For I shall unveil my meaning and abandon obscure
> and riddling speech.

We cannot be certain of the meaning of the word *paroidos,* which I
translate as "obscure" (*LSJ* gives "obscurely hinting," "singing
indirectly"; England, "distorted" or "distorting"), since it is the
only occurrence of the word before Aristotle. But Euripides seems
here to be calling attention to the doubleness of the language used
so far in the play by allowing Clytemnestra a striking word to say
in effect, "You cannot use words with two referents anymore,
Agamemnon." Hence this speech marks the crisis in the ritual
language of the play, as the deceptive coherence between marriage
and sacrifice openly breaks.

Clytemnestra now reveals that this is Agamemnon's second
crime against a child of hers. Euripides invents for Clytemnestra a
first marriage with Tantalus; this marriage had produced a child
that Agamemnon murdered when he took the unwilling Clytemnestra, by trickery, as a bride. Until this moment Clytemnestra
has nevertheless played the proper wife. Here Euripides ignores

the hereditary curse on the family of Atreus and locates past violence pointedly in the institution of marriage. The play also stresses that Helen's betrayal of her marriage inaugurated the threat to the institution and provided a cause for a war with the barbarians; Aeschylus in the *Agamemnon,* in contrast, emphasizes Paris' breach of hospitality as the primary cause of the war. Agamemnon's action now renews the threat to a marriage made originally, like Helen's, under the shadow of violence. Agamemnon says that at the occasion of Helen's marriage Tyndareus used the ruse of the oath taken by the suitors to forestall temporarily a disastrous outbreak of reciprocal hostility and allowed Helen to choose a husband wherever the winds of passion swept her (*IA* 69); the use of wind imagery here perhaps further links Helen's marriage with Iphigenia's dilemma and the present windlessness at Aulis.

At this point in the play, then, Agamemnon's ruse is exposed, the pathetic and domestic tone of these "wedding" scenes has won much sympathy for the innocent Iphigenia, Achilles is committed to the marriage and not to the sacrifice, and the entanglement of, and identity between, the two motifs appears irresolvable. The problem is compounded in the following scene, when Achilles is seized with a genuine *erōs* for his bride (1410–11). Iphigenia may also, as she blushingly observes Achilles for the first time and hears of his heroic willingness to sacrifice himself in her defense, be moved to act by an emerging love for the young hero.[16] Euripides' staging here perhaps reflects an increasing Athenian romanticization of wedding scenes also depicted on contemporary vase paintings, in which a youthful groom and a shy bride gaze at each other under the influence of a winged Eros.[17]

In the end Iphigenia abruptly interrupts the stichomythia with a speech masterful in its formal structure and rhetoric.[18] She tran-

---

[16]For the most recent treatment of the romantic implications of this scene, see Smith 1979.

[17]See Sutton 1981, esp. 164, 177, and 184–88.

[18]For a discussion of the rhetoric of Iphigenia's speech, see Schmitt 1921: 39–41, and for a summary of the interpretative controversies on this speech, see Schreiber 1963, esp. 44–49. The formal structure of the speech alone helps to counter the views of critics such as Funke 1964, who see Iphigenia here as confused or as hypnotized by her father's rhetoric (on this point see also Snell 1968: 498). For a detailed criticism of Funke, see Mellert-Hoffmann 1969: 68–90, esp. 85.

scends the dilemma created by the entanglement between the fictional marriage become almost real and the sacrifice needed to inaugurate the war. Echoed in detail by both the chorus and the final messenger (if the text is genuine), she welcomes each detail of the sacrificial rite as if she were indeed entering upon a marriage. At her entrance she was crowned as a bride by her mother; now, like Macaria,[19] she is to be crowned as a victim (1477–79):

> Distribute wreaths. Here is my hair to crown. Bring holy water for washing.

As the voluntary sacrificial victims in Euripides often claim, Iphigenia asserts that her act will be for her *paides, gamoi,* and *doxa* (children, marriage, and reputation, 1398–99). She will offer *kleos* (fame) to her mother as a compensation for her death (1440). Her subsequent directions, however, are atypical. She insists that the chorus dance in celebration for her (1480–81) in Artemis' meadow (1463), as she planned to do herself at her own *proteleia* for the marriage with Achilles (676). She commands her mother not to perform the traditional mourning and burial of the sacrificial victim, but to sing a paean (1437–38, 1442, 1467–69). Paeans could be sung and/or danced on the occasions of marriages, battles, or banquets either as a gesture of thanks for an evil avoided or as propitiation of the protective deities par excellence, Artemis and Apollo.[20] The paean here seems to retain this ambiguity of occasion and function: at a marriage or at the inauguration of battle, for celebration or propitiation.

The sacrificial altar of Artemis will substitute for Iphigenia's tomb (1444). Earlier she was doomed to be a bride of Hades (460–61, 540, 1278), an image typically used of female sacrificial victims in tragedy. Now she gives her body not to Achilles or Hades, but

---

[19]For the wreathing of Macaria, see *Heracleidae* 529; for the sacrifice as an equivalent of children and a source of *kleos,* see *Heracleidae* 591–92 and 534; and for Macaria's request for burial, also made by Polyxena in the *Hecuba* but not by Iphigenia, see 588–89. Macaria also models her act on the bravery of her father and love for her brothers. Polyxena sacrifices herself voluntarily as a gesture of freedom by one who is now a slave. The motif of the wreath and the winning of *kleos* are absent in her case.

[20]See Calame 1977: I, 147–52.

to Greece and to Artemis (1395–97). By refusing a tomb she suggests, at least, the possibility of survival or deification.[21] Iphigenia formally rejects marriage with Achilles and accepts her role as sacrificial victim in order to make the war possible and thus to save Greek marriage from the barbarian threat. She will not allow Achilles to fight for her *sōma* (body) as the Greeks will for Helen's (1417–20). If she is motivated by an emerging *erōs*, it is the controlled *erōs* appropriate to marriage, which the chorus celebrated earlier in the second stasimon (543–89), not the uncontrolled passion that swept Helen into a marriage first with Menelaus, then with Paris. Iphigenia acts for marriage and claims that she will receive its equivalent in recompense for her action. She departs exhorting her mother to mend her marital quarrel with Agamemnon (1454), whose action she calls involuntary (1456). Indeed, she brings to her acceptance of the sacrifice much of the form and content of her lost marriage, and her imagination has undoubtedly been stimulated and shaped by her preparations for it. The structural overlap between the two rites, so insistent throughout the plot, thus survives in the finale, with its strange mixture of violence, joyous submission, and a movement to a new existence that her mother should not mourn.[22]

In the beginning Agamemnon invents a false marriage in order to accomplish an involuntary and unpropitious sacrifice of his daughter. The early scenes, by playing on the formal similarities between the two rites, emphasize his cruel deception. The middle scenes, although they expose the fiction of the marriage, ironically make this fiction so real a possibility that the entire myth of the Trojan war stands in jeopardy. Achilles is about to subvert his talents to a private rather than a public cause. He envies Greece his bride (1406). In a final shift the false marriage becomes the basis for the resolution of the conflict and the return to the myth. In this scene, then, Iphigenia is not, as some critics have argued, merely mesmerized by fear and the rhetoric of her father into accepting

[21]*Sesōismai* in 1440 may also, as England 1891 points out on his line 1441, ironically anticipate Iphigenia's rescue by Artemis.

[22]On the relation between the separation of mother and daughter and that of Demeter and Persephone, see Cavander 1973: 8 and 13 and my discussion later in this chapter.

her self-sacrifice.[23] Instead she makes the sacrifice voluntary and propitious and psychologically acceptable to herself by visualizing it as marriage. If the final scenes are genuine, she tames unbridled *erōs* and *eris*, then goes to her death untouched by hostile hands. Whereas Helen has destroyed her marriage, Iphigenia makes her act a sacrifice for marriage, a means of reconciling her parents and of restoring *erōs* to its proper place. The *eris* of the army, which was exploding in *stasis* (sedition) and an uncontrolled surge toward a ritual lynching, is redirected to war. As Plato claims (*Rep.* 470b), war is the opposite of *stasis*, internal violence such as we see in later scenes of the play, where Achilles' own Myrmidons are the first to turn against him when he attempts to defend Iphigenia (1351–53). In contrast, war channels internal violence outward by ritualizing and subduing it to serve an ostensibly rational cause.[24] Through her extravagant merging of marriage and sacrifice, Iphigenia thus resolves the conflict between civilized feeling and private interest, which would deny her death, and political reality—the conflict between marriage, a private institution, and sacrifice, at first a private ritual for marriage but finally a *proteleia* to serve the interests of the community. The reason for the repeated, ironic emphasis on ritual detail in the play now becomes clear; out of ironic disparity there emerges a desperate source of salvation. The restoration of sacrifice and marriage, rituals shared by all Greeks despite their political differences, is tantamount to a symbolic restoration and definition of Panhellenic culture.

The Choral Odes: The Panhellenic Perspective of Epic and Epithalamium

The choral odes, which focus exclusively on the themes of marriage, war, and sacrifice, form a connected cycle of songs that reflect and extend in lyric form the tensions created in the ritual

---

[23]See note 18 above. For the dramatic preparation for Iphigenia's change of mind, which Aristotle found unmotivated, see Knox 1966. For an excellent discussion of the intense psychological relation between Iphigenia and her father, see Green 1979, esp. 154, 158, 179, 184.

[24]See Bataille 1962, esp. 64 and 76; and Vernant 1980: 25.

language of the play. As in many other late Euripidean plays, the chorus is detached from the action by being composed of foreigners—in this case young Chalcidian matrons who have come to sightsee at Aulis—and the relevance of their songs to the action is oblique. At the same time their greater detachment from the action allows them to offer a more public and Panhellenic perspective on it,[25] and the separate poetic sphere that emerges in their lyrics creates a strong pressure for a return to the traditional epic version of the Trojan war. This pressure is relieved by gestures made by Iphigenia and, to a lesser degree, Achilles and (whether or not he speaks truthfully) Agamemnon. The idealistic perspective and themes presented in these odes are precisely those adopted in Iphigenia's final lyrics.

The parodos, as many scholars have observed, has a strong Homeric flavor. To the eyes of the chorus, the army of Greeks is composed of demigods or *hēmitheoi* (172–73). This term, almost nonexistent in Homer, looks beyond epic diction to the role of these heroes in Greek cults, and hence may serve subtly to prepare for the later claim to divine status by Iphigenia herself.[26] Most of the major heroes of the Trojan war are here surveyed as they engage in orderly and beautiful activities. A catalogue of names closes with a detailed look at the brilliant Achilles, decorated with a string of epic epithets, winning a race. The ode looks backward to the causes of the war and the story of Paris and Helen, and forward by implication to Iphigenia's sacrifice, for the grove of Artemis is called *poluthuton* (abounding in sacrifices, 185).[27] Even without the disputed catalogue of ships that recalls *Iliad* 2.493–760,[28] this ode suggests the opening movements of a Trojan epic. It comes immediately after the prologue, in which Agamemnon is attempting to undo the war by preventing the sacrifice of his daughter. The epic tone of the ode creates a strong counterpressure for a return to past myth and a more glorious world than that of the *stasis*-ridden army and its leadership presented up to this point

[25]On this point see Mellert-Hoffmann 1969, chap. 1.

[26]See Nagy 1979: 159–61 on *hēmitheoi* in epic diction (Iliad 12.22–23) and in cult.

[27]England 1891 cites Vitelli as the first to notice the ironic and anticipatory quality of this adjective.

[28]Textual problems make this section of the ode difficult to read with certainty.

in the play. The impressionability of the blushing young women also prepares for the effect Achilles apparently has on Iphigenia, when the embarrassed and sheltered girl sees the hero for the first time. The chorus creates an expectation for a heroic Achilles, and it is important to remember that the Achilles whom Iphigenia sees is precisely the armored, larger-than-life hero of the parodos, not the more complex figure who appears in the scene with Clytemnestra.

The first stasimon (543–89) comes between the scene in which Agamemnon tells Menelaus that he now must sacrifice Iphigenia, and the first meeting of Agamemnon, Iphigenia, and Clytemnestra. It deals with the nature of *erōs* and the roles appropriate to each sex. Immoderate *erōs*, like that of Helen, leads to *eris*. The women of the chorus yearn instead for the good *erōs*, that self-controlled, moderate love appropriate for young married women like themselves. They praise good education and *aidōs* (modesty). Women should hunt *areta* (moral excellence) in the concealed sphere of love and marriage (568–70), whereas men have infinite ways to serve their city (570–72). The ode stresses the connection between marriage and war by observing the disastrous consequences of uncontrolled erotic behavior. It provides a model for correct behavior, a display of true *aretē*, and the *aidōs* and other fruits of a good education that by the end of the play are apparent to some extent in Achilles and certainly in Iphigenia. The ode shares the characters' own criticisms of their immediate situation, but it also emphasizes the motif of the marriage now abandoned by Agamemnon but still a reality for his wife and daughter, and it opens the possibility of an active pursuit of *aretē* by a virtuous woman. Iphigenia's final action embraces and transcends this choral advice as she publically wins *kleos* and acts for the community (an unusual achievement for a woman, if not for the sacrificial virgins of tragedy). Yet she does so in a feminine manner, through concealed *erōs* (see 569) and for the cause of marriage.

The second stasimon (751–800) follows the first scene between Agamemnon and Clytemnestra, in which Agamemnon's plan to sacrifice Iphigenia is running smoothly, and precedes the complicating appearance of Achilles, when the fictional marriage threatens to undercut the Trojan expedition. The ode again returns to the theme of Helen and her myth and offers a prophetic vision of the destruction of Troy and the losses to be experienced by the Trojan women. The sufferings of women bracket and undercut the achievements of war, just as the sufferings of the innocent Iphigenia threaten to undercut the expedition entirely. The rape of Leda by Zeus in disguise as a swan and the birth of Helen, recounted after the prophecy of the Trojan disaster, seem mere myths from the Muses' tablets, tales bearing no relation to painful reality (790–800, especially 797–800: *en deltois Pierisin / muthoi . . . ēnengkan para kairon allōs*).[29] The ode, by questioning its own myths, questions its relevance to the world of the play's action and perpetuates the tension between odes and action. For the first time the reality of the action begins to impinge on the ideals concerning marriage and war established in the earlier odes. Yet the breadth of historical perspective offered in the ode, encompassing the past and now insistently the future, continues to reinforce a sense of the inevitability of the myth.

The famous third stasimon (1036–97) begins with the radiant marriage of Peleus and Thetis, a wedding paradigmatic in Greek tradition for its glorious ceremony, replete with the presence of the gods themselves and their divine music, songs, and gifts.[30] This marriage, the centaurs arrive to predict, will produce Achilles, the most glorious warrior to fight at Troy. It also, although the chorus does not say so here, gave rise to the fatal contest of beauty among the three goddesses that led Aphrodite to promise Helen to Paris. (The connection between the beauty contest and the marriage motif is implicit in Iphigenia's lyrics at 1294–1309, where the contest is set in a meadow where the nymphs pluck flowers.) Out of this glorious marriage (not, by most accounts, a happy one), an apparently appropriate theme for an epithalamium at the marriage of Achilles and Iphigenia, come war, strife, and the destruction of marriage through uncontrolled *erōs*.

[29]On this kind of passage in Euripides, see Pucci 1977.
[30]On the third stasimon see Walsh 1971 and Parry 1978: 186ff. Neither attacks the difficult problem of the epithalamic conventions used by Euripides here. The meager surviving fragments of Greek epithalamic poetry make the latter task uncertain at best. Among later poems, Catullus 62 and Theocritus 18 are particularly helpful. Cavander 1973: 138–39 remarks that this stasimon could almost be read as a victory ode to Achilles.

Very little epithalamic poetry survives from before or during the classical period. But both this fragmentary evidence and later epithalamia indicate that the ode borrows heavily from the epithalamic tradition, while the prophecy about Achilles concerns the rearming made famous in *Iliad* 18. A fragment of Sappho thought to belong to an epithalamium (141 LP)[31] includes the motif of wine-pouring at a wedding attended by the gods also present in this ode. The references to music and dance and to the promise of offspring are also epithalamic. It is impossible to say whether a prophecy of this kind was typical in songs about mythical weddings. Catullus' treatment of the wedding of Peleus and Thetis, with its prophecy by the Fates concerning Achilles (Catullus 64), may have borrowed from this ode or from a larger tradition represented also in Aeschylus (frag. 284 Mette, after Plato *Rep.* 383). In the Aeschylus fragment Thetis speaks bitterly of Apollo, who sang prophecies about Achilles at her wedding and then went on to kill him at Troy. Interestingly, Catullus 64 stresses Achilles' destructiveness, whereas Euripides' ode concentrates on the visual image of the armor. Indeed, the descriptions of both the marriage and the shield have a pictorial, distant quality that contrasts with the troubled marriages and the mob violence of the action. The tone is more reminiscent of lyrics such as Sappho's fragment on the arrival of the bride Andromache at Troy (44 LP). The epithalamic themes and the hint at Achilles' future role in epic again augment the pressure for a return to an ideal and ordered social life and a Panhellenic poetic perspective on events.

The epode continues to hint at epithalamic motifs: the emphasis on the relation between the girl and her mother, the purity of the bride (here a quality of the sacrificial animal), and the comparison of the bride to a natural object (animal, plant, or flower). The chorus regrets the loss of *aidōs* and *aretē,* without which there will be no common struggle for men (*koinos agōn brotois,* 1096), and laments Iphigenia's fate in language that densely intertwines the girl and the sacrificial victim (1080–88):

> — σὲ δ' ἐπὶ κάρα στέψουσι καλλικόμαν
> πλόκαμον Ἀργεῖοι, βαλιὰν

[31]For a discussion of this fragment, see Page 1955: 124.

The *Iphigenia in Aulis*

ὥστε πετραίων ἀπ᾽ ἄντρων
†ἐλθοῦσαν ὀρέων†
μόσχον ἀκήρατον, βρότειον
αἱμάσσοντες λαιμόν·
οὐ σύριγγι τραφεῖσαν οὐδ᾽
ἐν ῥοιβδήσεσι βουκόλων,
παρὰ δὲ ματέρι νυμφοκόμον
Ἰναχίδαις γάμον.

But you—the Argives will wreathe your head with a beautiful band, like a pure, dappled heifer come from rocky mountain caves, and then bloody your human throat— a victim not raised to the tune of a pipe or the crude whistling of shepherds, but nurtured by her mother's side as a bride for the sons of Inachus.

Again, the realities of the action threaten to impinge upon the lyric ideals expressed by the chorus. At the same time, marriage and sacrifice become inextricably intertwined in a manner that anticipates the resolution of the play.

Immediately before this ode Achilles has agreed to champion Iphigenia; after it Clytemnestra and Iphigenia try to persuade Agamemnon not to sacrifice his daughter. By singing about epithalamic themes, the chorus emphasizes the multiple ironies of the situation. Achilles and the doomed Iphigenia, a sheltered girl who is in no respect an appropriate victim to pay for Helen's crimes, will never hear a wedding song. Yet the effect of the prophecy in the ode is simultaneously to deny to Achilles' intervention in favor of Iphigenia a mythical status comparable to that accorded his Iliadic wrath.

In her final scene Iphigenia's words appropriate and transform into action the promise of the odes by closing, even if illusorily, the gap between the past, with its poetic ideals for marriage and war, and the present world of the action. Her lament at 1279–1335, which moves from concern with family and self-pity to an awareness of her own dilemma in the larger mythical/historical context, ultimately makes more believable the final transition to public self-sacrifice. And, if the text is correct, the chorus is finally persuaded to join in this inspiring ritualized and lyric performance, perhaps even leaving an empty stage for the doubting Clytemnestra. Here the wispy, distanced perspective of the odes becomes a model for the heroine's fragile idealism and offers an appropriate lyric dimension both to Iphigenia's persona and final act and to the myth and its traditional conclusion.[32] The odes, like Iphigenia's lyrics, do not deny the brutality of the events about to ensue, but their form and beauty translate it to another level.[33] Myths and rituals thus become relevant to reality, despite the questions raised in the second stasimon concerning both myth and war's victimization of women. The very anachronism of the odes in a world in which tragedy, not epic, was the dominant art form hints at the unworldliness of Iphigenia's transformation; and in fact Iphigenia's sacrifice is not mentioned in Homer. The further the action in the corrupt political world of the play veers from the predicted sequence of the myth, the less relevant the ideals of the odes seem to become. Yet because the distance of the chorus from the action actually makes the odes more and not less relevant to an interpretation of the play, an analysis of the play must take into account both the distance between odes and action and their crucial and climactic point of intersection.

Marriage and Sacrifice

An interpretation of Iphigenia's ritual and poetic synthesis of marriage and sacrifice can be considerably enriched by an understanding of the social, religious, and literary context for these rites and the hidden structural similarities between rites upon which Euripides has built his plot. As Vernant has argued, marriage and sacrifice are homologous rites: "You could say that marriage is to sexual consummation what sacrifice is to the consumption of meat."[34] Whereas the eating of sacrificial meat ensures the physical

[32]Arrowsmith in Merwin and Dimock 1978: ix and xii argues that Iphigenia becomes a model of epic *aretē* in this play.

[33]Bonnard 1945 (anticipating Walsh 1971 and Green 1979) has an extensive treatment of the relation between the tragic action and the odes in this play that has influenced and complements my own. On the choral lyrics in general, see also Schreiber 1963, esp. 15–24; Schreiber is helpful on the way in which the parodos counteracts the expectations created in the paradosis (19–20).

[34]Vernant 1980: 138 = 1974: 149. Vernant's pun on consumption and consummation is impossible to translate effectively. See also Detienne 1977.

continuity of existence, marriage ensures the continuity of human life over time. Marriage, sacrifice, cooked food, and the *oikos* stand in Greek culture in structural opposition to promiscuity, bestial allelophagy, raw food, and living in the open. The *IA's* literary exploitation of the homology between marriage and sacrifice has precedents in Euripides' own *Alcestis* (see the later discussion in this chapter) and in the mock epithalamium that Cassandra sings before her "marriage"/sacrifice with Agamemnon in the *Trojan Women*.[35] Segal has also argued that in Sophocles' *Trachiniae* marriage and sacrifice, though not precisely homologous, are simultaneously invaded by the poison of the uncivilized and erotic centaur Nessus; the closing scenes of that play, in contrast, make a parallel restoration of both institutions.[36] Heracles' first sacrifice is interrupted by the workings of the poisoned robe; then he suddenly murders Lichas and bellows in unpropitious agony. But the play closes with his sacrificial death on Mount Oeta, where the rites are performed in an orderly and propitious manner. The marriage, disrupted by the intrusion of Heracles' mistress Iole into the household, is restored by Deianeira's courageous self-punishment and the marriage, however dubious, between Hyllus and Iole.

Yet the homologies between marriage and sacrifice go even deeper. Both rites involve a voluntary death, real or symbolic, designed to ensure social survival. Both seek to gain a propitious future through violence, loss and submission to a social order. Participation in a sacrifice signifies membership in a society and, by implication, submission to its rules and requirements and an entitlement to a share in its benefits. Marriage requires a comparable incorporation into the social order. The bride and groom yoke themselves in marriage for the production of legitimate children. The initial stages of each ritual mark the separation of the participants from their former state. The bride bathes and cuts her hair. The sacrificers, after washing their hands, cut off and dedicate a few hairs from the sacrificial victim and sprinkle it with water. In sacrifice the animal is made to gesture in consent to its demise; similarly, plays such as Aeschylus' *Eumenides* and *Suppliants* em-

[35]See Zeitlin 1965 and Lebeck 1971. Aeschylus in the *Agamemnon* describes Cassandra's death with sacrificial imagery.
[36]Segal 1975 and 1981.

phasize the importance in marriage of *peithō* (persuasion) and/or Aphrodite as a necessary counterpart to *bia* (violence).

The Greek bride, unlike the Helen of this play (68–71), rarely had any choice in her marriage. She was trained through ritual and other instruction from girlhood to submit to what could often be a frightening transitional experience. At Brauron, for example, some women of Euripides' audience (if women were present in the theater) were educated for the transition to marriage with a myth of sacrifice similar to that of Iphigenia in this play, and Iphigenia's cult was in fact intertwined with that of Artemis at Brauron. An Attic myth explained the dancing of prepubescent girls as bears in the *arkteia* for Artemis at Brauron as recompense for the killing of a she-bear. In one tradition Artemis demanded as an additional recompense the sacrifice of a virgin, for whom an Athenian substituted a goat dressed as a girl. As Henrichs has argued: "The Brauronian ritual commemorated the preservation and continuation of human life at the cost of animal life, and in the context of the female sex and prepuberty."[37]

Other myths and texts stressed a symbolic connection between marriage and death, a connection no doubt reinforced by structural parallels between marriage and funeral rites.[38] Artemidorus argues in his *Interpretation of Dreams* that "marriage resembles death and is signified by death. . . . For a virgin to dream of marriage indicates her death; for all that happens to one who marries happens also to the dead" (*Oneirokritika* 2.65). An important Greek myth of marriage, which played a central role in the ritual life of Greek women, is the story of Persephone's rape by Hades, her stay in the underworld, and her final achievement of new divine honors and partial reunification, after experiencing sexuality, with her Olympian mother. Iphigenia's experience echoes in part that of Persephone's

[37]Henrichs 1981: 207. For such female initiation rituals generally, see esp. Brelich 1969a and Burkert 1966b.

[38]For the marriage as death motif in ancient Greek literature, see esp. Rose 1925 and Segal 1981: 180–83 and 447 n. 86 on this motif in the *Antigone*. Redfield 1982: 188 and 190 with further bibliography notes the structural parallels between marriage and funeral rites. On the importance of the Korē plot in tragedy, see Guépin 1968: 120–42. He makes a distinction between *kathodos* dramas, in which a virgin dies, and *anodos* dramas such as the *IT* or the *Helen,* in which the female protagonist returns from a world of death and sterility.

marriage/death and separation from her mother followed by the promise of new divine honors. The epithet used of Iphigenia early in the play, "the bride of Hades," was common in funerary practice and in funerary epigrams for girls who died young, and played on the analogy with Persephone. Hippolytus' experience in the *Hippolytus* is also modeled on the Korē myth. Like Persephone, he suffers violent separation from a sacred meadow associated with chastity. Hippolytus' rejection of Aphrodite, however, makes the necessary and violent transition to sexuality actually rather than symbolically fatal. Nevertheless, the play closes with the establishing of a cult for unmarried girls; at their marriage they will cut their hair for Hippolytus and commemorate in song Phaedra's story and Hippolytus' refusal of Aphrodite. Hippolytus will be remembered, and his and Phaedra's myth will presumably aid the young women in confronting their difficult transition to marriage. Characters from Greek tragedy such as Medea (*Medea* 230–51) and the woman (Procne?) in the following fragment from Sophocles' *Tereus* (524 N = 583 R) also frequently emphasize the violence of the transition to marriage, and make it clear why this transition could be experienced as a symbolic death:

> I often consider how we women are nothing. When we are young, in our father's house, I think we live the sweetest life of all men; for ignorance brings us up delightfully. But when we have reached maturity and know more, we are driven out and sold, away from the gods of our fathers and our parents, some to foreigners, some to barbarians, some to strange houses, others to such as deserve reproach. And finally, after a single night has united us, we have to praise our lot and pretend that all is well.

Euripides' *Alcestis* and *Helen* capitalize on the mythical associations between marriage and death. Alcestis' promised sacrificial death for her husband (74–76) recreates the primal experience of the bride. In consenting to this self-sacrifice Alcestis finally gains a second marriage, which is blessed by a proper balance of roles. Admetus wins praise for his hospitality and is no longer stigmatized by his unmasculine lack of courage to face death. The heroic Alcestis is once more a housewife, delivered veiled and silent into her husband's hands by Heracles with the traditional marriage gesture of *cheir epi karpōi* (hand on the wrist, 916–17, 1115–19; the same gesture was used in depictions of rape and by Hermes Psychopompus).[39] Admetus' error forces him to experience a living death and a feminized housebound existence without Alcestis; indeed, it is through sharing the female's ritual experience of marriage as "death" that Admetus comes to a greater acceptance of death and a new life. The associations of this story with the Hades/Persephone myth are reinforced by the name Admetus, which is an epithet of the ever-hospitable Hades himself.

Helen and Menelaus in the *Helen* use the ruse of a mock funeral, which shares certain features with the Spartan marriage rite, to escape from Egypt and return finally to a propitious and real marriage, now that the fiction of Helen's voyage to Troy has been exposed.[40] Both the *Odyssey*, which closes with a symbolic wedding between Odysseus and Penelope (the wedding music conceals the death of the suitors), and the *Helen* involve a "remarriage" and a recovery of identity by a Trojan war hero, in part through his symbolic entrance into a female realm and feminine experience. Odysseus experiences both the underworld and the anonymity of the island of Calypso with its underworld associations, is reborn to the human world on Phaeacia, and goes on to rescue Penelope from an enclosed world that is unchanging and almost without growth.[41] In the *Helen* the associations created between Egypt and Hades and the threat of a marriage with Theoclymenus enrich the complex associations between marriage and death in the play. Other treatments of the marriage and death theme involving virgins, such as Antigone's symbolic marriage after death with Haimon in the *Antigone* or Cassandra's mock epithalamium for her coming marriage/sacrifice in the *Trojan Women*, end ironically not in rebirth and fertility, but in sterility and death. Yet the importance of the remarriage theme in the *Odyssey*, the *Helen*, and the *Alcestis* provides further evidence that the marriage pattern, with its sym-

[39]For a discussion of the motif in art, see Sutton 1981: 181 and 184, with further bibliography, and Mylonas 1945.
[40]See Plutarch *Lycurgus* 48.15.5 and *Helen* 1087–1620 passim. On marriage rites as an example of the transformative powers of culture, and on the woman as the acculturating partner in marriage, see Redfield 1982: 185 and 194.
[41]See Foley 1978 and Segal 1962.

bolic death leading to birth, could offer a model for rebirth and recovery in the wake of a military or social crisis.

The action of the *IA*, insofar as it deals with the heroine, reflects not only Greek myths of marriage such as the Demeter/Persephone story, but also the pattern of separation, transition (often including a symbolic death), and incorporation characteristic, as van Gennep has shown, of initiation rites such as marriage.[42] The reference to the sacred meadow, the scene of Persephone's rape, the emphasis on a journey to another place, the painful separation of parents and child, and the joyous submission, under the influence of *erōs* and the rhetoric of the father, to a marriage become propitious sacrifice reflect larger mythical and actual social patterns.[43] Ironically, the ideal bride and the ideal sacrificial victim become one, as the education for marriage provides the mode of transition to voluntary death.

In the *IA*, however, the homology between sacrifice and marriage expands to include war, the cause for which Iphigenia is to be sacrificed. As Vernant has argued, woman functions in relation to marriage as man does in relation to war.[44] Each sex, like Achilles and Iphigenia in this play, turns away from family life to accept a changed status for the benefit of the community. The woman accepts the control of a stranger to produce children, the man risks his life for the community. Each necessarily involves the kind of control or sublimation of desire emphasized in the *IA*. Indeed, Burkert has argued that the sacrifice of a virgin before battle precisely symbolizes this need to sublimate *erōs* for war, an *erōs* that is in danger of returning in a violent and uncontrolled form after battle.[45] In the period of the epics, marriage is both a cause of war and a means of making alliance or reparation. As Vernant argues, "although war may end in marriage, marriage may also be at the origin of war and may cause it to spring up again."[46] This point is repeatedly emphasized in the *IA*, especially in the choral odes: Helen is the cause of the war, and Iphigenia must die to repair this

[42]Van Gennep 1960 (1909).
[43]See note 10 above.
[44]Vernant 1980: 38.
[45]See Burkert 1972: 70–85, esp. 79, and Bataille 1962: 90–91 and 109–10.
[46]Vernant 1980: 21.

violation of marriage; marriage is the occasion for prophesying the birth of Achilles and his heroic death at Troy, and for the beauty contest that led Paris to Helen. In the Athenian *polis*, however, marriage had become in fact a private matter between citizens, and separate from issues of foreign policy. This contemporary situation is indirectly reflected in the strong tension between private and public, the marriage of Iphigenia and the war, found throughout the *IA*. The resolution of the play is thus an anachronistic return to myth and to the archaic reciprocity and complementarity between marriage and war, private and public, to be found in an epic or Panhellenic context.

The gesture of Iphigenia, then, not only reconnects with its myth a plot that has threatened to run out of control but also reintegrates the religious institutions of her society. Iphigenia's marriage/sacrifice is undertaken with a hint of rebirth or survival that is ratified, if the play closed this way, by Artemis' substitution of a deer for Iphigenia, a substitution that marks a propitious return to normal and civilized practice. This conclusion echoes the resolution of the earlier *Iphigenia in Tauris*, which closes with the transfer of a cult of Artemis from the land of the Taurians, where human sacrifice is performed in honor of the goddess, to Halae, where an animal victim will be substituted for the human. It is worth noting, before we read Iphigenia's gesture in the *IA* as merely ironic, that all positive resolutions of Euripidean plays are achieved either through a deus ex machina or by a strategy based on ritual. In the *Iphigenia in Tauris*, for example, Iphigenia and Orestes use the pretense of a rite of purification for Orestes, who cannot be sacrificed to Artemis because he is a polluted murderer, to escape from the land of the Taurians and to civilize Artemis' cult. In such dramas ritual offers a possibility for salvation that is simultaneously a deception and a gesture of truth: although Iphigenia lies to Thoas about Orestes' identity and her true purpose, and Orestes has already been ritually absolved of his crime by Apollo, Orestes' voyage in the *IT* does finally succeed in purifying him of his matricide.[47] Both he and Iphigenia, through being willing to pity, to forgive, and to risk death for each other,

[47]For treatments of ritual in the *IT*, see Wolff 1963, Sansone 1975, and Strachan 1976.

are psychologically as well as physically freed of the oppressive Trojan past. Furthermore, the resolution is achieved precisely through a realization that appearances do not offer a reliable view of the gods. In the *IT* Iphigenia is able, by refusing to believe that Artemis demands human sacrifice, to accept her aid and to make her ritual into a form of fiction and education. Such deception is seen as necessary to life.[48]

In the *Iphigenia in Aulis,* rituals also offer the possibility for a deception that becomes for Iphigenia a positive psychological and symbolic reality (a sacrificial marriage), mitigated perhaps by a concluding divine rescue, and Artemis' seemingly heartless prophecy offers a script for the reunification of Greece. The achievement of a resolution through ritual implies a restoration of the social order, which is based on those rites, and a re-creation of proper contact with the gods that transcends time and place. In this and other Euripidean plays the strategy for salvation comes from a woman, a person whose imagination is shaped by poetic tradition (see the feminine view presented in the choral odes), by ritual and marriage, not by politics. In Aristophanes' *Lysistrata* women also simultaneously represent the interests of the private and religious worlds and of Panhellenism, external causes that transcend those of the strictly male world of the *polis.*[49] Indeed, the contribution of women to the Greek *polis* was confined to the religious realm, where they were extremely active in public and private ritual. The resolution reached in such plays as the *IA* and the *Lysistrata* is not a strictly political one, but involves the remaking of what Turner calls *communitas,* a spirit that binds together socioreligious life yet is beyond social structures; a spontaneous emotion, often experienced through the sacred, that makes an individual feel at one with his community, its experiences, and its memories: "Spontaneous communitas is nature in dialogue with structure, married to it as a woman is married to a man."[50] The location of *communitas* outside the social hierarchy often requires, in reality as well as in fiction, that its representative be a woman.[51]

[48]See Wolff 1963: 127.
[49]For a discussion, see Foley 1982a.
[50]Turner 1969: 140.
[51]Ibid., 184.

Hence when we read as strictly ironic a plot that is resolved through ritual, we should be fully aware of the magnitude of the cynicism of such an interpretation. Such an ironic reading throws into question not only the myth and the author's interpretation of it, but the entire socioreligious system. Marriage and sacrifice, whose essential function is to unite human beings in society and to ensure social continuity, become simply instruments of deception. Certainly Euripides' treatment of the myth opens the possibility for an ironic reading of the climactic merging and restoring of marriage and sacrifice. Iphigenia dies for an army seized by an uncontrolled lust for violence. Her desire to prevent Achilles from dying for a woman (herself, 1392–93) is ironically undercut by his later death for Helen, the original corrupter of the marriage rite.[52] Clytemnestra, rejecting Iphigenia's Demeter/Persephone scenario in which the mother becomes partially reconciled to separation from her daughter, remains to the end intent on revenge and unreconciled to her marriage (see the disputed lines 1455, 1457, 1616–18). The history of Clytemnestra's marriage, based on repeated violence and violation of trust by Agamemnon, undermines Iphigenia's romantic and youthful faith in her father's rhetoric, in marriage, and in Greece. On the other hand, the play opens with a disastrous and ever-widening gap between public and private, an inability in Agamemnon to accept *tuchē* (fortune) and the demands of leadership (see especially 16–33). Through ritual and the fictions that ritual offers for restoring the social order, Iphigenia closes this gap and accepts what *tuchē* brings.

Ritual and the Politics of Panhellenism

In terms of the rest of the action of the play, Iphigenia's gesture of conversion to her marriage/sacrifice is not as isolated or as unexpected as it might at first appear. All the major characters are fully implicated in the tensions raised by her dilemma, and all except Clytemnestra are drawn into participation in the sacrifice

[52]See Dimock in Merwin and Dimock 1978: 8.

on Iphigenia's own terms. Like Iphigenia, all except Clytemnestra bow to a growing recognition of necessity and, however questionable their motives may be, move beyond selfish individual concerns to a fuller involvement with the community as a whole.

The myth of Iphigenia in all known versions before this play requires her sacrifice before the Greek army can go to Troy. Artemis demanded a sacrifice in one case because Agamemnon shot a sacred deer, in another in return for a promise by Agamemnon to sacrifice the most beautiful thing that the year produced, in a third case because of a hereditary curse on the Atreidae.[53] In Aeschylus' version many considerations press Agamemnon to perform Iphigenia's sacrifice: Zeus' command to avenge Paris' violation of hospitality through his abduction of Helen, a prophecy from Calchas announcing Artemis' demand for the sacrifice, the eagerness of the army, and his own desire to go to Troy. The chorus notes both his hestitation to kill his own daughter and his rapid conversion to accomplishing the act in a spirit of mad insensitivity to his own fatherhood. In the *Iphigenia in Aulis* Artemis offers in Calchas' prophecy not a command but a choice. The Greek army can go to Troy *if* Iphigenia is sacrificed; otherwise it will have to return home (89–92). In this play, then, divine forces intervene only in the form of Artemis' oracle, which offers the army a choice; in the form of the windlessness that makes the war impossible without the sacrifice; perhaps in the form of *tuchē;* and in the final miracle, if it occurred. The action of this play is thus unusually secularized, allowing the audience to concentrate on the moral issues raised and the choices made in response to them. Without the oracle, however, the return to ritual order and an idealized Panhellenism would have been impossible; the heartless oracle surprisingly provides a structure that allows for a transition from an atmosphere dominated by political corruption and a mindless *eris* to one less secularized and more oriented to public concerns.

The play opens with Agamemnon regretting his ambition and choosing the second alternative offered by the oracle. Succumbing to his love for his child, he is in the process of rewriting (*meta-*

[53]See Schreiber 1963: 66–71 for the mythological sources of this passage.

graphō, 108) the traditional script by revoking and rewriting his original letter summoning Iphigenia to Aulis.[54] Euripides' plays normally begin with an iambic prologue outlining the mythological background and the situation of the character delivering the prologue. Here, if the order of the manuscript is genuine (see the appendix to this chapter), the play opens atypically with anapests followed by the expected iambic prologue giving the mythological background, and the paradosis then concludes with anapests. The unusual structure of the paradosis seems to underline in a forceful and surprising way the nature of the plot, which unfolds until the final scene as a series of attempts and failures to change the myth as it is represented in the prologue and to save the innocent Iphigenia. The metatheatrical image—Agamemnon as a writer or rewriter of myth functions for the moment as the poet's double—is in keeping with the later passages in the play that emphasize, through references to a conflict between *onoma* and *ergon,* the impossible doubleness of the language, ritual, and plot of the early scenes, in which the marriage and the sacrifice remain in unresolved conflict.[55] The unexpected intervention of the standard prologue and the seemingly awkward transition between anapests and iambics can, in my view, be explained precisely by the fact that Euripides has an artistic purpose in adopting this odd form for the paradosis and for delaying the expected iambic prologue. He wishes his audience to recognize Agamemnon's iambic speech as a Euripidean prologue; hence the speech retains the form of such a prologue, rather than being a natural reply to the old man, which would be appropriately made in anapests.[56] The delayed prologue, which outlines and then casts suspicion upon the traditional myth,

---

[54]*Metagraphein* means "to correct a draft or rewrite." Although it occurs only here in tragedy it is clearly the correct technical word for what Agamemnon is doing. The use of *hupographō* at *Heracles* 1118 may be similarly metatheatrical. Here Heracles cannot believe what Amphitryon is telling him about his madness. But since the mad Heracles in fact bears little relation to the Heracles who first appears onstage in the play, two incompatible traditions confront each other in a similar fashion, because the mad Heracles is imposed on the earlier sane Heracles.

[55]On the *onoma/ergon* conflict raised in the case of Achilles, who has lent his name but not his consent to the marriage, see 128, 910, 938–39. For Clytemnestra's challenge to Agamemnon on this subject, see 1115–16.

[56]The *Andromeda* prologue may have contained anapests, as does the prologue of the *Rhesus,* a play that may or may not be by Euripides.

is then sandwiched between the unusual or unique anapests, which are reserved for the new, *anti*mythical plot that Agamemnon is in the process of devising. In other words, Euripides is here manipulating and overturning the audience's expectations about meter and the prologue form to anticipate the contradictions in plot and language that persist throughout the play. And he does so in a manner entirely consistent with the iconoclastic manipulation of dramatic form that characterizes all his late work.

In the early scenes the characters continue to vacillate in their concern for the innocent Iphigenia; ultimately Iphigenia draws all except Clytemnestra under her sacrificial mantle and her Panhellenic idealism. Agamemnon, a former victim of gross political ambition, as Menelaus points out, is initially proud of his unheroic change of mind to pity (396–401). He brings to bear in his argument with his brother all the hindsight of Aeschylus' chorus in the *Agamemnon:* the war is fought for an unworthy adulteress, and the army's eagerness for violence is sick and dangerous. Agamemnon's novel concern for his family even more surprisingly converts the formerly uxorious Menelaus. In contrast to portrayals of pairs of brothers in most other tragedies, their rivalry turns to brotherly concern and a convergence of interest. Menelaus adopts every word of his brother's position (473–503) and goes on to share in his brother's next reversal.[57] Clytemnestra later persuades Achilles to abandon his destiny in Troy to protect Iphigenia, even though she is merely his bride in name. The traditionally action-loving Achilles at first hopes to be able to avoid a violent confrontation with Agamemnon and to repersuade the king, who has succumbed to fear of the Greek army and Odysseus, to save his daughter; he then shifts to active championship of his prospective bride but finally accedes to her wishes. Iphigenia, unlike other sacrificial victims in Euripides, does not immediately consent to her sacrifice. She loves life passionately. But persuaded by her father's rhetoric of Panhellenism and the inspiring presence of Achilles, who describes the state of the Greek army, she redirects the plot to the myth with her final change of mind. She rejects the offer of Achil-

[57]Bogaert 1965 has in my view argued successfully against Parmentier 1926 and Meunier 1927 that Menelaus' change of mind is meant to be genuine.

les, who promises to stand by her should she change her mind once more at the altar (1424–29).

As Strohm has shown, Euripidean debates normally end in a stalemate; neither character persuades the other.[58] The tragedies in large part emerge from the clash between the passions and incompatible ideas of the characters, or from the unwillingness of a central character to change his or her mind. Changes of mind in Greek tragedy are rare outside Euripides.[59] They are usually associated with softness, the ambivalence of *peithō* (persuasion), femininity, and magic. In no other Euripidean play are changes of mind as pervasive as in the *Iphigenia in Aulis*. Particularly untragic and remarkable are the willingness to empathize with and adopt another's point of view and to give up desire (Menelaus), ambition (Agamemnon), or life so rapidly for another person.

The play offers no clear internal standards for judging these rapid shifts of mind.[60] It dwells on Agamemnon's former ambition and his fear of the army, on Menelaus' self-centered desire for a wife who willingly pursued adultery, on Achilles' pomposity and egotism, and on Clytemnestra's good-willed yet narrow and bourgeois point of view. Yet all these characters, with the possible exception of Clytemnestra, are capable of positive inspiration and of undertaking considerable risks and losses to save the life of Iphigenia. They do not lose sight of what it means to kill the girl for a dubious cause. The very corruptibility and ordinariness of the

[58]Strohm 1957: 3–49 passim.

[59]Knox 1966 has the most important discussion of this issue, although Schmitt 1921: 15–28, esp. 24–27, and Snell 1968, esp. 497, contribute to the discussion. Snell emphasizes the dramatic contrast between Agamemnon's indecisiveness and Iphigenia's willingness to make a decision. Knox argues that Iphigenia's change of mind is well prepared for by the pervasive pattern of mind change in the play and motivated by the Panhellenism theme. He puts Iphigenia's change of mind into perspective by a discussion of other plays, noting the rare changes of mind in Aeschylus (the Erinyes in the *Eumenides*) and Sophocles (the *Philoctetes*) and the more frequent though more isolated changes in Euripidean drama. The rapid shifts in the *IA* reflect the instability of the world of the play. Paradoxically, Euripides here represents a truly heroic action springing not from stubborn resolution and ideal *phusis* (as in Sophocles) but from a change of mind (232).

[60]See Snell 1968: 498–99 on the uncertainty faced by Euripidean characters in a world without definite external standards for morality.

characters make their ability to act to a greater or lesser degree beyond their own self-interest more striking and remarkable.

The characters' openness to pity creates in the audience a desire for Iphigenia to be saved and a strong distaste for the cause to which she is to be sacrificed. At the same time, the domestic, sometimes almost comic, tone of certain scenes, like the contrast between the action and the odes, which dwell on the myth and the glories of heroic *aretē,* evokes a sense that the move to save Iphigenia creates an alternative considerably inferior to the original myth. Iphigenia's naive urgency for her father's return home from a responsibility she does not understand (656–60) evokes strong sympathy; but her very naïveté serves to emphasize further Agamemnon's failure to live up to his role as a leader. The thought that Achilles' brilliance is to be expended in protecting Iphigenia from his own army, and not on the battlefield of Troy, is at the very least discomforting.

Regardless of how the audience evaluates the motives of the characters, however, no one can in the end change the myth. The play confronts and questions the ethics of war and revenge, sets private and public concerns in conflict, and ultimately bows to the necessity of the Trojan venture; the combined force of *tuchē,* the oracle, and the Panhellenic army is irresistible. Agamemnon, though his fear of the army and Odysseus may be despicable, is apparently justified in feeling that the arrival of Iphigenia renders her sacrifice inevitable. True, Achilles states that the army is impatient *either* to go to Troy *or* to disband (804–18), but that is before the army learns of the prophecy.[61] Menelaus, although he suggests killing Calchas (519), apparently bows to Agamemnon's fear of Odysseus. And it seems unlikely that the army would be vulnerable to the arguments for pity that have persuaded a brother. The army's dangerous mood is confirmed in Achilles' report of his own experience in trying to defend his bride; Achilles' heroic resistance to the facts is clearly useless. Agamemnon refers to the Aeschylean image of *anangkēs zeugmata* (yoke of necessity, 443) at

[61]Here I disagree with those such as Dimock (Merwin and Dimock 1978: 9) who stress the willingness of the army to depart and thus condemn Agamemnon for his decision. For the role of *tuchē* in the play, see esp. Ferguson 1968 and Bonnard 1945.

the moment of Iphigenia's arrival; before that, he apparently felt free to play an untraditional role.[62] According to Iphigenia, Agamemnon sacrifices his daughter *akōn* (unwilling) and sane (1456). The individual characters in the world of this play, though corruptible, do not fall victim so much to their own desires and hereditary madnesses as to the violence and sickness of the very Panhellenic cause (the Greek army and Greek marriage) for which Iphigenia chooses to die.

Once Iphigenia's arrival has made her sacrifice inevitable, the effort to save the girl is balanced by a gradual movement back to the myth and to the behavior associated with these characters in earlier treatments of the myth. Even the correct, well-meaning matron Clytemnestra, who remains unmoved by the Panhellenic cause, evolves into the vengeful and plotting character found in Aeschylus. The agonized father and reluctant leader mouths the rhetoric of Panhellenism, thus bringing the rhetoric of the play closer to the mood of the lyrics, and offers to his daughter at least a convincing picture of the *eugeneia* of his ancestors (painted as uniformly noble in this play, 29–30, 321, 473–74, 504–5, 1233, 1457), which he himself lacked in earlier scenes.[63] Agamemnon, supported by Menelaus, now appears to undertake the venture to Troy as if it were a public rather than a private venture.[64] If the ending of the play is genuine, he leaves for Troy eager and unrepentant. The pompous and self-centered Achilles, who has previously been all too willing to leave the hard work to women and children and obsessively concerned with his reputation, rises, un-

[62]The questions of Agamemnon's vacillating character, the political pressures upon him, and the sincerity of his adoption of the rhetoric of Panhellenism have been endlessly debated. For a summary of some major views, see Conacher 1967a: 261. Extensive discussions are found in Friedrich 1935, Frey 1947, Wassermann 1949, Vretska 1961, Funke 1964, Snell 1968, and Mellert-Hoffmann 1969.

[63]The theme of Panhellenism is not exclusive to the odes before Agamemnon's speech. Menelaus introduces the theme into the rhetoric of the play at 370, and, as Mellert-Hoffmann 1969 points out in chap. 1, there is no reason not to take Agamemnon's statement here as a sincere expression of his views, which were temporarily overwhelmed by his private concern for his daughter.

[64]See Strohm 1957: 137–38. Strohm is excellent on the imprisoning effect of circumstances in the play and on the static nature of the action, which, despite counterintrigues, keeps returning to the original crisis until Iphigenia's final gesture (137–46).

der the influence of Iphigenia and her dilemma, to a height of inspiration and generosity that his perfect education has previously failed to instill. To Iphigenia at least he must appear a true epic knight in shining armor. Iphigenia herself fully transcends her previous naiveté and love of life in her choice to die for what appears to her to be a noble cause. But her act comes as a culmination to broader shifts in the plot, not as an isolated anomaly. This mysterious convergence of the action toward the epic promise of the lyrics (Clytemnestra excepted) and toward the traditional ending to the myth at least in part reinforces a sense of the inevitability of her sacrifice and the significance of her conversion.

The *IA* opens with a Girardian "sacrificial crisis." The leaders of the army have been locked in a competitive struggle for power, or "mimetic rivalry": "The world of reciprocal violence is one of constant mirror effects in which the antagonists become each other's doubles and lose their individual identities."[65] Social hierarchy is collapsing; the leaders reject or are inadequate to leadership. Cultural distinctions such as those between the sexes (as when Agamemnon threatens to usurp Clytemnestra's role in the marriage ceremony) begin to be blurred. Mob violence is imminent; the army is gripped by *erōs* for war and revenge. In accord with the Girardian scenario, Iphigenia's sacrifice restores (and even recreates, if she is deified) the religious system and ensures social unanimity. Although the oracle left the choice for the expedition to Troy up to the Greeks, the chorus in 1402–3 finally attributes the violence of the human community exclusively to Artemis and *tuchē:*

> Your decision, young woman, is noble. But *tuchē* and the goddess's oracle are sick.

Yet the audience cannot so easily ignore the extended experience that the play offers of the uncontrolled politics of Panhellenism and the play's repeated questioning of its own myths (see especially 72, 790–800). Clytemnestra, if the text is genuine, finally refuses to be convinced by the messenger's proffered resolution of Iphigenia's situation (1615–18):

[65]Girard 1978a: 186.

[99]

O child, you have been carried off by one of the gods? How shall I address you? How can I not call these lying tales made up [*paramutheis-thai tousde matēn muthous*] so I will cease from bitter grief for you?

The *IA*, then, comes close to a Girardian exposure of divine violence as a mere projection of human violence upon the gods, and thus to challenging the religious system. Furthermore, the counterplot to rescue Iphigenia threatens to destroy the sacrificial system from another angle absent from earlier tragedy. It poses a politics of love against a politics of revenge. Love and pity begin to dissolve mimetic rivalry and ambition. The whole Panhellenic venture and the social hierarchy are threatened not by violence but by love, by the altruistic desire to save the innocent Iphigenia. The ultimate irony of the ending, then, is the restoration of the sacrificial system, after it has been almost exposed and rejected, when love is harnessed to imitate and serve the cause of revenge.

In the *Iphigenia in Tauris,* the civilizing ritual substitution of animal for human sacrifice in the cult of Artemis is accomplished through the willingness of Iphigenia, Pylades, and Orestes to forget vengeance and to sacrifice themselves through love. The cultural and religious order is finally reestablished not simply through ritual, but through a love that is also reflected in the divine sphere by the joint action of the siblings Artemis and Apollo.[66] The original sacrifice, harmlessly reenacted, becomes a model for redemption; the violence of the past, the story of Pelops as well as of Iphigenia, becomes an illusion in the light of repeated divine rescue of the victims. In the *IT,* ritual becomes a structure through which learning and growth beyond violence take place; the past and the present are reconnected through ritual, a ritual that must ultimately be continually reenacted (like myths in drama) as a means of recapturing the crucial memory of the original violent event. In the less optimistic *IA,* the cultural and religious order is reestablished neither by the generative violence threatened in the earlier scenes and enacted in the *Bacchae,* nor, as in Aeschylus, by secular justice—clearly not an alternative in Euripides' world. Iphigenia turns

[66]See Wolff 1963: 127 for Euripides' use of the principle of ritual substitution in the *IT,* Sansone 1975: 288–93 on the sacrifice of Iphigenia as a model for the redemption of Orestes, and Caldwell 1974 on psychological doubling in the play.

the threatened lynching into an orderly and voluntary ritual (in Aeschylus the sacrifice was involuntary and hence unpropitious) through her youthful love for her father[67] and his ideals, and perhaps through an emerging love for Achilles. Ultimately, by its return to the old sacrificial system, this play finally obscures in large part the hint of an attack on the ethic of revenge and reciprocal violence in favor of voluntary sacrifice and love that Girard finds in the New Testament.[68]

Lack of certain knowledge about the concluding scenes makes a definitive interpretation of Iphigenia's marriage/sacrifice impossible. The text up to the point of Iphigenia's departure creates an expectation that the final scenes will confirm for Iphigenia something more than the burial accorded to her predecessors in voluntary sacrifice. Furthermore, the tradition prior to Aeschylus and to Pindar's *Pythian* 11 also allowed for the substitution of an animal or double for the innocent girl.[69] The foreshadowing of Iphigenia's rescue and survival is so strong that the disputed final scenes are hardly necessary to an interpretation of the play. In fact, the disputed extant text fulfills our expectations by placing the same emphasis on the sacrificial moment that it has up to this point. Critics of the exodus find problematic the abrupt transition from Iphigenia's departure to the messenger speech, the fragment of Aelian (*De natura animalium* 7.39) suggesting that Artemis herself appeared to make a speech as deus ex machina, and various other minor textual difficulties.[70] On the other hand, earlier scenes do prepare us for a divine intervention, when Clytemnestra supplicates Achilles, whom she determines in desperation to treat as a god and savior (911; in 973–74 Achilles agrees to accept the role of god). The failure of the human savior implicitly paves the way for a divine rescue.

Indeed, Euripides' plays tend to close with a series of irresolvable contradictions held in a fragile balance. The poet wrote the *IA*

[67]On this point see Green 1979: 179.

[68]See Girard 1978b.

[69]See Henrichs 1981: 198–203 on earlier versions of the Iphigenia myth. The *Cypria* and Hesiod frag. 23 allow for Iphigenia's survival.

[70]On the problem of the exodus see, aside from the commentaries, Page 1934: 192–204 and Cecchi 1960. If Artemis did appear, it is difficult to imagine how one would justify Clytemnestra's subsequent role in the myth.

at the close of the Peloponnesian War and at a period of renewed external threats to the Greeks; some of his contemporaries were seriously offering the politics of Panhellenism as a mode of political salvation.[71] Nevertheless, Iphigenia's sacrifice and the rhetoric of Panhellenism do not finally change the realities of her world. The violent Aeschylean scenario cannot be fully transformed by individual gestures of pity and self-sacrifice. And the play cannot, through the merging of marriage and self-sacrifice, achieve more than a symbolic resolution of the conflict between public and private interests that opens the play. In a sense the play brings an action dependent on the uncontrollable mob politics of injustice, found in plays such as the *Orestes,* into conflict with a counteraction that asserts the capacity of the individual for redemption and for learning through poetic tradition and ritual, found in the earlier *Iphigenia in Tauris.* The gap between the ordered and brilliant Homeric army of the parodos and the eroticized mob of the action is not closed, although Achilles finally presents himself to Iphigenia as a model of *aretē.* The irredeemable plot, the divine demand for the sacrifice of an innocent girl for the corrupt Helen, is hardly made bearable by Iphigenia's vision and a gesture of divine pity— the substitution of a deer—and the hint of deification. Nevertheless, when politics are irredeemable, ritual and poetry offer a timeless scenario for a positive and necessary deception and for a politics of love that dissolves even while it consents to a politics of revenge. Through Panhellenic rituals and poetic forms (especially the epic and the epithalamium), Iphigenia's resolution to her dilemma bypasses, even while it is undercut by, the violent politics of the Greeks.

Appendix: Lines 1–163

I believe that the prologue of the *IA* (1–163) has artistic merit in its present form and that the arguments against its authenticity are not sufficiently telling.[72] On textual and structural points Knox's

---

[71]See Dimock in Merwin and Dimock 1978: 4 on Gorgias' proposal at the Olympic games around the end of the fifth century of a Panhellenic crusade against the Persians as an alternative to intrahellenic strife.

[72]Older scholarship on the paradosis, such as England 1891, Page 1934,

defense remains the most forceful, but Bain's recent attack on Knox needs some discussion.[73] Bain argues that Knox has not provided a convincing defense against the three most central objections made against the paradosis by previous scholars.

The first objection concerns the awkwardness of the transition from anapests to iambics. Knox defends the formal and unrealistic nature of Agamemnon's iambic reply to the old man by reference to Greek messenger speeches, which also go far beyond a narrow and naturalistic reply to the questioner. Bain objects to the analogy on the grounds that the messenger speech is designed to inform *both* the audience and those onstage, whereas the prologue primarily informs the audience even when other characters are present onstage. I do not find this objection compelling. The true circumstances of the situation have been kept secret from all but four members of the Greek army, and Euripides is, as often, introducing a plot that will temporarily run counter to the established myth. Hence I defend the unnaturalistic transition from anapests to iambics as a deliberate attempt to make Agamemnon's iambics seem to the audience like a delayed prologue. Even detractors of the paradosis in its present form generally admit that neither the iambics nor the anapests alone constitute an adequate introduction to the play as a whole, and the rarity of anapests in a Euripidean prologue is hard to evaluate given our limited knowledge of his corpus and the innovative nature of the dramatist.

The second objection is that lines 105–7 and lines 124–6 are contradictory and that consequently the anapests and iambics cannot be by the same hand. Knox defends their consistency by arguing that the statement *hōs echei tade* ("this is the way things stand") at 106 is ambiguous: either Achilles and the army think that

---

Friedrich 1935, and Fraenkel 1955, largely concludes on the basis of difficult transitions in the text that the prologue is the work of two or more authors, one of whom may or may not be Euripides.

73The trend among recent scholars (such as Valgiglio 1956, esp. 179–82, and 1957; Schreiber 1963; Ritchie 1964; Mellert-Hoffmann 1969; Willink 1971; Knox 1972; and van Pottelbergh 1974) has been to defend the prologue in its present form or substantially in its present form. Willink, for example, defends the prologue but reorders it 49–96, 1–48, 97–114, 115–63. For a reply, see Bain 1977: 11–14. Knox and Mellert-Hoffmann offer the most thorough defense. I here concentrate on defending Knox against Bain 1977, who offers the only full-scale return to the views of earlier scholars. Mellert-Hoffman's views have received brief criticism in a review of her book by Diggle 1971.

Iphigenia is coming to Aulis but do not know that the marriage is false, or Achilles and the army know nothing about the summoning of Iphigenia. The old man at 124 interprets Agamemnon's words to mean the former, and Agamemnon then makes clear that the latter is in fact the case. Bain argues that the average spectator would not notice the initial ambiguity, and that it would be pointless for Euripides to raise such an ambiguity only to resolve it twenty lines later.

Again, Knox seems to me to take the stronger position. But it is important to note that the phrase *hōs echei tade* comes at the end of Agamemnon's explication of the entire situation at Aulis and almost certainly refers to the army's ignorance of more than the false marriage. As we discover later, the army and Achilles know neither about the marriage nor about Calchas' prophecy concerning the sacrifice. In fact only Agamemnon, Menelaus, Calchas, and Odysseus know anything about the situation. Iphigenia's arrival in camp will, Agamemnon immediately realizes, stimulate Odysseus to reveal Calchas' prophecy to the army and ensure Iphigenia's sacrifice. The old man's chastisement of Agamemnon at 133–35 seems to indicate that this is the first he has heard of the sacrifice. But Agamemnon's phrase, because it is so general in its application, does not exclude the possibility that Achilles knows of the marriage, but not that it is false. The old man is asking for a clarification of line 105. Euripides makes Agamemnon's phrase ambiguous because for the moment he wants to retain the possibility that Agamemnon can save Iphigenia and to make Agamemnon's sudden shift of mind to condemning his daughter dramatically plausible and surprising. But he cannot leave Achilles' situation ambiguous, since the dramatic effect of the Achilles-Clytemnestra scene depends on the hero's ignorance of the marriage. Hence the two passages are neither redundant or contradictory, and each prepares the audience to respond to a pivotal scene.

The final major objection is that Agamemnon has no plausible motive for reading the letter to the old man and for switching to anapests to do so. In contrast, Iphigenia in the *IT* has a convincing motive for reading a letter. Knox conjectures that the old man will need to know the content of the letter in order to handle a delicate mission diplomatically. This is an imaginative motive, but unnecessary. The reason given in the *IT* for entrusting the message to the messenger is to ensure its arrival even if the message is lost or damaged. Euripides' audience would hardly require him to quote from his earlier play, once he has there established a convention concerning letter-reading with a plausible motive (if the conventions of the Greek stage require such naturalistic motivation, which I doubt). The reading of the letter also provides Euripides with an opportunity to stress Achilles' ignorance in preparation for his later scene. But in my view the shift to anapests here serves primarily to mark a formal and clear transition to Agamemnon's antimythical plot.

Finally, it should be emphasized that Euripides' striking manipulation of dramatic form in this passage is typical of his dramaturgy as a whole.[74] The chapter on the *Phoenissae* offers many examples. The conclusion of the *Medea* offers another. Here the audience expects the house doors to open to reveal the bodies of the children. Instead, Medea surprisingly appears with the children on the roof or on the machine in the chariot of the sun. The lack of so much of the Euripidean corpus makes metrical examples harder to evaluate. The use of lyrics for the messenger speech of the Phrygian slave in the *Orestes* underlines in a formal way the unusual nature of that speech; the slave is unable to report the exact nature of Helen's "death" to the audience and parodies Aeschylus' Cassandra (although here the enslaved Trojan cannot speak Greek). As will be seen in the chapter on the *Bacchae*, the use of trochaic tetrameters for Dionysus' "messenger speech" at *Bacchae* 616–41 may be another.

[74]For further discussion, see Arnott 1973 and Zeitlin 1980. See also note 56 above.

]3[

The *Phoenissae*

In the central scene of Euripides' *Phoenissae* (834–1018), the prophet Tiresias enters to inform Creon that the city of Thebes will not survive the attack of Polyneices and his allies unless Creon's younger son, Menoeceus, the last of the pureborn sown men of Thebes, is sacrificed to appease Ares;[1] Creon's elder son, Haimon, is unavailable because he is betrothed to Antigone. For many generations Ares has nursed his wrath over the slaughter of the dragon, and he now demands a sacrifice or *sphagia* (*sphagenta*, 933) as restitution for the crime that founded the city. Creon, instantly abandoning the patriotism that he previously professed, resists Tiresias' proposal by plotting to send his son through the battle lines into exile. But Menoeceus, after seeming to acquiesce in this plan, deceives his father and departs alone to sacrifice himself at the dragon's den.

The sacrificial death of Menoeceus has been interpreted by some critics as the central action and positive climax of a play in which all the characters except Menoeceus, Jocasta, and Antigone display inappropriate or untraditional attitudes to family and city.[2] Others

A shorter version of this chapter was first delivered in the spring of 1980 at a Princeton University conference in honor of J.-P. Vernant.

[1]On voluntary sacrificial action in Euripides, see Schmitt 1921, Roussel 1922, Strohm 1957: 50–63, Burnett 1971: 22–26, Vellacott 1975: 178–204, and, exclusively on the *Phoenissae*, Rebuffat 1972.

[2]For generally positive interpretations of Menoeceus' sacrifice, see especially Voigt 1896, Reimschneider 1940, Pohlenz 1954, Strohm 1957, Garzya 1962, de

have found yet another example of Euripidean irony in the isolation of this act of selfless heroism from the rest of an "episodic and overstuffed drama" (as the author of one ancient argument to the play called it).[3]

Both groups of critics are partially correct, for the play seems to offer two discrete and mutually exclusive readings of Menoeceus' action, which means one thing in the light of the choral odes and Tiresias' speech about the need for the sacrifice, and another from the perspective of the rest of the stage action. The choral odes, as Grube pointed out, seem designed to frame closely Menoeceus' action: no other Greek tragedy crowds three stasima into four hundred lines at the center of the play, with one brief ode as a tag.[4] These odes, as many critics have seen, form a continuous song cycle.[5] They offer a consistent and connected reading of the history and prehistory of Thebes. The chorus celebrates Menoeceus' action as continuing the series of confrontations between Theban kings and mythic monsters that has already pitted Cadmus against the dragon and Oedipus against the Sphinx. Menoeceus' patriotic sacrifice atones for the original crime of violence that founded the city and has continued to haunt it ever since. This original action, presided over by the goddess Athena, also had sacrificial overtones, as the use of the word *chernibas* (sacrificial waters, 662) at the killing of the dragon implies.[6] Tiresias' report that the gods require Menoeceus' sacrifice probably surprised the Athenian audience, for

---

Romilly 1967, Rawson 1970, Arthur 1975, and Burian in Burian and Swann 1981. Arthur, Rawson, Reimschneider, and Schmitt 1921 especially emphasize the themes of family and fatherland first discussed by Hartung 1843: 442–44.

[3]For recent interpretations of Menoeceus' death as ironic, see esp. Vellacott 1975 and Conacher 1967a: 241–42. Vellacott (203) argues that Euripides uses scenes of voluntary sacrifice to show that war justifies every crime and creates a quasi-religious authority that masks barbaric emotions. Mastronarde 1974 makes a more cautious pessimistic interpretation; as he remarks (215 n. 21), could Euripides have invented Menoeceus' sacrifice only to debunk it?

[4]Grube 1941: 371.

[5]On the odes, see esp. Kranz 1933: 228ff.; Reimschneider 1940 passim, esp. 15ff. and 28ff.; Arthur 1977; and Parry 1978: 166–73. Burian in Burian and Swann 1981 follows Arthur in linking his interpretation of Menoeceus to the odes.

[6]Vian 1963, esp. 232–34, shows that the founding acts of Cadmus follow a predictable mythical pattern, which includes a sacrifice to propitiate the local deity.

the episode is generally agreed to be a Euripidean innovation.[7] But
it is *not* surprising in the light of the choral odes, which locate it in
a historical context shaped by divine forces.

The death of Menoeceus, as Ludwig has shown, also marks the
center of a symmetrically ordered plot.[8] Jocasta's prologue is an-
swered in the closing scene by the laments of Oedipus, Antigone,
and Creon; these framing scenes emphasize the troubled history of
the house of Laius. Antigone's lyrics in the next scene, the *teichoskopia* (the viewing from the wall), match her lyric laments, initially alone and then with Oedipus, near the end of the play.
Jocasta's failure to reconcile the brothers Eteocles and Polyneices in
a long debate receives a reply in the messenger's description of
their fatal duel. The central episode, the death of Menoeceus, is
framed by Creon's and Eteocles' plan for the coming battle and the
messenger's report of that battle. Yet despite these axial symme-
tries and the central place given in the action to Menoeceus' death,
the chorus alone gives his gesture the recognition and praise that it
deserves (1054–66).[9] In contrast, the messenger who describes the
battle between the Argives and the Spartans gives Menoeceus a
mere three lines in a subordinate clause (1090–92):

> When the child of Creon had died for his country, standing on the
> tower tops and piercing his throat with a black-bound sword to save
> the land, . . .

Creon's later intent to mourn his son properly is forestalled by the
absence of Jocasta, who has left the palace in an attempt to prevent
the duel between her two sons, and again by the arrival of the
messenger announcing the deaths of Jocasta, Polyneices, and Eteocles. Menoeceus' body may well have lain untended and un-

---

[7]For the question of Euripides' invention of the Menoeceus episode, see esp.
Schmitt 1921: 88–93. Vian 1963: 206–15 has inconclusively contested this view.
To argue that Menoeceus performs a comparable function in the myth to Melanip-
pus, Megareus, and Haimon might argue for the creativity and aptness of Euripides' invention rather than for the actual existence of a Menoeceus in the tradition. See also Zielinski 1924: 202.

[8]Ludwig 1954, esp. 130–35.

[9]Macaria's sacrificial death in the *Heracleidae* also receives no further notice, but
her act is publicly celebrated before her death.

mourned onstage for some part of the ensuing scene, a visual reminder of a heroic death ignored throughout the remaining dramatic action.[10] Although Menoeceus has won an *onoma gennaion* (noble reputation), Creon, as he mourns his son, stresses not his glory, but the pain he has brought to his father (1314).

More important, throughout the remaining action it is unclear in precisely what sense Menoeceus' self-sacrifice has succeeded in ensuring the safety of the city. The initial battle between the Thebans and the Argives ends in a draw, owing to the intervention of Zeus' thunderbolt on the side of Thebes (1180–88). This clearly divine influence on the battle apparently represents the mark of Menoeceus' sacrifice on the action. But the war is by no means over at this point. Though Thebes is saved, the Argives have not been defeated, and Polyneices and Eteocles eventually offer to decide their conflict by individual combat. They kill each other, but Thebes then defeats the Argive army because, unlike the enemy, the Thebans keep their shields during the duel. This act of *promēthia* (forethought, 1466) hardly suggests a further imprint of divinity on the battle.

Yet even this battle apparently does not complete the saving of the city, despite Tiresias' emphasis on the death of Menoeceus. Tiresias says before the battle that the best strategy for rescuing Thebes, for which the sacrifice of Menoeceus was a *substitute* or alternative (*allē mēchanē sōtērias,* another means of salvation, 890), would have been the explusion of *tōn Oidipou* (the offspring of Oedipus, not "those around Oedipus," 886), who are possessed by a *daimōn* and about to destroy Thebes. In the *Phoenissae,* Oedipus has survived his sons, and after the battle Creon plans to carry out Tiresias' previously unheeded advice by exiling the ancient king from the land. Nevertheless, Creon's belated act of patriotism is suspect from several angles.[11] First, the Creon who was unwilling

---

[10]Mastronarde 1974: 213 n. 4 and 502–3 argues, contrary to the usual interpretation of 1317, that Creon does not enter with Menoeceus' body. He asserts that Creon has left it at home and has come to search for Jocasta to perform the proper mourning ritual. The text seems far less clear than Mastronarde implies.

[11]For bibliography on Creon's order to banish Oedipus and its relation to Tiresias' oracle, see Mastronarde 1974: 225–28. Creon's detractors outnumber his defenders. The literary tradition, though it insists on the death of the brothers, does not require the banishment of Oedipus. If Euripides meant Creon's act to be a

to carry out Tiresias' suggestion and sacrifice his son to save
Thebes, and who is willing to abandon Eteocles' instructions to
complete the marriage of Antigone and Haimon, executes here a
plan proposed neither by Eteocles nor by Tiresias, who gave no
instructions concerning Oedipus himself. In Tiresias' speech the
sacrifice of Menoeceus was an alternative *pharmakon* (cure) to ensure the safety of the city (893). Oedipus' curse has been fulfilled,
and the offspring of Oedipus have been removed from the city by
their mutual death. At the point in the play where Creon decides to
exile Oedipus, the Argives have already been defeated and Thebes,
at least for the moment, "saved." Oedipus himself has already
won from the audience some sympathy for his plight. It cannot
help but feel that Creon may be distorting and stretching the
words of the prophet in order to consolidate his own advantage
and power, and that the piety of Menoeceus has in fact set no
abiding example for the rulers of Thebes.

Finally, Menoeceus departs with these words (1015–18):

> If each man would take his available goods and devote them to the
> common good of his country, cities would experience fewer evils
> and would be fortunate in the future.

Thebans, however, share such selfless patriotism only to the degree that they do not have power. Jocasta anticipates these sentiments in her debate with Polyneices and Eteocles, who scarcely
listen and themselves make way for the Creon whom we see making apparently self-serving fiats at the end of the play. If Menoeceus' idealism has achieved precisely nothing in reconciling
public and private interests, how can his ritual death have contributed to the city's actual salvation?

The difficulty in establishing a satisfactory reading of the death
of Menoeceus, then, seems deliberately compounded by Euripides. Menoeceus, having died gloriously according to the account of the chorus, but with uncertain effect in the action, leaves
the audience in doubt as to what meaning to confer on his ritual
sacrifice.

---

late but correct response to Tiresias' earlier warnings about the house of Laius, he
certainly has left open the possibility of doubt and ambiguity.

Conacher locates this puzzle in the play's "series of paradoxical confrontations of the world of myth (in which the pattern of events is determined by some external and supernatural force) and the 'real' world of Euripidean drama, whose events are usually presented as the result of human passions and human folly."[12] Conacher's suggestion, although it needs to be made more precise, offers a useful starting point for an analysis. In the *Phoenissae* Euripides, as we have suggested, creates a contrapuntal relation between the action and the choral odes. That is, the chorus of foreign women sings a history of Thebes in mythical terms, a history in which the acts of divinities leave a clear and unquestioned trace. In the action of the play Tiresias' prophecy, Menoeceus' death, the thunderbolt, and the influence of *tuchē* still reflect divine interest, but it is human plans and passions that actually propel events. Nevertheless, as in all Greek tragedy, no events in either realm are determined entirely by the gods (nor, I think, by men), and the course of the action and the display of character are not strictly naturalistic.

An examination of Menoeceus' death, then, must proceed from two directions. As in the case of the *IA*, we shall consider the sacrifice first from the perspective of the stage action and then from the perspective of the odes. Finally, insofar as a corrupt text allows, we shall explore how the counterpoint established between the world of myth created in the odes and the naturalistic world of the action shapes our interpretation of the sacrifice.[13]

[12]Conacher 1967a: 233, criticized by Mastronarde 1974: 112, who objects that this attempt to separate myth and reality is impossible in Greek drama; myth is what the poet makes it, and reality is the stage world created in the play. For further discussion of divine and human causation in the play, see esp. Treves 1930, who finds that the play consistently denies divine care for men and justice; as well as Arthur 1975: 39–42; Mastronarde 1974, esp. 284–86; and Burian in Burian and Swann 1981: 5–6, all of whom stress that the end specified by myth is largely reached in the action of this play, if not in the Theban past, by human means.

[13]It is difficult to offer a coherent literary interpretation of a text that has aroused so much controversy. Extensive discussion of textual issues is beyond the scope of this book. Nevertheless, a convincing reading of the play can indirectly contribute to a defense of the received text. Mastronarde 1974 has eloquently defended the greater part of the text against the extensive attack of Fraenkel 1963. A similar defense by Erbse 1966 has recently been attacked by Reeve 1972. Haslam 1975 (contested by van der Valk 1982) and 1976 has brought papyrological evidence to bear on the question. The exodus and problems on individual passages are discussed in later notes. For a history of the textual controversy on the *Phoenissae*, see esp. Mastronarde 1974 and Arthur 1975.

The action in fact reveals a consistent strategy governing an apparently inconsistent and overcrowded plot. Those in political power at Thebes nearly succeed in allowing private interests to overcome the public welfare. They constantly and deliberately threaten to undermine the myth with their self-serving expediency. Creon, for example, tries to prevent Menoeceus' sacrifice. Eteocles is unwilling to meet with Tiresias and almost refuses to adopt the traditional battle plan; the brothers forestall their father's curse by delaying their fatal duel. Menoeceus' sacrifice, coming at the center of this wildly veering plot, redirects the action to its myth and gives it a remarkable symmetry. The brothers complete their duel, the enemy is defeated, and the family of Oedipus is permanently removed from Thebes. Finally, whereas Jocasta's initial attempt to save the city by reconciling the brothers fails, Antigone, though probably unable to bury her brother, takes advantage of Oedipus' exile to make the second successful selfless gesture of the play, this time for family rather than city, as she accompanies her father to Athens. Women and children act in this play for the higher interests of the city, the family, and the gods, all of which are abandoned by those in power but kept in the audience's awareness by the choral lyrics. The words and actions of Menoeceus, Jocasta, Antigone, and the chorus, like those of Iphigenia in the *IA,* symbolically close the gap between action and odes, again despite an overall impression that these isolated idealistic actions have in no sense cured the politics of Thebes.

The Action

A late Euripidean play can be as important for the play that it is not as for the one that it is, an effect frequently called parody. His *Electra,* for example, disproves to Orestes' old tutor the credibility of the footprints and the lock of hair that sufficed to identify Orestes in Aeschylus' *Libation Bearers* (*Electra* 524–44). In the *Orestes,* as Burnett and Zeitlin have shown, Euripides makes multiple and often contradictory allusions to earlier poetic texts and especially to Aeschylus' *Oresteia,* thus creating an uneasy juxtaposition of the novel and the familiar that more often under-

mines than reinforces the surface meaning of the action.[14] Sophocles responded to Aeschylus' interpretation of the Orestes myth, as
Aeschylus did to that of Homer and the lyric poets. But Euripides
heightens the effect well beyond what one normally finds in a
traditional literature. The *Orestes* does not derive its unity from a
coherent *muthos,* consistent characters, or even themes that work
together. Indeed, the action has no fully independent meaning but
develops in large part through its critical response to earlier texts.

The *Phoenissae* is equally insistent in invoking and abusing tradition, though not to the same effect as the *Orestes.* Although much
of the epic, lyric, and tragedy dealing with Thebes and the house
of Laius is lost, there are clear allusions in the *Phoenissae* to the
Iliad, to Aeschylus' *Seven against Thebes,* to Sophocles' *Oedipus Rex*
(if the text at this point is genuine), and to Euripides' own *Erechtheus.* The grammarian Aristophanes observes in his hypothesis to
the *Phoenissae:* "This plot, with the exception of Jocasta, is set
down in Aeschylus' *Seven against Thebes.*" The plot of the *Phoenissae,* then, apparently resembles that of Aeschylus' *Seven* more
than that of any other tragedy known to Aristophanes. Revivals of
Aeschylus were occurring at this period, and Aeschylus' works
had already achieved a unique and privileged status as classics, to
which the parodies in the *Electra* and *Orestes* are clearly responding.
The *Phoenissae,* while reacting both specifically and in terms of
typical scenes to the entire earlier tradition, seems to invoke most
extensively the literary tradition represented in Aeschylus' *Seven.*[15]
Reading the *Phoenissae* against this literary tradition can help to
illuminate the role of Menoeceus in what appears to be a disordered and inconsistent plot and to make it clear why the radical
surgery performed on the text by generations of philologists is not
in principle necessary.

In the *Seven* the chorus states that the oracle of Apollo warned
Laius that if he had no offspring the city would be saved (742–49).

[14]Burnett 1971 and Zeitlin 1980. My own discussion of the action of the *Phoenissae* was enriched by an oral report given by John Heath in a seminar of mine at
Stanford.

[15]Most critics of the play give passing attention to a comparison of the two plays
and have briefly acknowledged Euripides' most obvious references to the *Seven:*
Phoen. 748–52 and the emphasis on the family Erinys at 624 and 700.

In this final play of Aeschylus' trilogy, the city is indeed finally saved when Eteocles and Polyneices end the line of Laius by their mutual slaughter and when the arrogant, impious Argives find their match in the Spartoi, the autochthonous sown men who devote themselves with praiseworthy modesty to the mother earth who bore them. A conflict between state and family and between male and female stands at the center of the drama. Two confrontations between Eteocles and the women of the city, who form the chorus, frame a shield scene in which Eteocles symbolically defeats the enemy and entraps himself in the family curse as he announces the deployment of warriors at the seven gates of the city; a final disputed scene involves the mourning of the brothers and a conflict over the burial of Polyneices.

In Euripides' *Phoenissae,* as in Aeschylus' play, Thebes is apparently "saved" by the extinction and expulsion of the race of Laius from Thebes (see Tiresias' oracle) and by the heroic death of a sown man, Menoeceus. A conflict between city and family, male and female, similarly pervades the plot. At points Euripides seems to encourage expectations for a reprise of an Aeschylean version of a scene, only to dash them. The Pedagogue, for example, leads us to expect a chorus of women as troublesome and disorderly as they were in Aeschylus, whereas Euripides' chorus is in fact orderly and distant. Elsewhere the poet at first refuses to provide an Aeschylean shield scene but later grants it in an unexpected form, and he makes Antigone obliged to give Polyneices a burial that she is apparently unable to carry out. From this perspective the action of Euripides' play must be interpreted as much in the light of its omissions, additions, and failed promises as in the light of the actual development of the action onstage, which is far from necessary and probable at any point.[16] Accordingly, we shall begin by

[16]Wilamowitz 1903, esp. 588, Kitto 1954, Ebener 1964, and Conacher 1967a doubt the unity of the drama and emphasize the lack of necessity and probability in the action. Others have identified various sources of unity in the play. Podlecki 1962 finds unity in the repetition of themes and images concerning light and darkness, beasts, victory, and the joyless dance; Grube 1941 and Valgiglio 1961 find it in the emphasis on the fate of Oedipus and his sons. Reimschneider 1940 argues (esp. 19) that the hero of the play is Thebes and that the drama unfolds as a series of conflicts between the destroyers of the state and its defenders; Menoeceus' sacrifice is thus the climax of the drama, which finds closure in the death of the destructive sons of Oedipus and in the expulsion of Oedipus, the innocent bearer

examining the action as a scene-by-scene response by Euripides to the known literary tradition and especially to the tradition as it is represented in Aeschylus' *Seven*. This analysis will show that the play acquires its meaning in large part by calling attention first to its often outrageous differences from, and finally to its similarities to, these earlier poetic texts.

Eteocles and Jocasta open the *Seven* and the *Phoenissae* respectively by offering a plan to save the city. (Compare the similar energetic patriotism of Theban rulers such as Oedipus at the opening of the *OT* and even Pentheus in the later *Bacchae*.) As a general maintaining control and planning effectively for the safety of the city, Eteocles aligns himself with the pure patriots, the sown men of Thebes. Only later does he emerge fully as the Cadmean son of Oedipus, the victim of the family curse. Whereas the Aeschylean Eteocles views the hysterical prayers of the chorus of women as inimical to the city's interests,[17] in the *Phoenissae* a woman, Jocasta, who has, contrary to the known tradition, survived up to the moment of the battle between her sons,[18] steps in to rectify the irresponsible behavior of the male members of her family. Whereas

---

of *miasma*. Strohm 1957 finds structural coherence in a series of *Responsionen*: the two *agōnes* between the brothers, the exile of Polyneices and Oedipus, the two appearances of Antigone, and the doubling of the role of the brothers and Menoeceus. Rawson 1970: 125 finds the play a demonstration that selfishness and selflessness toward family and fatherland appear in different forms, but that fatherland is always to be set above all other values. De Romilly 1967, esp. 116, has a similar view. Arthur 1975 argues that the play, and especially the sacrifice of Menoeceus, shows that self-interest and justice cannot coincide; hence the final scene shifts the dilemma outside the limits of the *polis* and individualism. Mastronarde 1974: 286ff. states that the play shows a series of failures to act effectively and thus reflects an essential pessimism about the conditions of human existence. Yet he believes the play is in some sense unified by its repetition of themes (such as betrayal and reconciliation, exile, family, and city) and by showing the full complexity of the downfall of Thebes in human, divine, historical, public, and private terms. Burian in Burian and Swann 1981 (published after this chapter's presentation as a paper) shares my emphasis on the self-destructive and willful pursuit of selfish ends by Creon and the brothers.

[17]On the confrontation between Eteocles and the chorus of women and the importance of the gods to which the women pray, see Benardete 1967.

[18]In the Lille Stesichorus fragment (P. Lille 76a, b, c), the unnamed mother of Eteocles and Polyneices seems temporarily to settle the quarrel between her sons, though almost certainly at the time of the original division of the inheritance. The dialogue here may have inspired Euripides' characterization of Jocasta in the *Phoenissae*, particularly in the mother's emphasis on the survival of the fatherland.

Eteocles in the *Seven* tries to minimize in his speech the role of the family Erinys, Jocasta, as often in Euripides, brings the skeletons out of the closet at once. Family has played the determining role in the disasters of Thebes. She emphasizes from the first the fatal meaning hidden in the names of her husband and children (26, 56–58), rather than allowing this meaning to emerge, as in the *Seven,* in a terrifying and magical fashion.[19] Laius conceived Oedipus in a drunken fit (21–22) and intentionally insulted Oedipus at the crossroads (37–42); Eteocles and Polyneices mistreated their father, who cursed them in a state of sickness (63–68); Eteocles broke his word to Polyneices (71–76). The rulers of Euripides' Thebes have deliberately and consistently subordinated the interests of both family and state to their own desires, and here they abandon the safety of the city to a woman.

Jocasta's prologue, in typically Euripidean fashion, establishes an innovative direction for the myth and lays the basis for a more explicit parody of tradition in the second scene, which clearly urges the audience to view Euripides' Antigone in relation to the *Iliad*'s Helen and Aeschylus' chorus of women in the *Seven.*

Neither the entrance of the chorus nor the promised debate between Eteocles and Polyneices immediately follows Jocasta's prologue. Instead there is a scene from the private world sufficiently surprising and apparently irrelevant that a few scholars have excised it without convincing textual grounds;[20] this is the *teichoskopia,* in which Antigone and the Pedagogue observe the Argives deployed for battle from some raised vantage point above the stage, just as Helen and Priam in *Iliad* 3 observe the Hellenic army from the walls of Troy. In Aeschylus' *Seven,* Eteocles' initial monologue is followed by the appearance of a scout who has just been among the enemy and who reports to Eteocles that they have been casting lots to decide at which gate each of the seven will be

[19]Mastronarde 1974: 29–31 sees in the references to naming in the prologue a possible parody of Aeschylus.

[20]There are other examples in Euripides of scenes that intervene between the prologue and the chorus, but this one surprised critics as early as the author of the second argument, who finds the scene poorly integrated into the action of the play. After Morus and Hermann, the major critics of the *teichoskopia* (although not all propose its excision from the text) are Schroeder 1906, Verrall 1895: 233–39, and Dihle 1981.

stationed. The nearly hysterical chorus of women then enters, terrified by the sounds of war into abandoning their homes to pray on the protected acropolis. In the *teichoskopia* of the *Phoenissae* the Pedagogue has performed nearly the same functions as Aeschylus' scout. He has just been among the enemy to make a truce with Polyneices (95–98). But here he reports, not to the ruler, who will shortly emerge as a general without foresight, but to a young and innocent girl. Adopting the Aeschylean Eteocles' emphasis on the proper place for women, the Pedagogue is repeatedly scrupulous that no one in the city see Antigone making her momentary foray outdoors (89–95); the place for well-brought-up young women is at home (193–201). Here, however, Eteocles' stress on the internal safety of the city and the proper role of women in time of war is reduced to a fussy concern over the niceties of Athenian morality. In contrast, although Hector in *Iliad* 6 is similarly surprised to find his proper wife Andromache out of doors, Homer's magisterial Helen moves up to the wall for her *teichoskopia* in *Iliad* 3 with the freedom of a near goddess. The old men at the wall do not comment on her behavior but are so awed by her beauty that they think a war fought for Helen to be without blame (*Iliad* 3.156–58).[21]

Antigone voices prayers comparable to that of Aeschylus' chorus and echoes their fear for the walls. She, too, is in terror of being captured in war. She prays, however, not in the apparently inappropriate manner of Aeschylus' chorus, but to gods whom a proper young virgin would invoke, Hecate and Artemis (109–10, 151–53, 190–92). Yet despite her use of the same excited dochmiacs and polysyllabic adjectives as Aeschylus' chorus of women (see the compound adjectives with *leuko–*, *pan–*, and *chalko–* in particular),[22] Antigone looks at the war from a different perspective. Aeschylus' chorus invades public places in terror of the ever-

[21]The scholiast on line 88 remarks on the sex/age reversal between this scene and the Iliadic *teichoskopia,* and on Antigone's inappropriate exit from the house later in the play.

[22]See *Phoen.* 114, 119, 120, 149, and Aesch. *Seven* 160, *Persians* 415, *Suppliants* 334 and numerous *pan* compounds. Parry 1978, esp. 167 and 173, argues that the mythohistorical odes of this play are Aeschylean yet deny the power of the past to shape the present.

encroaching sounds of war. Euripides' Antigone is dazzled by the sunlit panorama that she sees from a safe distance (117).[23] Whereas Helen authoritatively identified the figures on the battlefield for Priam, the naive Antigone cannot interpret fully what she sees before her and has to be enlightened by the old Pedagogue. Tydeus' armor appears strange to the girl; the Pedagogue must explain that these arms are merely an Aetolian custom (138–40). Whereas Helen cannot see her brothers, and ironically does not know that they are dead, Antigone sees her brother (ironically soon to be dead and united with her as she wishes, 163–67)[24] as a glorious but imprecise outline on the plain (161–62, 168–69).

The Euripidean battlefield acquires its epic brilliance less from the identification of well-known and bona fide heroes, as in *Iliad* 3, than from the subjective vision of an impressionable young girl. The Pedagogue's laconic statements undercut Antigone's questions and their glamorous expectations of battle. Yet Antigone's vision also domesticates the scene before her. The strange armor of Tydeus makes less impression than the fact that Antigone recognizes in him Polyneices' brother-in-law (132–38). Parthenopaius is a curly-haired young man with threatening eyes, a tame version of his ambiguous Aeschylean predecessor (145–50). The orderly, circular progression of Antigone's survey of the battlefield and its terrain, as she picks out the heroes and remarks on their armor, does not uncover a significant relation between heroes and gates such as are found in Aeschylus. The scene becomes an epic-style digression that avoids hints about the future and thus does not contribute to developing a sense of tension and inevitability. The scene closes with the Pedagogue's rushing Antigone offstage to avoid an encounter with the arriving chorus, who he fears will be a source of gossip (*philopsogon*, 198) and confusion (*taragmos*, 196).

This expectation of trouble from the female, which was impor-

---

[23]Podlecki 1962 and Arthur 1975: 44–46 note the emphasis on brightness in this scene. Barlow 1971: 57–60 stresses the subjective nature of the scene and the contrast between Antigone's innocent vision and the politics of the play, as well as the use of *skiagraphia* (a technique of contemporary painting), which suggests, along with the description of the images, that Antigone's knowledge of the world has come primarily from art.

[24]On this point see Mastronarde 1974: 223 n. 16.

tant to the characterization of Aeschylus' chorus, proves consistently irrelevant to Euripides' women in the *Phoenissae*. Euripides' foreign virgins proceed in measured trochees to evoke the peaceful world of Delphi, a world in which they are dedicated to dance and sing as a *choros* (236) for Apollo. This chorus, unlike Aeschylus' chorus of native-born women, is almost a chorus by profession. The women express a sympathy for Thebes based on a remote common ancestry (243–49) and on the journey they shared with Cadmus from Tyre to Thebes; but their hope is to extricate themselves from the present disaster in which they have been unwittingly trapped (237–38). They bring to the present situation a distanced and wide-ranging mythological perspective that includes not only the history but also the prehistory of Thebes.[25] Only in their final ode do they become involved in the action of the play to the point of adopting the anapests and dochmiacs of Antigone's *teichoskopia* and the dochmiacs of Aeschylus' first chorus in the *Seven*.

At this point in the play, then, the first two movements have gained at least part of their force from what seems to be a deliberate contrast with the literary tradition represented in Aeschylus' *Seven* and in epic. Jocasta has temporarily usurped the traditionally male role of rational concern for the city. Antigone takes on a role strikingly similar to that of Aeschylus' involved and native-born chorus but avoids its hysterical tone and its apparently inappropriate movement into external spaces barred to respectable women. This scene, Eteocles' later refusal to detail his battle plan, and the messenger's description of the actual battle ultimately give the conflict an open-ended, almost naturalistic quality. Epic is evoked,

[25]Whatever the complex reasons for Euripides' choice of this chorus, the combination of foreignness and remote kinship allows it to offer a wide-ranging perspective on the action. Rationalizations of Euripides' choice of a Phoenician chorus begin with the naive suggestion of a scholiast on *Phoen.* 202 that the chorus can speak more freely to rebuke Eteocles if it is composed of foreigners. Among many later views, Rawson 1970: 112 (see also Goossens 1962: 621) argues that Euripides has chosen an exotic chorus of Phoenician exiles as a deliberate contrast with Aeschylus' closely involved chorus. Rawson and Rebuffat 1972 find a further motive in recent Athenian relations with Carthage. Rebuffat argues that Menoeceus is sacrificed in a deliberately Phoenician fashion. Arthur 1977: 166 views the Phoenician maidens as representatives of Thebes' literary past.

as it is frequently elsewhere in the play, to offer a nontragic version of events. The Aeschylean moral drama about beleaguered Thebes and its arrogant and doomed besiegers fades through Antigone's impressionistic view and the parallel of the Iliadic *teichoskopia,* where the celebration of individual glory suppresses doubts about the rightness of the war. Indeed, the Pedagogue now pointedly attributes justice to the enemy (154–55). The role of the *teichoskopia* has not fully emerged, however. For the Aeschylean parallel also prepares for Antigone's later role in the play when she, like Aeschylus' chorus, will rush immodestly into public spaces inappropriate to proper young women in order to help dissuade the brothers from their duel and to express her traditional concern with lamenting the brothers and the burial of Polyneices. Finally, Euripides' chorus of foreign women enters and, contrary to the expectations of the Pedagogue, expresses devotion both to the interests of the city and to the orderly performance of ritual and song.

A remarkably timid Polyneices now enters the city in terror of every sound (263–71, especially 269), like Aeschylus' chorus.[26] Just as Jocasta has assumed the role played by Aeschylus' Eteocles as the figure most concerned with the fate of the city, Polyneices now shares the perspective of the hysterical and endangered Aeschylean virgins. He expresses regret that he no longer belongs in the central spaces of the city that reared him (367–70). The characteristic reversal of roles continues. Men are now dangerous and antiheroic invaders of the central spaces of the city, whereas women soberly concern themselves with public issues. Aeschylus' Eteocles continually attempts to keep the enemy *outside* the walls, especially by the way he interprets their shields, and suppresses any internal surrender to emotion in time of war.[27] In contrast, Euripides' Polyneices brings within the walls the *dikē* he claimed on his shield in the *Seven* and tries with some success to establish his claim to that *dikē*. Jocasta and her son stage an emotional re-

[26]The scholiasts on *Phoen.* 275 and 395 inaugurated a scholarly distaste for Polyneices' weak and unworthy character here. Schmid in Schmid and Stählin 1940: 580 n. 5 finds his entrance almost comic.

[27]On the important relation between inside and outside in the *Seven,* see esp. Bacon 1964.

union. Just as the Phoenician women have been deprived of the
opportunity to dance in peace for Apollo at Delphi, the family
quarrels have deprived Jocasta of her normal female role in presid-
ing over the marriage of her son (344–49). She mourns in black for
sons yet alive (322–26; Andromache in the *Iliad* similarly mourns
for the living Hector), thus adding to the sense of political corruption in the city an image of ritual dislocation. But here again
politics, not the women of Thebes, are primarily responsible for
the disruption.

Eteocles enters second. The ensuing *agōn* between the brothers
delays, as he reminds us, Eteocles' Aeschylean role of marshaling
the Thebans at the walls (448–51; note, too, his haste to end the
peace conference, marked by the transition to trochaic tetrameters
at 588).[28] Jocasta domesticizes the debate by urging the brothers,
as if they were unruly children, to look each other in the eyes—
after all, they are not seeing a Gorgon's head (454–59). Jocasta
soon exposes Polyneices' claims to justice as treason (569–85), but
the ambitious Eteocles makes no claim to justice, arguing simply
that no sane person would surrender or share the power that all
men seek (499–525). After ignoring Jocasta's attempt at mediation,
the brothers close their debate by deliberately choosing to destroy
each other. Both will deploy their forces at the gates to ensure this
meeting (621–22):

P. Where will you set yourself before the walls?
E. Why do you ask me this?
P. So that I may station myself there to kill you.
E. Desire of this holds me also.

This expectation that the brothers will soon meet their fate is
shortly to be disappointed, for they do not confront each other
until after the battle.

Aeschylus' *Seven* derives its suspense entirely from the shield
scene and from the increasing horror the audience feels as it becomes certain that brother will unwittingly be forced to meet
brother in battle, thus fulfilling Oedipus' curse. Euripides' first

---

[28]Later Eteocles' haste turns his dialogue with Creon into rapid stichomythia.
See Mastronarde 1974: 139.

major scene has debased and domesticated the confrontation of the brothers. Supernatural forces play no obvious role in this conscious choice for self-destruction; the scene is hardly the centerpiece of the drama. The audience can only wonder, among other things, what tour de force will allow the plot to develop shape and moral significance. At the same time, the debate indirectly questions the premises of Aeschylus' shield scene. Aeschylus' Eteocles defeats the enemy first through *language;* by the end of the shield scene there is no need for an ensuing messenger speech to make it clear that Thebes will win and that the brothers will destroy each other. In the *Seven* the words of a good interpreter of signs have magical power, and Eteocles exercises that power through *klēdonomanteia,* the power to read and interpret such signs. Whereas the shield scene of the *Seven* asserts a positive connection between sign and truth, language and reality, Euripides' Eteocles insists on the lack of connection, and Jocasta, who defends an Aeschylean position, fails to persuade her son.

Polyneices' claim to justice presumes that true argument is *haplous* (single and simple, 469) and needs no *poikilōn hermēneumatōn* (subtle interpretations, 470), whereas the unjust argument, being sick, needs drugs (471–72).[29] Jocasta, in undercutting Polyneices' claim to *dikē,* essentially dismantles his insistence on a straightforward relation between his language and truth. Eteocles, on the other hand, argues that language is conventional: words do not mean the same for all, nothing is the same or equal for men except the name, and the fact implied by the name is not so (499–502). Eteocles uses this argument to support his amoral claim to power. In her mediating argument Jocasta finds the principle of equality in *nature* as well as in cities or in the minds of different men (535–48). That is, for Jocasta language has a basis in reality itself. The *isotēs* (equality) for which she argues, as many scholars have shown, has its origins in pre-socratic concepts that equate the

---

[29]For discussion of the rhetoric of the speeches of the brothers, see esp. Mastronarde 1974: 100ff. and Arthur 1975: 104–13. Polyneices' speech has a rhetorical correctness lacking in Eteocles'. For Polyneices' claim about language, see Aesch. *Hoplōn Krisis* frag. 176 N: *hapla gar esti tēs alētheias epē.*

political and the natural and, as Heraclitus shows, in language itself, for both nature and language exist through *logos*.[30]

Jocasta's rhetoric rationalizes Eteocles' celebration of the myth of autochthony in the *Seven:* against the arrogant, impious, and unjust Argives stands gate by gate a series of sown men as devoted to their mother earth as they are virtually indistinguishable. In asserting that mortals have no private possessions but care merely for those of the gods, Jocasta also echoes the egalitarian arguments of Solon and other Athenian statesmen, both sophistic and pre-sophistic, and thereby reconciles myth and *logos,* the traditions of autochthony and contemporary scientific arguments for equality and against tyranny (although Sophists such as Thrasymachus in Plato's *Republic* argue that tyranny is "natural"). Her position defends the principles upon which both Aeschylus' Thebans and Euripides' Menoeceus die. She fails to persuade her sons; and she even puts her own argument in partial jeopardy by suggesting that some words, such as *to pleon* (profit), have *onoma . . . monon* (a name only, 553). The brothers leave the stage after some wordplay on the name of Polyneices, "the man of many quarrels" (636–37), which, in the context of their openly unfraternal quarrel and their professed views of language, further undercuts the possibility that words can determine reality in this play.

Although Euripides has apparently made an Aeschylean shield scene impossible by Antigone's *teichoskopia,* by the brothers' deliberate and outrageous choice to destroy each other, and by Eteocles' attack on the relation between sign and reality, the following scene continues to tease the audience with the possibility that the deployment of the warriors at the seven gates may yet gain some novel significance. In this scene Eteocles, apparently forgetting his promise to meet his brother at a gate, considers several alternative military strategies (712–34). The blatant anachronism of these suggestions, which all derive from fifth-century warfare, serves to underline the deviation from tradition. Creon has to persuade the

---

[30]For discussion and references, see Arthur 1975: 113–17 and Mastronarde 1974: 103ff. For a brief reference to the views of language in the passage, see Pucci 1980: 80–82.

hasty and imprudent ruler, so different from his competent Aeschylean counterpart, to adopt the Aeschylean strategy (737–56).[31] Finally, as Eteocles prepares to leave the stage he curtly refuses to waste time with a description of the deployment of the warriors at the gates, a description that would evoke the Aeschylean shield scene in the minds of the audience (748–52):

> These things will be. Going to the seven-gated city I will arrange the captains at the gates, as you suggested, matching our citizens with equal opponents. It is a waste of time to give the name of each captain, since the enemy is encamped beneath our very walls.

But Eteocles does not simply refuse to play the role of his Aeschylean counterpart. He temporarily usurps functions performed by others in Aeschylus' *Seven* and in Sophocles' *Antigone,* and performed after rather than before the battle: he leaves instructions concerning his own and Polyneices' burial, Antigone's marriage with Haimon, Creon's role as ruler, and his father, Oedipus (757–77). (The later *Oedipus at Colonus* follows Euripides in having Polyneices request burial before the battle.) Unlike his Aeschylean counterpart, Eteocles cannot resist concern with the *oikeia,* his private interests, as well as with, or even over, the *koina* (common interests, 692). Although the dividing line between public and private interests is always difficult to establish in the case of a royal house, Euripides' Eteocles makes a point of separating these interests and hence draws attention to the clash between public and private that was developed earlier in the *agōn* with Polyneices. Indeed, the ironic disparity between his present concern for family matters and his earlier willingness to "let the whole house go to ruin" (*erretō propas domos,* 624) is patent. At his departure for battle Eteocles again remembers his hope to meet his brother face to face—but this time, although no lots have been cast as in Aeschylus,

---

[31]See Garlan 1966 for parallels between fifth-century military tactics and Eteocles' suggestions here (see also Goossens 1962: 617). Garlan sees in this scene and the battle scene a close parallel to the military dilemma presented by Agis of Sparta when he approached the walls of Athens in 411 and 410. The Athenians chose passive defense of their ramparts rather than active defense of the surrounding territory. Depending on the date of the play, Euripides is either commending the city's prudence in 411 or warning her to restrain her bellicosity after 410.

he hopes that chance will offer him this opportunity (*moi genoito,* 754; see also 755). Like Aeschylus' Eteocles, he calls for his armor, although he does not, as Aeschylus' Eteocles probably did, arm onstage (778–81). In the *Seven,* the call for arms emphasizes the sudden transformation of the hero into a warrior irrevocably set on the killing of his brother. In the *Phoenissae,* the armor is a useless prop, another red herring whose significance cannot be fully appreciated without a knowledge of the Aeschylean text.[32] Eteocles hopes to depart with *dikēi nikēphorōi* (justice that brings victory, 781); here, if the text is correct,[33] he lays claim to a virtue to which he, unlike Aeschylus' Eteocles, has earlier admitted he had no right.

Finally, Eteocles leaves to Creon the confrontation with Apollo's representative Tiresias, whereas in other known Theban plays (Sophocles' *Antigone* and *Oedipus Rex,* Euripides' later *Bacchae*) the patriotic ruler undertakes it himself. Eteocles calls attention to this deviation from dramatic tradition by remarking that, because of previous bad relations between himself and the seer, he fears that Tiresias might refuse to deal with him (772–73). In the following scene Creon, faced with the sacrifice of Menoeceus, then readily abandons his equally traditional role as advocate of the claims of the state over those of family. Eteocles leaves the stage without *knowing,* in the sense that only the gods can offer true knowledge, how to save the city.[34] The scene between Creon and Eteocles thus unfolds entirely as a series of lightning-fast rejections or usurpations of the roles played by Theban rulers in times of crisis in the plays of Aeschylus, Sophocles, and, no doubt, others. Zeitlin, in a discussion of Euripides' *Orestes,* argues that Orestes borrows frantically from a "closet of masks" belonging to characters in earlier poetry and drama.[35] Through these masks Orestes tries at one moment to escape from his myth, at another to replay familiar roles in a world that has rejected them and whose culture is frag-

[32]On the arming of Eteocles in the *Seven,* see Schadewaldt 1961. For further discussion with bibliography, see Taplin 1977: 158–61, who disputes Schadewalt's previously accepted views.

[33]This line may be interpolated, since it is missing in a papyrus fragment. See Haslam 1976: 7–8.

[34]See Mastronarde 1974: 194.

[35]See Zeitlin 1980.

mented beyond the point of recovery. The process expresses the hero's crisis of identity in a world without paternal role models.

Euripides' Eteocles in undoubtedly also a volatile personality, but the similar raid on the "closet of masks" in the *Phoenissae* serves a different end. The deliberate perversion of traditional roles undertaken by the brothers distracts the audience from any mounting concern for their nature and welfare as individuals and calls attention instead to an erratic development of the plot, an emerging sense of ritual dislocation, a pattern of inversion and transformation of male and female roles, and a pervasive split between public and private concerns. Without myth, without divine pattern, without the claim of language to mirror reality, Euripides' tragic poetry threatens to descend from the realm of philosophy, where necessary and probable events cohere in a well-selected *praxis,* to the randomness of history (see Aristotle's contrast between poetry and history at *Poetics* 1451b). Indeed, as Tiresias will shortly confirm, Eteocles' inadequate leadership puts Thebes on the brink of an antimythical disaster and thus creates the necessity for Menoeceus' intervention.

In fact Eteocles' promise of a battle between the seven pairs of champions with their squadrons (749–50) is never fulfilled. The arrangement of gates and shields is reported by a messenger *after* the battle, and at surprising length, given Eteocles' earlier scorn for the enterprise. Aeschylus' famous kledonomantic ritual between ruler and scout, in which the language and action of the ruler shape the ensuing battle, becomes in the messenger's account an almost exclusively naturalistic encounter between the two armies.[36] Eteocles, in the course of a military encounter that essentially ends in a

---

[36]For a defense of the battle scene, many parts of which have been excised by textual critics, see Mastronarde 1978 and Mellon 1974: 152–54. Mellon argues that the shield scene does not repeat the *teichoskopia,* that it satisfies the audience's expectations for the Aeschylean scene, and that Euripides wishes to separate this static description from the narrative that follows. Adopting these arguments as well, Mastronarde comments on how the shield scene orients the audience pictorially for the following action (an orientation made nearly impossible by the omission of these lines) and defends the artistic value of the text for its relation to the safety of the city theme in the play. He stresses that neither the possibly parodic relation of this passage to Aeschylus nor a few textual obscurities argue for interpolation in a passage that Page 1934: 21 admits to be written in a generally Euripidean style.

draw, moves from gate to gate (1163–71), never directly confronting Polyneices.[37]

Although we know little about epic treatments of the battle of the Seven, we do know that in the *Thebaid* there were, as here, two phases to the battle rather than one as in Aeschylus. The first included the attack on the city, the death of Capaneus, and the single combat between the sons of Oedipus; the second, the battle between the remaining champions and the victorious sortie of the Thebans.[38] Yet as in later versions, the fraternal duel belongs to the first phase. Euripides apparently also draws on epic tradition in his choice of the name Periclymenus (1157), the one Theban champion mentioned besides Eteocles, and in his selection of Adrastus rather than the Aeschylean Eteoclus, Eteocles' near double in name, to represent the enemy.[39] Perhaps the poet, in preparation for the role of Menoeceus, deliberately avoids the mention of Aeschylus' autochthonous Theban champions and makes a point of separating the fate of Thebes from the duel of the brothers reported in the second messenger speech.[40] The messenger's report has minimal and cryptic correspondences with the Aeschylean shield scene. Tydeus' shield with its fire-bearing Prometheus (1120–22) recalls that of Aeschylus' Capaneus, which shows an unarmed man bearing fire to burn the city. The giant portrayed on Capaneus' shield may invite remembrance of the immense size of Aeschylus' champion of the same name (1131–32), and his hubristic challenge to Zeus' thunderbolt as he mounts the walls of Thebes conflates the images represented on the shields of Aeschylus' Capaneus and Eteoclus (1172–76). If anything, the comparison with Aeschylus' Capaneus functions to divert attention from the symbolic power of the image on the shield to the diminished threat of Euripides' champion. Adrastus' child-snatching Hydra (1135–38) recalls Parthenopaius' Cadmean-bearing Sphinx in the *Seven;* yet the Hydra, unlike the Sphinx, has no special meaning in the Theban context. The only

[37]On the relation between gates and warriors in the *Seven,* see Zeitlin 1982.
[38]For a discussion of the *Thebaid* battle, see Vian 1963: 203. For epic coloring to the language at 1067–1283 and its effects, see Barlow 1971: 73 n. 46 and 106 and Arthur 1975: 134–39.
[39]See Zeitlin 1982: 73–82 on Eteocles and Eteoclus.
[40]See de Romilly 1967: 115 on this second point.

shield identical to those described in the *Seven* is that of Amphiareus (1111–12), and it is a blank one.

Attempts to interpret Euripides' description of warriors, gates, and shields as symbolic have been notably unsuccessful, and the lack of significant pattern becomes a statement in itself. Individual shields may hint at a possible message. The horses on Polyneices' shield, the mares of Potniae who ate their master (1124–27), suggest civil strife and contrast with the controlled steeds of Amphiareus in the *teichoskopia* (171–74) or of Eteoclus in the *Seven* (461–64).[41] Capaneus' boast and the figures on several Argive shields—the earthborn giant Argus, the Hydra, and the fire-bearing Prometheus—meet an appropriate defeat from the thunderbolt of Zeus. Yet the enemy makes no consistent challenge to the gods. Parthenopaius' neutral blazon shows his mother Atalanta heroically defeating the boar. The choral odes before the messenger's description of the battle scene have prepared for such ambiguity by emphasizing the presence of monsters within, not merely outside, the city, and Eteocles has made it clear that justice is no longer claimed by the Theban side. Hence Zeus himself must intervene to establish a distinction between friend and enemy, inside and outside, made in Aeschylus' version by Eteocles himself as he sets Hyperbius' blazon of Zeus and his thunderbolt against the challenger Hippomedon's hubristic image of a fire-breathing Typho. Whatever hints the messenger's speech provides, the speech as a whole remains as teasingly inconclusive and unreadable as Amphiareus' blank shield. As in the *agōn* between the brothers, the relation between signifier and signified and between image and reality remains opaque or purely fortuitous. If Euripides is borrowing here from epic versions of the scene, the choice, as in the *teichoskopia,* is not a neutral one, but a deliberate effort to avoid the tragic implications of the scene offered by Aeschylus. The effect is to highlight the decisive external intervention of the thunderbolt of Zeus, the presumed mark of Menoeceus' sacrifice upon an action that threatens to take an arbitrary and antimythical course.

[41]On the horses, see Mastronarde 1974: 199, de Romilly 1967: 110, and Arthur 1975. Arthur argues (132–34) that through the shield devices the assault on the city becomes civil strife (the mares of Potniae turned savage and ate their master Glaucus), and that the shield devices resonate with the dragon theme of the choral odes.

The *Phoenissae*

The return of Eteocles' squire as a messenger after the battle might at first suggest to the audience that Eteocles is dead. In fact only some time after the messenger speech is there any account of the expected fatal meeting between the brothers. Having failed to fulfill their promise to meet each other and thereby carry out their father's curse during the battle, they have belatedly chosen to confront each other in a duel.[42]

In Aeschylus, Eteocles' decision to meet his brother at the seventh gate stirs horror in the chorus of women and a deep fear that fraternal blood will pollute the land of Thebes. In Euripides' *Phoenissae* the armies ratify their leaders' decision (1238–39), they are only briefly touched by shock at the fraternal encounter (1369–71, if these lines are genuine), which evokes horror in the family only. There is contrast, too, for example, between his army's advice to Polyneices to set up a trophy of victory to Zeus (1250–52) and Jocasta's earlier reproach to her son at 571–72: "What trophies can you dedicate to Zeus?" No one mentions pollution; Oedipus' curse is forgotten. Indeed, the duel scene is dominated by the enthusiastic partisanship of each army for its respective champion and unfolds with all the formal features of an epic duel, including a Homeric simile (1380–81). Duels in Euripides proceed as they do in the *Iliad*:[43] the arming of the warriors is followed by a prayer, the encounter is often decorated by a simile, and the contest unfolds in a sequence of confrontations involving spear, stone, and sword. The setting is usually a truce between the two armies. Extant epic duels are inconclusive, failing through treachery or divine intervention to settle the issue for which they were undertaken. Here the duel is inconclusive (1424, 1460–79) not because death is forestalled, but because both brothers die. As in epic, the duel serves as a prelude to another battle, here won by the Thebans only because *promēthia* led them to retain their arms as they watched the contest (1466–72). Both Eteocles' use of trickery (the

[42]Von Fritz 1962: 209 argues that the duel of the brothers is now unnecessary, since the city has apparently already been saved. Hence we cannot, with Reimschneider 1940: 38ff., fully defend Eteocles for his proposal of the duel on patriotic grounds, or sentimentalize his death with Treves 1930: 187. If the brothers had not completed their duel, however, Oedipus' curse would have remained unfulfilled, and the play would have concluded in an antimythical fashion.
[43]On the challenge to single combat, see Mellon 1974: 154–56. On the epic quality of the duel, see Arthur 1975: 134.

Thessalian *sophisma* at 1407–8) and the Thebans' wearing of arms during a truce discredit the city and deprive its victory of a moral dimension. The duel is terminated not by superior strength or skill, but by Eteocles' own greedy restlessness to despoil his brother (1416–24); and the brothers' final expressions of familial sentiment toward Jocasta and Antigone make no amends for their previous self-serving attitudes but simply create new and dangerous responsibilities for their sheltered sister. To an audience familiar with tragic versions of the confrontation between the brothers, the almost morally neutral (as in epic?) treatment of the fratricide must have seemed striking and perhaps even shocking. Because Homeric duels end inconclusively, the tragic outcome to the duel of the brothers in Euripides has an unexpected quality, as if a tragic resolution is finally being imposed on a conflict that has long threatened to delay or even preclude its traditional outcome.

In the final scenes Oedipus' late banishment offers yet another opportunity for bringing several aspects of the literary tradition into conflict. Antigone cannot both accompany her father into exile and pay the penalty for the burial of her brother. Lines 1666–82 make it clear that she abandons her resolve to bury Polyneices, for the bodies of both brothers are onstage well guarded by Creon and then almost certainly removed by him; her change of mind in the final lyrics concerning the burial is probably spurious.[44] Creon offers no reason for his denial of burial to Polyneices except the command of Eteocles, who was acting out of hatred for his brother. As in the case of Creon's unnecessary exile of Oedipus, a Sophoclean patriotism is suspect from a man willing to abandon

[44]Lines 1743–46 have been condemned by nearly all commentators. Antigone is unlikely to have reversed her decision without explanation in the final lyrics (as opposed to iambics). The interpolation may reflect a resistance to abandoning the burial of Polyneices by Antigone or, as in the case of some later commentators, a failure to understand that Creon has forced Antigone to give up her original intentions. No defender of these lines can explain how Antigone could accomplish her plan, given Creon's superior power and his knowledge of her intent. Abandonment of the burial motif is shocking but not entirely surprising from a poet who was capable in his own *Antigone* of allowing Haimon to rescue Antigone and have a son by her. For a good discussion, see Conacher 1967b, esp. 98–99, who replies effectively to Meredith 1937 and Kitto 1939. My interpretation of the role of Antigone would be the same if the text were genuine, however. Aeschylus, too, if the ending of the *Seven* is genuine, leaves the burial issue unresolved.

the city to save his son Menoeceus, and even his loyalty to kin is ultimately limited in every case to his own immediate family. Thebes remains indifferent to the religious issues involved in Polyneices' burial, and Antigone can pursue her commitment to kin only in exile. Despite the uncertain text,[45] the final scene apparently provides Antigone an opportunity to compensate for her failure to live out her by now familiar role. We shall examine later her heroic affirmation of loyalty to Oedipus.

[45]Critics have found numerous inconsistencies, interpolations, and textual difficulties in the exodus of the play (1582–1766). Important discussions, in addition to those in the commentaries, can be found in Wilamowitz 1903, Friedrich 1939, Kitto 1939, Valgiglio 1961, Fraenkel 1963, Diller 1964, Erbse 1966, Conacher 1967b, Mastronarde 1974, and Mellon 1974. Erbse and Meredith 1937 alone defend the entire exodus, including 1737–66. The following major features have disturbed commentators: Creon's silence from 1356–1584, his abrupt exit, and his failure to give explicit commands concerning the disposal of the bodies; Oedipus' dull and confused *rhēsis* at 1595–1624 (see note 51 below); Oedipus' trochaic tetrameters at 1758–63 (clearly borrowed from Sophocles' *OT*); and Euripides' inclusion of the conflicting motifs of exile and burial (see note 44 above). I agree with critics who defend the exodus as genuinely Euripidean. Those who wish to eliminate one of the two motifs, burial or exile, must excise large parts of the earlier text, which clearly prepares for an appearance by Oedipus and an expanded role for Antigone. On this point, see esp. Conacher 1967b: 94–95 and Mastronarde 1974: 227–36 and 522. There are dramatic precedents for Creon's long silence, and his abrupt departure poses few difficulties. His business is finished, and his major motive throughout has been an overriding concern for his sons. (See Robert 1915: I, 444 on Creon's motives, and Mastronarde 1974: 494–500 on Creon's role in the exodus.)

I remain uncertain about the final lyrics from 1737–66, with the exception of 1743–46 (see note 44 above), which should almost definitely be deleted. The absence of these lines from the Strasbourg papyrus, which quotes the rest of the lyrics, is certainly damning. Obscurities in the text from 1747 to 1757 do not necessarily argue against these lines; as Meredith 1937: 101 says, "Genuine interpolation may be platitudinous, bathetic, or frankly absurd: it is not usually *obscure*." The dialogue between Antigone and Oedipus does not contradict the exile motif; it simply reintroduces Oedipus' hesitation to accept Antigone's company in exile and reasserts the importance of the maiden's role in ritual and religion, a major theme in the play. These lines effectively divide Antigone forever from the world of the Phoenician maidens of the chorus (see my later discussion). The final lines of the chorus do remarkably break dramatic illusion in their request for victory. And Oedipus' trochees, though it has been argued that they make an effective parody of Sophocles in a play riddled with such allusions, are awkward both because they address an imaginary Thebes and because Oedipus insists on reintroducing the Sphinx issue closed by Antigone at 1732. Other characters in tragedy make apostrophes to invisible audiences, however (see Mellon 1974: 148 n. 4), and Oedipus is an eccentric character throughout the exodus.

Euripides' allusions, designed inconsistencies, and red herrings baffle expectations for the outcome prescribed by myth.[46] The allusions to epic apparently further emphasize Euripides' refusal to adopt previous known tragic interpretations of the myth. Each scene, though it may have internal coherence, has an oblique or indecipherable relation to the last: Polyneices and Eteocles agree fairly early to meet face to face in battle but fail to do so until much later; Eteocles adopts the Aeschylean strategy of placing seven warriors at seven gates, then fails to remain at one gate; Eteocles refuses to provide a shield scene, but a messenger later fills the gap. The bizarre redundancies and inconsistencies in the action, excised by generations of philologists, appear to be part of a deliberate and comprehensive iconoclastic strategy. Polyneices alone claims justice; Eteocles refuses to meet Tiresias; the brothers delay their duel; and Creon, whose patriotism is continually made suspect, apparently shockingly succeeds in preventing Antigone from burying her brother. This persistent devotion to narrow interests challenges the mythical tradition, which ensured the survival of Thebes and the extirpation of the house of Laius. The gestures of Jocasta and Antigone do not affect the public world, which scarcely notes the sacrifice of Menoeceus. Thus the play's failure finally to resolve the expected tragic tensions between religion and politics, male and female, and family and state seems not so much inevitable as the result of deliberate neglect. Like the *adikos logos* (unjust argument) described by Polyneices (470–72), Euripides' plot seems in need of subtle drugs and a sophisticated hermeneutics.

The Effect of Menoeceus' Sacrifice
on the Action

By the end of the play, the plot has in fact largely achieved not only the conclusion represented in the tradition adopted by Aeschylus, but also the precise axial symmetry or ring composition

[46]For Euripides' tendency to break out of the limits of traditional myth, see esp. Zeitlin 1980. See also Goffmann 1974, esp. 345–77, on the technique of "breaking the frame."

identified by Ludwig. The action opens and closes with family concerns; the debate of the brothers is matched symmetrically by their fatal duel; and the central moment is the death of Menoeceus, heightened and framed by a concentration of choral odes. In this sacrifice divine command and human action coincide, as they initially fail to do elsewhere in the action. In terms of the Aeschylean plot, the intervention of Menoeceus offers a temporary substitute both for the death of the brothers and for Eteocles' ritualized deployment of the Spartoi against the enemy.[47] Here, however, only one sown man is singled out from Aeschylus' nation of autochthonous warriors to devote himself consciously to his mother earth. If Menoeceus' sacrifice was, as most scholars think, a Euripidean addition to the myth, in the *Phoenissae* Thebes is "saved" through the poet's intervention. The death of Menoeceus is indeed, as Tiresias characterized it, a *pharmakon* (893), a cure that salvages a plot in which the characters are, as Oedipus was said to be when he cursed his sons, sick (66), or unable or unwilling to listen to a divine voice. Tiresias refuses to speak directly to Eteocles, and Creon refuses until after the battle to follow his advice (919). Even if Euripides did not invent the character of Menoeceus, he has designed his role so that it appears to be an external intervention, a true *mēchanē sōtērias* (a way of providing safety, 890, like the god on the *mēchanē* or machine) to save a Thebes that would otherwise have fallen, against tradition, to its enemies.

In other plays involving a voluntary sacrifice, the community that is to benefit from the sacrifice performs it in response to a supernatural command. Here the sacrifice does come, as in Girard's model, as a resolution to a social crisis in which the characters, like the leaders of Thebes in this play, have descended into "mimetic rivalry." Creon, fearing precisely this kind of communal demand for the sacrifice (970) should the people hear of Tiresias' prophecy, tries to send Menoeceus into exile, thus blocking a Girardian solution to the social crisis of the play that is almost enacted in Euripides' later *Iphigenia in Aulis*. Indeed, in the version of the tradition given by Apollodorus (3.6.7), Tiresias gives the

---

[47]On previous views concerning Menoeceus' sacrifice, see notes 1–3 and 16 above.

oracle to the Thebans rather than to Creon and requests a voluntary sacrifice before the gates. As a result Menoeceus' self-sacrifice, an act of deception against his father, is accomplished in complete and extraordinary isolation from the community. Not only do we know that in other plays a youthful sacrifice is in essence a communal ritual; in addition, in the *Phoenissae* Tiresias enters with an allusion to his role in Euripides' own earlier play, the *Erechtheus,* in which Praxithea volunteered to sacrifice her daughter to save Athens (852–57). The reference to the earlier play serves mainly to underline the unusual and distorted pattern to the sacrificial action here.[48] The Thebes of this play is a world that fails to perform its own sacrificial cure and hardly recognizes Menoeceus' gesture when it occurs.

Sacrifice, as was argued in Chapter 1, is an act of communication between god and man. It is also an act that defines a political community. Only citizens participate in the act and share, on preestablished principles of distribution, in its benefits. In so doing citizens give and share in a gift that is no longer their own, but the gods'; by participating in sacrifice they tacitly indicate their submission to the community, its rules, and its hierarchies. Thucydides compares the relation of citizens to their city with that of guests at an *eranos,* a collective meal at which each guest brings a share (2.43).[49] Jocasta and Menoeceus envision the relation of men to wealth, political power, and community on principles that precisely echo this model of sacrifice; a man's life and wealth belong to the city and the gods (555–67, 1015–18). Ideally, sacrifice is organized to conform with both the religious and political organization of the community and enacts the unity between the two realms. As is emphasized in Jocasta's inability to preside at her exiled son's wedding, her mourning garb at the *agōn* between the brothers, and the failure to bury Polyneices, ritual in the *Phoenissae*

[48]Vellacott 1975: 195–98 finds the reference to the *Erectheus* ironic: the sacrifice in that play offers ambiguous help to the country, three daughters (his sole heirs) die instead of one, and Erectheus is engulfed in a chasm. The conclusion thus casts doubt on Praxithea's original patriotic speech (very similar to that of Menoeceus in this play) and atypical willingness to sacrifice her child.

[49]For a discussion of these issues in the play and parallels with Thucydides, see de Romilly 1967.

is severed from its proper relation to the community, even while Menoeceus' gesture miraculously preserves it.

Positive deceptions performed in a ritual context are not unusual in Euripides. In the *Iphigenia in Tauris,* Orestes and Iphigenia use the cult of human sacrifice dedicated to Artemis to escape their terrible past and to bring back to Greece a cult of Artemis in which human sacrifice is only a memory; here the plot explicitly declares inadequate the conclusion offered by Aeschylus' *Oresteia* (*IT* 961–75) and provides a novel solution to the dilemmas faced by the house of Atreus. In both the *IT* and the *Phoenissae* the sacrificial rite becomes a source of healing. What appears to be a deviation, an arbitrary intervention, or an addition to an already completed myth is in fact the origin of salvation. Yet in the earlier play Orestes and Iphigenia recreate a sense of community through their ritual deception, whereas Menoeceus' secret gesture emphasizes his estrangement from his fellow men.

Menoeceus' action substitutes for the deus ex machina traditional in late Euripidean drama. Yet, because it comes in the middle of the play and not at the end, the audience experiences simultaneously the return of the myth to its traditional course and the seemingly marginal effects of the sacrifice on the politics of Thebes. As the deliberate actions of the characters finally begin, as in most Greek tragedy, to serve rather than undermine a tragic pattern, traditional material willfully abandoned in the earlier scenes surprisingly reappears in a new context. The messenger follows his mention of Menoeceus' sacrifice with the shield scene earlier rejected by Eteocles; Eteocles, in proposing the duel with Polyneices, offers for the first time patriotic motives for his belated action (1223–35). Creon, however questionable his motives, finally assumes his traditional stance as city defender in banishing Oedipus and in refusing burial to Polyneices. Antigone emerges from seclusion to attempt the full roster of roles offered her by tradition as well as to undertake with Jocasta the mediating role of Aeschylus' chorus. Yet none of the characters seems to act in direct response to Menoeceus' gesture; we do not even know whether the brothers know of it. And, as if to emphasize the incurable state of Theban politics, Euripides closes the play with the denial of burial to Polyneices and a departure to survival in exile. The difficulty of locating precisely the effects of the sacrifice on the action has led some scholars to argue that the myth finally reaches its expected conclusion by strictly human means.[50] Yet tragedy never represents human actors as puppets of the divine, and the fulfillment of a divine pattern is perceived only after it has been achieved. Oedipus, if all his lines are genuine, closes the play by recognizing at some length the role played by divine forces in his life.[51] Tiresias' prophecy, the thunderbolt of Zeus, and the central placement of the Menoeceus episode in a plot in which the characters have previously threatened to escape their fate seem to argue for the power of Menoeceus' sacrifice to redirect, however mysteriously, the action to its mythical tradition.

Menoeceus' Sacrifice and the Choral Odes

Menoeceus' choice to sacrifice himself establishes the single point of intersection between the song cycle of the chorus in the first four odes and the action of the play. As Menoeceus enters the action of the play he also steps out of the action and into a separate world established by the choral odes and by Tiresias' divine command, a world that offers a coherent interpretation of his sacrifice. From this perspective, Menoeceus' autochthonous heroism as the last pure sown man atones for the violence done to the earth-born dragon at Dirce, where Cadmus, seeking water for the sacrifice of a heifer, encountered and killed the monster with the help of Athena. Ares, god of war, and Earth, who bore the sown men, both demand a reparation for this crime. Menoeceus' sacrifice must be understood in relation to the act that founded Thebes and to the pattern of its entire history, which unfolds as a series of violent confrontations between the rulers of Thebes, Cadmus and Oedipus, and a series of mythical monsters that are defeated with the help of divine interven-

---

[50]See notes 12 and 42 above.

[51]The genuineness of all or part of Oedipus' *rhēsis* at 1595–1624 has been questioned on grounds of textual difficulties and style. But Oedipus' speech is apparently meant to be a subjective interpretation of his experience by an old man confined to years of silence and obscurity within the palace. For a sympathetic treatment of this speech, see Mastronarde 1974: 525–26, despite the textual difficulties discussed at 526ff.; Mellon 1974: 128–33; and Meredith 1939, esp. 100–105.

The *Phoenissae*

tions. The battle between the brothers reenacts that of the Spartoi, and Oedipus' defeat of the Sphinx contrasts with Menoeceus' surrender to the dragon. As Arthur has argued in the most recent and detailed treatment of the song cycle of the odes, the lyrics offer an interpretation of the chronicle of Thebes, moving gradually from prehistory to the present, juxtaposing past and present events, and discovering significant patterns and parallels between apparently unrelated actions.[52] After Menoeceus' death, however, the women of the chorus lose their foreignness and their detachment and become absorbed into the action of the play.

The Phoenician women describe themselves as offerings (*akrothinia*, 203; see 214–15) dedicated to Apollo and hence attuned to the language of their god; they anticipate and echo the perspective of Apollo's seer Tiresias and the sacrificial role of Menoeceus. Throughout the odes a structural contrast is developed between the Apolline world at Delphi and the peaceful era of Thebes' prehistory, on the one hand, and the world of Ares at Thebes, the world in which the chorus is now trapped, on the other. The maidens open the parodos by evoking a vision of the world to which they intend to go at Delphi, a world of music, dance, and perpetual celebration where they will wet their hair with pure water and serve their god in an environment of light (222–25). There Dionysus is tamed and earth-born dragons are destroyed; nature, god, and man live and act in apparent harmony (226–38, 645–75). Early Thebes is also idealized. The walls of the city rose to the music of Amphion's lyre; Cadmus married the divine Harmonia, or the principle of social unity, at a wedding attended and blessed by the gods.[53] Earth gave forth water and fruit to the city,

[52]See Arthur 1972. My discussion owes much to her argument and is therefore briefer than it would have been otherwise. Arthur's general thesis is that the odes provide the link between the themes of fatherland and family, between the heroics of the past and the present disgrace (164). The odes develop the theme of the curse of civilization that orders and controls all the major action of the drama (174); the play is pessimistic, for violence is incorporated into the founding of the city itself (184–85), and the defenders of the city are also its destroyers (182). Order and chaos reach rapprochement only in the environment of ritual control at Delphi (169). Parry 1978: 166–73, esp. 167, argues that since the action is so remorselessly focused on realpolitik, the odes polarize as much as synthesize the different temporal dimensions of the play and what they represent.

[53]See Vian 1963: 142–43.

[137]

and the maidens of Thebes once danced for a Dionysus apparently untainted by the violent elements of his myth that we know from the *Bacchae*. Even the mention of Semele's death by the thunderbolt of Zeus is here suppressed. Menoeceus' sacrifice finds a place in this world made by and for the beautiful dances of maidens, a world of ritual activity and poetic permanence in which violence is repressed or given meaning as part of a divinely inspired order.

In contrast, the world of Ares in which the chorus currently finds itself, and in which Thebes was previously caught during the attack of the Sphinx, is repeatedly called unmusical (785, 791, 807, 1028), unproductive of happy maiden songs and dance, and productive of lament (784–800, 1033–42).[54] The city, founded at a terrible price, always threatens to regress to the mutual slaughter or the volatile aspects of autochthony enacted in the original battle of the sown men (801–17, 1296–98). The sown men are for the city a *kalliston oneidos* (821), a brilliant reproach, a source of glory and safety for Thebes in war and a threat to its internal equilibrium. The land of Thebes itself also persistently threatens to avenge the violation of the earth accomplished at its origin. The chorus, then, offers a vision of the city's history unique among extant Theban tragedies; the city is portrayed as having been founded on a unity of opposites, on a tension between violence and harmony, to which two kinds of dance and song and ritual performances respond. Delphi offers ritual control of violence like that represented in the sacrifice of Menoeceus, whereas the world of Ares represents the uncontrolled mimetic competition of the political world. The problems of the Labdacids are absorbed into a larger picture of the history of the city itself; the chorus, whose journey has repeated that of the founder Cadmus to Thebes, broadens the relation of the present to the past.

Aeschylus' chorus of native women enters the action of the *Seven* to try to prevent Eteocles from fighting his brother, and then to lament the bodies of the two brothers, perhaps accompanied by Antigone and Ismene. At precisely the same moment in the action of the *Phoenissae,* when the messenger brings the news

---

[54]On the theme of distorted dance and song in the play, see especially Podlecki 1962, esp. 369–72, and Arthur 1975: 52–53.

of the impending duel between the brothers (but after the death of Menoeceus), the chorus finally adopts the anapests and dochmiacs of Antigone's *teichoskopia* and the dochmiacs of Aeschylus' opening chorus and begins to share directly the fears of Antigone and Jocasta (1284–1306). Antigone and Jocasta then assume the role of Aeschylus' chorus, attempting to dissuade the brothers from their duel, and the Phoenician maidens relapse into silence. They do not fulfill their promise to lament the brothers (1301–2), for their Aeschylean role has been usurped by Antigone and Oedipus.[55] Euripides' chorus seems to function to provide an alternative lyric perspective on the action and especially on the sacrifice of Menoeceus. The chorus becomes silent precisely at the moment when, as a result of Menoeceus' death, the action begins to move back toward the tradition from which it threatened to deviate and to regain the order of myth. The death of Menoeceus makes a temporary bridge between the action and the odes. After it, as we shall see, Antigone expresses in her lyrics some of the poetic ideals voiced by the chorus and tries to act in conformity with the kind of sacrificial ideal represented by Menoeceus, although this time she devotes herself to family rather than to state.

The Role of Antigone

Both Antigone in the *teichoskopia* and Aeschylus' chorus of native women use dochmiacs, prayers, and exclamations of fear to express their excited reaction to the enemy's encroachments. Like Aeschylus' chorus and the chorus of Phoenician women, Antigone belongs, as she stresses throughout the *teichoskopia,* in an enclosed peaceful realm apart from war and suffering. All of these women have as their primary positive function the performance of ritual and prayer (see 1265 and 1751–52 for Antigone's girlhood involvement in ritual). Like the chorus of Phoenician women, Antigone's initial perspective on the action is characterized by her literal as well as figurative distance from it, and by her ability to find order and brightness in the scene laid out before her. Both Anti-

[55]See Arthur 1977: 165.

gone and the chorus respond with sympathy through a sense of kinship to what they see before them; Antigone is full of love for her brother, and the Phoenician women see themselves as distant kin, through Io, to Thebes. Both are drawn into closer involvement in the action through their fear for the brothers. Like Antigone, Aeschylus' chorus, raising important ritual issues, confronts Eteocles to try to dissuade him from meeting his brother at the seventh gate.

When Jocasta hears of the threatened duel between the brothers, she deliberately wrenches Antigone from the enclosed virginal world of happy choruses and dance for which the Phoenician women are destined at Delphi into the unmusical world of Ares (1264–66):

> O child Antigone, come out before the house. Not in dances or in maiden pursuits does the decree [*katastasis*] of the gods advance for you now.

Whereas Menoeceus, from one perspective, steps into the world of the choral odes, Antigone steps from their world into the stage action of the drama and takes up the burden of their lyrics. From this moment on Antigone explicitly dances to the tune of Ares, not to that of Apollo or the benign Dionysus, as a "bacchant of the dead" (1489–90). Both Creon (1636–38) and Oedipus try vigorously to persuade Antigone to rejoin the world of virginal contemporaries that she has left. If lines 1747–52 are genuine, Oedipus suggests that, rather than accompany him into exile, Antigone should show herself to her companions, offer prayers at the gods' altars, or go to the hills of the maenads to find Bromios and the untrod haunts (*sēkos*, 1751–52; the chorus evokes similar haunts in the second stasimon).[56] But Antigone replies that she has entered the world of lament; the offering (*charis*) of dance that she once made in the *thiasos* of Semele, dressed in a fawnskin on the mountain, is without *charis* (*achariton*, without joy or grace, 1757) for her now.

Euripides apparently made three important additions to the ver-

[56]See note 45 above on the text here.

sion of the myth given by Aeschylus and probably to that in other poets as well: Jocasta's survival through the death of the brothers; Menoeceus' sacrifice; and the joint exile of Oedipus and Antigone *after* the death of the brothers, which comes as an alternative to the burial of Polyneices by his sister.[57] These three supplements to the literary tradition are the only sources of unambiguously positive action and rhetoric in the plot of the *Phoenissae*. Jocasta's argument finds fulfillment in Menoeceus' farewell speech and sacrificial death. Antigone finds in Oedipus' exile an opportunity for heroic action, a way to gain a place in the world of poetic *kleos,* which Menoeceus has already attained. Exile will be painful for her and for Oedipus. But if his prophecy about Colonus is a genuine part of the text, as I believe it is, Oedipus will leave behind his ignominious concealment in the palace at Thebes to win burial, and perhaps by implication a cult in Athens (1705–9), the site of the recent heroic sacrifice of Praxithea's daughter.[58] The family of Oedipus is not simply eliminated, as in Aeschylus, but survives in part to find a new role in exile. Oedipus' disaster may unexpectedly become a source of painful opportunity.

Ironically, Antigone's attempt to follow tradition seems to result in the only action of the play that fails to achieve the expected outcome, her burial of Polyneices.[59] This naive and sheltered girl lacks the disposition requisite to fulfill her Sophoclean (and perhaps Aeschylean) role; she decides to bury Polyneices as a result of his request (1447–50), not as a result of her own heroic inspiration. Her initial reaction to the fatal duel of the brothers is a sense of

[57]Robert 1915: I, 444–45 argues that Euripides invents Antigone's accompaniment of her father into exile. Conacher 1967a: 229 thinks that Euripides also invented the sympathetic Polyneices and Oedipus' presence in Thebes during the siege. Both choices undercut the clarities of the Aeschylean plot.

[58]There are no impressive textual or literary reasons for excising 1705–9. Oedipus does not contradict his position in 1687, for he has now decided to accept Antigone's offer and go into exile. There are parallels (Eurytus in the *Heracleidae* and Polymestor in the *Hecuba*) for human beings making the dramatic prophecies usually reserved for gods on the machine (in this case the play has no such *deus*). For a good discussion see Mastronarde 1974: 538–39.

Oedipus' cult at Colonus was known to the audience, which would probably assume that burial in Athens would include Oedipus' future worship as a hero there.

[59]See note 44 above.

abandonment over the loss of her promised marriage to Haimon (1436–37). Sophocles' heroine sternly reserves for her final exit her regrets concerning marriage. When Euripides' Antigone tries to act on a heroic model, the result is forceful but rather grotesque. After Creon thwarts her plan to bury Polyneices, she threatens to become a Danaid on her wedding night with Haimon (1675). Antigone's song of lament is called a *mousopolon stonachan* (a lament serving the Muses, 1499).[60] Commentators have remarked on the phrase, for the Muses traditionally have little to do with the world of lament and death. Yet this paradoxical phrase almost perfectly reflects Antigone's attempt to combine the bright vision of her past with her new role of lament. She appears to try to step to the tune of the choral odes in a world out of tune with her intent.

Yet, like Menoeceus, Antigone cannot bridge the gap between the world of Apollo and the world of Ares. Thebes rejects her awkward, if moving, attempt at heroism. Deprived of her traditional role and her earlier participation in the ritual life of Thebes, she persists in pursuing a second-best choice and a meaningful, more feminine destiny in her devotion to kin and private life. She determines to sacrifice herself and her marriage by accompanying her father into exile. I use the word *sacrifice* here to underline the symmetry, noticed by previous critics, between the actions of Antigone and Menoeceus.[61]

The end of the play, even aside from its severe textual problems, makes interpretation of Antigone's role particularly difficult. Antigone and Oedipus sing past each other, and at cross purposes. The babbling old man has no interest in his daughter's attempts at heroics.[62] He is preoccupied with the dark world of the past, the family curse and the glory of his old encounter with the Sphinx (1728–31), a glory already shown by the chorus to have been undercut by his later unwitting crimes. Oedipus thinks Antigone's choice to accompany him into exile is *aischra* (shameful, 1691) for a virgin. Antigone is impatient with her father's reminiscences about

---

[60]See Paley 1880 ad loc. on this phrase ("for, as explained on *Medea* 190, the Greeks seem to have regarded poetry, *mousa,* alien from grief and accordant only with joy") and my discussion of these issues in the *Heracles* chapter.

[61]See esp. Rawson 1970: 123 and Garzya 1962: 104.

[62]On Oedipus' character here, see esp. Mellon 1974: 128–33.

the Sphinx (1732–33) and insists that her choice of solitary lament and exile is *gennaia* (noble, 1692; see also 1680). Although Oedipus finally accepts Antigone's company in exile, he seems to contest her choice to the end. Furthermore, both Polyneices and Menoeceus have disparaged exile as a mode of life (388–407, 1003–5). The Phoenician maidens, on the other hand, look forward to serving Apollo in exile, and the journey from their homeland has reestablished for them the historical past and a sense of kinship with the Thebans. Antigone also chooses a life of exile and of reliving with Oedipus her city's past.

The play opens with the old Pedagogue helping Antigone mount up to a high vantage point from which to view the besiegers. This image of old leading young perhaps suggests a reversal of the proper sequence and function of the generations throughout the play. Later the blind Tiresias is led onstage from Athens by a daughter hitherto unknown in the dramatic tradition (elsewhere he is accompanied by a boy or, as in the *Bacchae,* walks alone). The play closes with a third image of old man and young girl; this time Antigone leads her father to Athens. Again the visual repetition may hint at the appropriate reordering of the disordered generations of the house of Laius reached at the end of the play; the young lead the old, and Oedipus and Antigone retrace the steps of Tiresias and his daughter to Athens.

Through the contrapuntal relation established between the action and the odes, Euripides opens an immense gap between the individual and the collective experience, between self-interest and the needs of the *polis.* The chorus and Tiresias' prophecy emphasize the roles of earth and her monsters, an intimate connection between culture and nature. Hence the chorus sees the confrontation between the brothers as one between two beasts (1296).[63] In the action, this language of poetry and prophecy is at first incomprehensible. Jocasta hears that Polyneices won his marriage to one of the daughters of Adrastus because of an oracle that predicted a confrontation between a lion and a boar (408–11). The

[63]Conacher 1967a: 248 notes the parallel between the brothers and the other Theban monsters here. Arthur 1975: 89 and Burian in Burian and Swann 1981: 14 view as ironic the naming of the brothers as beasts. In my view the reference underlines their final absorption into Theban myth.

prophecy was fulfilled by Polyneices and Tydeus. When hearing this story, Jocasta, despite her family history, remarks in puzzlement (412): "What does the name of beasts have to do with you, child?" In the same scene she is unable to make her sons view their situation in relation to the needs of the city. Until Menoeceus' sacrifice the action develops as if the past had no easily determined relation to the present. Only Jocasta, Menoeceus, the foreign chorus, and, later, Antigone and Oedipus can speak with the voice of the city, a voice in tune with history and myth.

In this play it is primarily the voices of women, of the very young and the very old, of those who stand outside or above the passions of politics, that remain in tune with the patterns of continuity in city and family life. They allow themselves in the face of an apparently resistant reality to be educated and directed by myth and ritual. The women in the chorus of the *Electra,* who are on their way to a festival of Hera, adopt a similar stance when they assert the therapeutic power of terrible myths even at a moment when such myths seem to stand little chance of being confirmed in reality (they doubt that the sun changed its course over Thyestes' adultery; see *Electra* 737–46). Whereas Creon, Eteocles, and Polyneices seem to fulfill their destinies largely through passion, Jocasta, Menoeceus, Antigone, Oedipus, and the chorus all look beyond the moment toward the gods, heroic action, the past, and the future. Jocasta in her prologue and in her speech in the *agōn* looks back to the founding of the city, and through the present to the larger patterns that link human life to nature and the gods. Menoeceus is willing to view his life completely in relation to that of the city and its history. Oedipus insists on reviewing his past and on understanding his destiny as part of a divine pattern. Antigone, the bright-eyed visionary of the *teichoskopia,* moves awkwardly but insistently to a selfless commitment to her natal family, which takes her away from marriage, her childhood companions, and her city. The Phoenician maidens dedicate themselves to Apollo and to a life of celebrating myth in a foreign land through dance, song, and prayer in honor of the gods. Their vision does not deny that the forces for continuity and for violent disharmony in a community are continually held in a precarious balance. Their poetry has a sacrificial perspective. Hence it finds meaning in Menoeceus' sacrifice, in a ritual that puts violence in a comprehensible context and transfers the ultimate responsibility for that violence into divine hands. For these virgins the act of Menoeceus produces a wish to bear children in his image (1060–61). If they can do so, and we have no reason to suppose otherwise, the death of Menoeceus leaves a heroic mark on the future.[64]

Herodotus recounts a series of stories in which a culture is seen to survive through women.[65] Women, even in exile and married to foreign husbands, imbue their children so strongly with the culture of their birth that the children remain more their own than those of their conquerors. At the price of exile, the lyric vision of the chorus and of Antigone moves beyond the boundaries of Thebes to Delphi and Athens, where ritual (there is no reference to politics in the mention of these places) has brought violence under control for the community.

In Aeschylus' *Oresteia,* the political and religious life of a city evolve together, although the final play separates the religious and secular realms and places the enforcement of justice in the male political sphere. For Euripides in the *Phoenissae* hope seems to lie outside politics in the same religious sphere (Delphi, burial in Athens) he is so often accused of condemning. Menoeceus' sacrifice will not cure the rotten politics of Thebes in any obvious sense, although his action sets the myth on course and temporarily ensures the safety of the city. For power is left in the hands of a leader whose patriotism is suspect, and the sacrifice of Menoeceus, hardly acknowledged by Thebes, remains primarily a source of grief to his father. Creon is not consoled by the *kleos* of his son; and his son, unlike some other sacrificial victims, did not act for public recognition. Ironically, the sacrifice that promises to affect the future is less that of Menoeceus than the private gesture for family made by Antigone. From the perspective of any one scene in the play, the search for salvation and a larger historical and divine pattern in events, like that presented in the odes, seems vain. This

[64]Kranz 1933: 256–61 argues that because a virgin *hierodoulos* cannot have children, this wish of the chorus makes no sense. The rules concerning virginity in Greek cult are far too complex for such an assumption, however. See Goossens 1962: 618 on the irony of bearing children to become sacrificial victims.

[65]For a treatment of these issues, see Dewald 1981.

impression is increased, no doubt deliberately, by the plethora of characters, the lack of alignment in the generations, and the redundant, random, or antimythical actions of the play. Yet ultimately the events of the play reveal a surprising logic and a choice, by those who depart from the city, for survival, for a destiny ultimately allied with ritual performance or a private devotion to kin and with a commemoration of the past in song. Many critics have seen in the *Phoenissae* (probably performed in 410) important links with contemporary Athenian politics: the recent return of the controversial Alcibiades from exile, the attempted mediations of Theramenes, the self-seeking and destructive factionalism of oligarchs and democrats.[66] Perhaps Thebes' miraculous survival in despite of its leadership reflects Euripides' own awe at Athens' continuing escape from destruction in the face of both internal and external violence and disruption.

As Goossens remarks of Menoeceus' sacrifice, "In relation to the *Heracleidae* and the *Erectheus,* there is a kind of terrible progression in the acceptance, in the poet's consciousness, of human sacrifice as told in the old legends becoming the symbol of the demands of patriotism" (my translation).[67] Certainly Menoeceus' death is presented as a cruel and ideally unnecessary one. Human sacrifice is clearly only a legendary and literary cure for the evils of political life. Yet when Euripides invents the human sacrifice of Menoeceus to redirect his sick plot to the outcome prescribed by tradition, he seems to make a marginal gesture of confidence in ritual and in the poetry that incorporates this sacrificial cure.

[66]For the most extensive discussions of the play in relation to contemporary politics, see Goossens 1962: 602–9 and de Romilly 1967.
[67]Goossens 1962: 617.

]4[

The *Heracles*

The peripety of the *Heracles* begins with a purificatory ritual that becomes a perverted sacrifice in which the divinely maddened hero destroys his own wife and children. The language of the play represents Heracles' crime not only as a perverted sacrifice but also as a monstrous *agōn* and as a terrifying unmusical song or Dionysiac ritual. The failure of the sacrificial ritual succinctly expresses a crisis in the relations between gods and men; the perverted *agōn,* a shattering of the relation between hero and community; and the unmusical Dionysiac song and dance, a disruption of the relation between singer and heroic subject without which choral celebration cannot proceed.[1]

As I argued in Chapter 1, sacrifice, *agōn,* and festal *molpē* (including dance, song, and, for Dionysiac festivals, drama) are fundamental to the conduct of Greek public life. All of these ritual forms function to unite men in a community, to define man's relation to the gods, and to control and contain violence internal to a community. Pollution sacrifice such as that initiated by Heracles in this

A shorter version of this chapter was originally presented at a workshop on problems in Euripides in Victoria, British Columbia, in October 1978. I wish to thank the participants in the seminar, the commentator, M. J. Cropp, and the organizer of the workshop, Professor S. E. Scully, for their comments.
[1]Arrowsmith 1954: 141–56 and, more briefly, Bond 1981 take note of the Dionysiac and athletic imagery used here but do not offer an interpretation of it. (See also Zeitlin 1970a: 102 on the Dionysiac imagery.) Girard 1977: 39–41, 44, and 47 is the only critic I have found who tries to explain the failed sacrifice.

play is a form of justice by which gods purify a murderer and/or his environment of the effects of violence and define and re-establish his relation to his society.

Similarly, Heracles' *agōnes,* the *agōnes* of war, and the Greek athletic *agōnes* ideally use physical force and competition in the service of civilization, not to undermine it as in this play.[2] The victor in a fifth-century *agōn* might approach a near-divine status at the moment of victory, but he must perform his feat in accordance with the regulations of his *polis* and for its benefit and glory as well as his own. Epinician poetry, mediating between victor and community, used the victor's success to create communal bonds.[3] Athletic games may originally have been performed, like the games for Patroclus in *Iliad* 23, as part of a funerary ritual for heroes that revitalized the community after an important loss. Meuli and Gernet, however, see affinities between justice and the games.[4] The former argues that the games originated in duels to determine for the community the party responsible for a third party's death; the violent combat forestalled further revenge. The latter less speculatively emphasizes the similarities between legal procedures and those of the Homeric games. Both views reflect a general coherence of archaic culture; indeed, *agōnes,* pollution sacrifice, and in addition all poetry that offers praise and blame can be compared with other means of dispensing justice.

Festivals in honor of the gods suspend the hierarchies and limits imposed on citizens in everyday life.[5] The result, as Plato suggests at *Laws* 653d, is a temporary release of potentially dangerous tensions and frictions. Tragic poets used Dionysiac rituals in particu-

---

[2]See Rudhardt 1958: 149–58 and Bilinski 1979. Both dance and agonistic contest fit the structural model Rudhardt proposes for sacrifice (see Chapter 1). For the correspondence between the cult of athletes and the cult of heroes, especially those of Heracles, see Fontenrose 1968 and Crotty 1982: Chap. 4.

The term *agōn* is, of course, a complex one, meaning not only a labor or contest of many kinds but also a struggle, battle, trial, assembly, speech, and so on. All these meanings ultimately come into play here as Heracles' struggles turn from physical to mental and verbal.

[3]See Crotty 1982, esp. chap. 2, on the epinician poet's mediating role between victor and community.

[4]See Meuli 1941 and Gernet 1955: 9–18.

[5]For a more detailed discussion of festival in Greek city life, see Chapter 5.

lar to symbolize the dangers inherent in this festal context.[6] Here the boundaries between god, man, and nature dissolve; but the resulting collective ecstasy may suddenly erupt into bestial revenge and kin murder. Greek drama, too, essentially entailed Dionysiac ritual performed in a civic context. Comedy celebrated the festal state with outrageous license and satire, but with a view to restoring social justice and fertility. Tragedy presented and interpreted the myths of a Panhellenic past for a democratic society in Athens; but the plays control and in fact ritualize their movement to violence, social inversion, and disorder. In both genres a new form of praise and hence of communal solidarity emerges from festal inversion or tragic disaster.

Why does Euripides make the central moment of the *Heracles* a ritual crisis of spectacular proportions? And how can an exploration of this question help interpret a play that has deeply puzzled critics for its radical shifts and disjunctions in the action, in the views adopted of the gods, and in the character of the hero himself?

The *Iphigenia in Aulis* and the *Phoenissae* involved sacrificial actions in which ritual offered a "cure" for a social crisis, as well as creating a bridge between odes and action, that is, between myth and tradition and the corrupt politics of Greece or Thebes. In the *Heracles* and the *Bacchae* the use of the sacrificial motif is more complex: first, a perversion of ritual results in unintentional kin murder; second, the sacrificial crisis is absorbed into a larger ritual crisis, which itself includes a perversion of *agōn*, of festal *molpē*, and of the poetic tradition itself. In the *Heracles* the choral odes no longer serve largely to create a counterpoint with the action. Instead, the events of the suppliant action and then of the peripety directly jeopardize the stance adopted by the chorus toward Heracles and the gods. The meanings of sacrificial ritual, of Heracles' labors, and of the encomiastic songs of the chorus stand and fall together. The chorus (and to a lesser extent the characters) evokes a pretragic hymnic and epinician tradition; throughout the suppliant action it struggles to praise and find hope in the absent

---

[6]See esp. Detienne 1979a: chaps. 3 and 4 and Segal 1978a for the fundamentally anticultural nature of such Dionysiac festival.

Heracles. The peripety silences this poetry of praise, for if the gods are irrational and unjust and the hero cannot be celebrated, choral poetry loses its function. It is left to Theseus and Heracles to find the environment and the terms on which the hero can survive and continue to win honor and praise.

The *Heracles* also raises with particular directness social and artistic questions central to all Greek tragedy. First, how can the heroic *aretē* of a Heracles be celebrated in an Athenian context? The crazed Heracles of the peripety can be said to represent a whole class of epic heroes whose violent achievement of *kleos* (fame) comes ultimately at the cost of their family's or community's survival. What place can such firebrands command in a fifth-century democracy, in which ideally the exploits of the individual contribute to the glory and survival of the group? What relation have the sufferings and disasters of such titanic creatures to those of ordinary mortals? In the *Heracles* Euripides systematically confronts almost the entire earlier tradition on Heracles and the contradictions it poses for a Thebes that finds no place for the hero.[7] Yet finally only Athens and tragedy, with its emphasis on sacrifice, violence, and suffering, can rescue Heracles from the "death" and anachronism with which he is threatened in the earlier scenes and create an untraditional spiritualized hero equal to the mutability of human life and valuable for the Athenian *polis*.

At *Poetics* 1448b–1449b Aristotle implies that tragedy descends from or logically succeeds encomium.[8] Poets were originally of two kinds: the serious poets who represented the deeds of noble men and who wrote hymns and *engkōmia* (praise poems), and those who preferred *psogoi* (blame poems) and the representation of the deeds of inferior men. Epic and tragedy were successors to or descended from the first group, and iambic satire, the *Margites,* and comedy from the second group. The connection between encomium and tragedy is not immediately obvious. Yet, as we shall see, it does begin to explain why the peripety of the *Heracles* should

[7]My argument is, though from an entirely different point of view, comparable to that of Wilamowitz 1895, who interpreted the play as questioning the tradition about Heracles. He, however, originally saw Euripides as attacking Heracles' "Dorian" heroism.

[8]On the limits of this formulation see Nagy 1979: 253–64.

entail the perversion of the encomiastic poetry of the suppliant action, and why the final scenes make a point of instituting honors for the humiliated hero in a new social context.

Our discussion of the *Heracles* will examine in succession the ritual and poetic crises of the play and the social, artistic, and psychological implications of each.

In the peripety Hera interrupts Heracles' pollution sacrifice, denies purification and hence justice to the hero, and stains him instead with a new *miasma* (pollution). In the concluding scenes, however, Theseus ignores the pollution that Heracles has acquired in the "sacrifice" of his wife and sons, offers to purify the hero, and promises to honor him perpetually with the sacrifices of hero cult. Ritual performance continues, but apparently without recourse to an Olympian superstructure. Heracles accepts his full dependence on other men rather than on himself and the divine; the slaughter of the children in place of animal victims ultimately allows the substitution of Theseus and the Athenian community as Heracles' heirs.

In the peripety Heracles' civilizing *agōnes* also become destructive to those whom they were meant to protect. The hero's first reactions upon awakening from his madness are to reject the labors and contemplate suicide. Again, Theseus finds a new context for Heracles' glorious *agōnes* and his heroic powers in Athens. In coming to terms with his weapons and his painful past, Heracles provides suitable closure for a mode of civilizing violence, his labors, for which a world now tamed has no further use.

Finally, poetic *kleos* itself enters the cycle by falling, like Heracles, victim to itself. By momentarily denying in the peripety its own capacity to praise any version of Heracles offered by the poetic tradition, Euripides' poetry ultimately amplifies its capacity to memoralize in an Athenian context a now transformed heroism. Paradoxically the ritual crisis itself becomes a cure for an anarchy that sets man against man and man against god. Sacrifice, *agōn,* poetry, and the whole festal context reconstitute themselves by the end of the play and harness violence on all levels. The mysteries of ritual become by association the mysteries of poetry, so that the profound cultural values violated in the peripety can regenerate themselves. The *Heracles* (like the *Bacchae*) thus contains an implicit recognition that tragedy derives from and serves ritual; tragic resolutions are achieved through ritual, and tragic heroes are made through sacrifice.

The Ritual Crisis

At the beginning of the play Heracles is reported to be in the underworld performing his final labor, the abduction of the dog Cerberus from Hades. Euripides here apparently changes the traditional order of the myth, putting the murder of the children after, not before, the labors.[9] In his absence the tyrant Lycus has usurped the government of a faction-ridden Thebes and has decided to confirm his rule by eliminating the family of Heracles. Heracles' family, his father, wife, and three male children, have taken refuge at the altar of the temple of Zeus Soter (48). The situation for the family seems hopeless. Megara, Heracles' wife, eventually persuades his father, Amphitryon, to abandon hope and accept death nobly. The family leaves the altar; Megara dresses the children in the garments of death (329) and addresses them as sacrifices (*ta thumata*) about to be made to Hades (453). At this moment Heracles returns from the underworld as a savior whom Megara describes as not inferior to Zeus (521–22). He removes the chaplets of death from the children's heads (562) and bids farewell to his labors (575). He kills Lycus, apparently bringing the rescue plot to a happy conclusion.

Heracles then undertakes to purify himself and the house of the slaughter he has just performed (922).[10] The *hiera katharsia* (purification sacrifices 922–23) are prepared; the basket is carried

[9]It is important to remember that in this play Heracles' labors are essentially over. For previous treatments of the Heracles myth and Euripides' probable innovations, see esp. Hendrickson 1929, Arrowsmith 1954: app. B, Wilamowitz 1959 (1895): II, 1–107, and, more generally, Galinsky 1972. Bond 1981: xxviii–xxx notes in disagreement with Wilamowitz that the evidence concerning the timing of the murder of the children in the tradition before Euripides is late and slim. Nevertheless, I strongly suspect that Wilamowitz is right.

[10]Bond 1981: 311–12 also assumes that both the house and Heracles would have been polluted by Lycus' corpse. He doubts that *miasma* would have resulted from such a lawful killing.

around in propitious silence. Heracles is about to carry the torch in his right hand and dip it into the lustral waters (928–29). At this moment he abruptly begins to go mad (see also 1144–45 for emphasis on the ritual moment at which the madness took Heracles).[11] The mad hero asks that the waters be poured out and the

[11]Bond 1981: 308, 310 (see also 318 on line 995) and Moulinier 1952: 88 share my assumption that Heracles' purification ritual is a full sacrificial procedure with animal victims, rather than a purification with fire and water like that performed by Odysseus when he purifies his house in the *Odyssey*. Wilamowitz 1959 (1895): III, 207 apparently interpreted these preliminaries as the whole purification ceremony. As Rudhardt 1958: 270 points out, evidence on the procedures in purification sacrifice comes almost exclusively from literature and art, and is thus difficult to evaluate. (See also Moulinier: 87–94.) In Greek tragedy the other important purifications of an individual and place polluted by murder involve the use of blood, or blood in addition to fire. Apollo in the *Eumenides* purifies Orestes with pig's blood (282–83), as does Zeus a murderer in an Aeschylean instance cited by Eustathius (ad *Il.* 1183, 18; see also Medea's purification of Jason in Apollonius Rhodius 4. 705–7). But these two tragic rites are performed by deities. In Euripides' *IT* Iphigenia plans to purify the strangers and the temple with both lambs (1223–24) and fire (1224, 1331–32); thus the only close tragic parallel is one in which animal sacrifice is part of the procedure (*phonōi phonon / musaron eknipsō*, 1223–24). In the *Heracles* the term *hiera . . . katharsia* (922–23) could be interpreted to include animal victims (see *IT* 1224–25, where, after the lambs are mentioned, Iphigenia brings the *katharsia* in addition to the fire of torches). Philostratus 2.23 describes a painting derived from the scene in the *Heracles*, showing baskets, basins, grain, firewood, and a sacrificial bull, as well as an altar heaped with dead children. The preliminary steps taken here are identical to those preceding animal sacrifices (see, for example, Aristophanes *Peace* 956–1017), and they are most easily understood as a shorthand way of indicating that an animal sacrifice is about to take place (especially given the presence of the basket, which would have no role in a rite confined to fire and water). In addition, the symmetrical shift from an animal to a human victim is the rule in tragic sacrifices (see *Agamemnon* and *Euripides' Electra, IT, IA*—in reverse—and *Andromache*). Rituals of purification in Greek literature involving fire or fire and sulphur only—for example, *Odyssey* 22.481–94 (fire and sulphur), *Helen* 865–72 (fire and sulphur), and *IT* 1216 (fire)—generally refer to the purification of a place rather than of a person. If this were the case in the *Heracles*, it would make no difference to my later argument about the failure of the sacrifice, which becomes a human "sacrifice" that pollutes Heracles, not his house (note Heracles' later fear of his own *miasma* before Theseus), but it would suggest that Heracles himself (rather than his house) is not polluted by the murder of Lycus. The text, however, provides insufficient detail.

Although Greek propitiatory rituals frequently involved sacrifices or offerings to non-Olympian deities (as in Sophocles' *OC* 466–92), a fact emphasized by many religious historians (see Stengel 1920, esp. 120ff., or Rohde 1925: 214 n. 168), the major tragedy passages dealing with ritual purification of an individual for murder involve Olympian deities (Apollo, Artemis, Zeus). Here the sacrifice is

baskets thrown away (941). The recent killing of Lycus seems to suggest the killing of another tyrant deserving of revenge, Eurystheus, the man for whom Heracles was forced to commit his violent labors (936–40). Thinking he is killing the children of Eurystheus, Heracles proceeds to "sacrifice" the sons whom he has just preserved from the same fate; he kills the second son as the child departs the altar to supplicate his father. Finally (994–95):

$$δεύτερον \ δὲ \ παῖδ' \ ἑλών,$$
$$χωρεῖ \ τρίτον \ θῦμ' \ ὡς \ ἐπισφάξων \ δυοῖν.$$

His second son taken, he rushed to add a third sacrificial victim to the other two.

The killing of the children is described not only as a sacrifice but as a final terrible *agōn* (1229: "Theseus, have you seen the *agōn* of my children?" See also the ironic *teknon . . . ekponēsō thanaton* at 580–81).[12] Heracles the *kallinikos* (victorious) destroys the victorious crown of his life, his children (*ton kallipaida stephanon,* 839; compare 355–56, *stephanōma mochthōn,* of Heracles' labors). The mad Heracles shakes his head like a racer at the starting gates (867). He mounts an imaginary chariot in an attack on Mycenae (943–49) and celebrates a victory feast in his own honor at Megara (955–57). Thinking he is at the Isthmus, he then wrestles with no one and declares himself victor (961–62). Heracles must become one of the beasts he has fought for so long (869–70). Lyssa's maddening of the hero is also described as an athletic contest and an *agōn.* She runs races against him (863). More ironic still, the term *agōn* is later applied to Hera's action against Heracles (1191 and 1311–12).

Finally, Heracles' murder of the children is described as a per-

---

made on the raised Olympian altar of Zeus, under which one of Heracles' sons cowers like a bird (see *bōmos* at 927 and 974, *bōmia* at 984, and *eschara* at 922; on *eschara* see Rudhardt: 270). Fictional purification sacrifices may well have borne little precise relation to actual practices, and we must interpret them accordingly. For example, there is no evidence, except in one vase painting probably influenced by Aeschylus' *Eumenides,* that purification with pig's blood was actually practiced at Delphi in the classical period. On this point see Moulinier 1952: 88–89 and Dyer 1969.

[12]On the potential irony here, see Bond 1981 ad loc. On the use of the term *agōn* in the play, see Bond on line 1189.

verted song and dance (871) and as a corrupt Bacchic ritual (891–95, 899, 1085). Lyssa institutes a dance without kettledrums or thyrsus (891–92) in order to kill the beautiful chorus (*choros de kallimorphos*, 925) of Heracles' children. Heracles becomes a Bacchus of Hades (1119). He pants and bellows like a bull (869–70), the animal most associated with Dionysus. The sacrificial libations of wine become the outpourings of bloody pollution (894–95). Hera is finally left to dance alone (1303–4, although the text is difficult), while the chorus laments and then falls silent.

The Perverted Sacrifice

After his slaughter of the suitors in the *Odyssey*, Odysseus purifies his house with fire and sulphur.[13] The gods stand behind his ritual. In the final book Athena steps in to protect Odysseus from the consequences of his justified revenge. Peace is made with the families of the suitors. The gods honor those who honor them. At the close of the suppliant action of the *Heracles* the chorus expects a similar outcome for the hero.[14] A perfectly sane Heracles has ex-

[13]Purification sacrifices alone rarely suffice in tragedy to deal with the problem of *miasma*. Theseus' offer to Heracles in this play seems remarkable, although the question of potential *miasma* is simply ignored in such plays as Sophocles' *Electra*. In the *Odyssey* the necessity for Athena's appearance to save the hero from the relatives of the suitors suggests even here that the ritual is only a partial solution to the problem.

[14]Burnett 1971: 159–67 argues that the suppliant action in the *Heracles* is unconventional: the characters lose faith in the gods, dress in black (not suppliant white), leave the altar voluntarily, and look to secular sources of survival. The champion of the state acts against, not for, the suppliants. Heracles is justly punished by the gods because he has become too godlike and acts to replace the gods as a savior of men. Strohm 1957: 55 ff. comments further on the atypical relation of the *agōn* (debate) between Lycus and Amphitryon and the suppliant action; Amphitryon does not make a plea to Lycus. No one in fact refers to the altar as a source of asylum. Strohm argues that as the concern of the suppliant in Euripides becomes more personal, emphasis on the religious importance of the altar and on asylum decreases. A further anomaly occurs in the final scenes, where, after the original suppliant action, Theseus responds to Heracles' new dilemma by acting as a strictly human savior to the hero. Zeitlin 1970a: 157–58 notes also the unusual use of a false suppliant action to lure Lycus to death (715) and the mad Heracles' rejection of his children as suppliants, thus accomplishing Lycus' intent at 601–2.

Although the exact conventions of suppliancy are more difficult to determine than is usually supposed, these critics seem correct in drawing attention to the

acted a justified revenge from the murderous usurper Lycus and possibly also from a number of the guilty Thebans; he acts decisively yet remains attentive to Amphitryon's advice (585–86).[15] The chorus reacts with a song celebrating renewed confidence in a just universe (734–814). The gods do care for men. Heracles is the son of Zeus.

Like Odysseus, Heracles initiates a correct ritual appeal to the gods to purify himself and his house. As a form of justice, pollution sacrifice serves to remove the stain acquired in the shedding of human blood and to reincorporate the murderer into his community.[16] Taking advantage of the moment of ritual communication, the goddess here offers in place of justice and purification a long-meditated revenge. (Note the ironic contrast between Heracles' labors as a form of purification at 255 and his new pollution at 1283–84.)

An Oxyrynchus papyrus says that for showing Heracles going mad in a play at the Dionysia Euripides was prosecuted (by Cleon) for impiety.[17] Although the story is almost certainly apocryphal, it apparently records ancient dissatisfaction with the treatment of Heracles in this play. The moment is indeed shocking. Sacrifice establishes the division between god and man, delineates a man's relation to his community, and, in a pollution sacrifice, makes god in part responsible for human violence. In the sacrificial crisis of the *Heracles* all these functions of sacrifice come into play, raising multiple questions about the ritual itself and about the relations among god, man, and community established through the rite. Euripides typically provides several possible answers to those questions, and none remains certain.

---

unconventional nature of the suppliant action here and to the play's reliance on a human savior; the unusual suppliant action corresponds with the unusual relation between men and gods developed throughout the drama. Yet we should recall, in relation to Burnett's tenuous argument that Heracles' family is justly punished for its lack of faith in the gods here, that the human intermediary is always the decisive factor in suppliant actions, and that the chorus, at least temporarily, continues to find in Heracles' successful return and vengeance evidence of divine support (see Zeitlin 1970a: 360).

[15]On the question of Heracles' revenge on Thebans other than Lycus, see Bond 1981 on 604ff. The text is unclear.

[16]See note 11 above.

[17]*POxy* 2400, vol. 24, 107–9, lines 10–14.

Iris, in offering justification for Hera's maddening of Heracles, implies that Heracles has overstepped the limits that separate the divine from the human. He has made the gods nothing (*theoi men oudamou*, 841). In other words, he threatens the gods' *timē* from men (honor expressed through prayer and sacrifice).[18] Surprisingly, even the gods themselves need the powers of the hero, for Heracles has fought on the side of the gods against the giants and shared in their victory celebrations (178–80, 1192–97), thus becoming part of the community of gods as well as the community of men. He is the product of a divine/human relation offensive to Hera (826, 1309). In the suppliant action the chorus and characters treat Heracles as such a near divinity. Parallels between the staging of Aeschylus' *Prometheus Bound* and the *Heracles* may further hint at the hero's unintentional threat to divine power. Both heroes are shown onstage bound to a pillar, and the roles of Iris and Lyssa may echo those of Aeschylus' Kratos and Bia.[19] By sacrificial logic, then, Heracles' ritual fails and he is punished by Hera because in his case the ritual no longer functions to divide the divine from the human.[20]

Iris' position is perfectly understandable. Hera's hatred of Heracles was well known.[21] In literary tradition Heracles quite often transgressed human limits, even going so far as to fight against the gods rather than with them (Pindar, *Olympian* 9). He became an Olympian after death. But Euripides has Lyssa contest Iris' argument (846–54). Heracles, she argues, has been a model of piety, a great benefactor whose reputation is well deserved. He alone has preserved the *timai* of the gods (852–53). She advises Iris to reconsider (847–48). Lyssa's defense is thoroughly borne out by the

[18]See Chapter 1 on sacrifice as *timē*. Bond 1981: xxvi in his discussion of line 841 quotes M. J. Cropp's argument that the lines mean "if Heracles escapes unpunished, the interests of mortals will be preferred to the interests of the gods (i.e. Hera)." Euripides, Bond argues, may also have had in mind the notion that nothing great comes to men *ektos atas* (without tragic disaster, Soph. *Ant.* 614).

[19]See Mullens 1939.

[20]Vernant 1980: 120 argues that pollution results from a failure to maintain the proper distinction between separate, especially divine and human, realms.

[21]Bond 1981: xxiv–xxv and 206–7 stresses that Hera's revenge on Heracles would have appeared well motivated to the audience, since it was familiar in the literary tradition. This point is perfectly correct, but in the circumstances of this play her action is nevertheless made to seem unjust and shocking, as is emphasized by offensive references to Zeus and Hera throughout the play (see esp. 1127).

Heracles we have seen onstage up to this point as he honors the gods, rescues his family and city from an unjust regime, and justly chastises Thebes for its betrayal of his interests.

Fearing the nobility of Heracles' children and their legitimate claim to the throne of Thebes (168–69), Lycus has determined to kill them to ensure his own authority (245–46). He does not respect the altar of the gods (240–46, 722–25), and he rules a Thebes dominated by *stasis* and indifferent to the claims and past benefits of Heracles (217–28). Hera makes the mad Heracles perform the crimes intended by Lycus. Threatened at the altar by Lycus, Megara has addressed the children as *thumata* (sacrificial victims, 453); Hera makes Heracles treat the children as sacrificial victims. Indeed, as Zeitlin has argued, the sacrifice of the children in this sense comes as no surprise: the combination of a suppliant plot and sacrificial imagery must be seen as proleptic of a later plot development also involving ritual (see also the *Helen* and the *Andromache*); sacrifice and suppliancy share the presence of the altar and the threat of imminent death.[22] Echoing Thebes' neglect of the hero's benefits, Hera ignores Heracles' past honors to the gods. Reenacting Lycus' fears for *his* regime, she apparently wishes to take revenge on Heracles because Zeus' adultery threatens her legitimacy as wife and because he has made the gods nothing (841). Whereas Lycus was prepared to violate the sanctity of the altar, Hera ignores Heracles' claims to justice and violates his correct ritual appeal to the gods. Although the parallels are not in every respect exact, Hera in essence offers to Heracles in an even more despicable form the (in)justice of Lycus and Thebes. By equating the justice of Hera and Thebes, Euripides hints at a Girardian identity of divine and communal violence. In this play neither the divine nor the human realm offers justice. In response to a just revenge, Heracles receives only revenge. The failure of Heracles' pollution ritual seems to reflect precisely the hostile divine and human reality in which he is trapped.

Sacrifice draws the boundary between god and man and defines the relation between the sacrificer and his community. The failure of a ritual of purification could symbolize the inability of a com-

[22]See Zeitlin 1970a: 125 and 346.

munity indifferent to the hero and ridden by *stasis* and loss of hierarchy to reintegrate the hero.[23] Yet critics of the play, taking their cue from Iris' blame of the hero, have struggled to find in the hero's own person an explanation for his disaster. Even Girard, who usually finds the explanation for sacrificial crisis and the ensuing explosion in the community, argues in the case of this play that Heracles' extraordinary capacity for violence undermines the sacrificial mechanism, in that his return to Thebes overloads the ability of ritual to control this violence. According to Girard, Heracles acts like a soldier who returns from war only to act violently against those whom he fought to protect. Douglas's cross-cultural analysis in *Purity and Danger* similarly emphasizes the danger of social explosion and the locus of impurities that can be found in transitional states or in acts, objects, and beings that lie between normal social categories.[24] Both views help to illuminate the ambivalent effects of *nostos* (return home) common throughout Greek myth. Yet Girard's observation more aptly describes Sophocles' explosive hero in the *Trachiniae,* who has already explicitly committed two of the three sins that Dumézil associates with Heracles' myth: disobedience to Eurystheus, for which he was punished with madness and the labors; the killing of Iphitus, for which he was punished with sickness (or in the *Trachiniae,* with slavery to Omphale in Lydia); and the sack of a city to capture Iole, which led to Deianeira's gift of the poisoned robe.[25] In Sophocles' play Deianeira cannot tolerate Heracles' challenge to her role as wife; Iole's

[23]Although the Thebes of this play is in a state of "sacrificial crisis," which might logically result in the mass lynching of a scapegoat figure, Girard 1977 himself emphasizes instead in his interpretation of the play the problem of Heracles' *own* pollution for the sacrificial system. Girard seems correct in stressing the ritual setting for the action, but the text does not directly attribute excessive violence and impurity to the hero.

[24]See Girard 1977: 39–41 and Douglas 1966, esp. 116, who stresses the use of ritual generally to control the passage of an individual from his old to his new status.

[25]Dumézil 1969 identifies Heracles' madness as typical of the Indo-European warrior. Yet in fact Euripides' Heracles has at the point of his entrance apparently committed none of the three sins Dumézil identifies in his myth. Burkert 1979: 93–96, attributing to shamanistic origins Heracles' role in bringing animals back to civilization and his intimate connection with sacrifice, finds a relation between shamanistic ecstasy and Heracles' madness at the sacrifice.

presence in the household will make a mockery of her marriage. The robe mortally wounds the hero while he is offering a sacrifice to celebrate his violent return to civilized life. In the final scenes the hero himself comes to see the logic of this particular punishment. He insists on completing his own sacrifice and responds to his disastrous surrender to *erōs* by insisting on the marriage of Iole and his son Hyllus. Agamemnon's return in Aeschylus' *Agamemnon* also results in a fatal sacrifice, this time of himself by his wife. But Agamemnon has already been tainted by his past crimes, his ritual slaughter of Iphigenia, and his violation of the gods' shrines at Troy.

Wilamowitz and others have insisted, without Girard's perceptive emphasis on the sacrificial setting for the disaster, that Euripides' Heracles represents a similar case.[26] For Wilamowitz, Heracles' Dorian heroism explodes in an excessive revenge on Thebes; the hero showed signs of incipient madness before committing his crime. Because Wilamowitz's specific arguments have been thoroughly discredited, later critics have based their similar views on the madness scene itself. The mad Heracles does indeed imagine the killing of his children as an act of long-suppressed revenge against Eurystheus and his children. The murders suggestively come as a climax rather than as a preliminary to the labors, and Iris notes that Hera waited until this point to attack Heracles (827–29). Should we then follow Kamerbeek in viewing Heracles' psychotic break as an understandable reaction to the strain of his overburdened life?[27]

Euripides seems to insist, however, that his Heracles is not the unstable and violence-prone hero well known in previous tradi-

[26]For an excellent refutation of the views of Wilamowitz 1895, see Kroeker 1938, esp. 114–24. In this he is followed by Bond 1981: xix, 206–7, and 285, who emphasizes Heracles' lack of *hubris* and the reasonableness of Heracles' revenge. Pohlenz 1954 attributes Heracles' madness to the shock of finding his family in danger; Blaiklock 1952: 122–40 explains the madness as an epileptic fit. Pachet 1972 more convincingly argues that the madness has a certain compelling dream logic despite its implausibility in the context of this play. Although Greek ideas of madness are difficult to evaluate, the notion of a strictly external cause for insanity seems in no way foreign to Greek thought. For recent general discussions, see Simon 1978: 89–154 and Vasquez 1972.

[27]Kamerbeek 1966, esp. 14. His views are a variation on those of Wilamowitz 1895 and similar to those of Verrall 1895, Murray 1913, and Pohlenz 1954.

tion. Everyone in the play repeatedly assumes that Hera is responsible for the madness (1127, 1180, 1253, 1263–64, 1310, 1311–12, 1393). Amphitryon speculates briefly on whether the blood of the slain could have made Heracles mad (965–67), as happens in the case of Orestes in Aeschylus' *Libation Bearers*. But Heracles has not at this point killed his own kin.[28] In the *Bacchae* Euripides makes Pentheus' madness psychologically understandable. Even the madness of Sophocles' Ajax seems a logical extension of his hubristic overconfidence and his obsession with honor and revenge; in the *Ajax* the hero goes mad while contemplating violent action, and the gods substitute animals for the intended human victims. But in the *Heracles* Euripides creates a sane and modest hero without an explicit record, like that of Sophocles' Heracles or Aeschylus' Agamemnon, of illegitimate violence.

If Heracles had indeed transgressed the limits between god and man or had in fact been the volatile and violent hero of tradition that he becomes in his state of madness, sacrificial logic could easily explain his disaster. The ritual setting can speak with an implicit language as precise as that of the explicit language of the text. Yet in this play the sacrificial explosion seems more logically to derive from the community of Thebes and from the goddess who enacts the plans of its tyrant. The failure of Heracles' ritual thus implicitly poses the same questions posed in the play as a whole; but it raises them without offering answers, drawing attention to the disjunction between the logic of ritual and the actual situation of the hero. What place can be found for Heracles in a world that has no place for his heroism? Not, certainly, in an unjust and indifferent Thebes, nor in a universe peopled by similarly unjust deities. Not for the violent individualist of existing literary tradition. Instead Euripides provides an untraditional Heracles, a model of paternal concern, piety, and justice. In descending into madness he seems to be pushed arbitrarily into his own literary reputation for violence and instability, and into a sacrificial scenario that belongs more appropriately to heroes such as Sophocles' Heracles or Aeschylus' Agamemnon. At the height of Heracles' disaster Lyssa's defense opens a moment of hope and pos-

[28]On this point, see Bond 1981 ad loc.

sibility. A just community could surely find a place for the Heracles of Euripides' play.

The Restoration of Sacrifice

Heracles' disaster seems irrevocable. He cannot live in Thebes, for his pollution has been redoubled rather than removed. Trapped between an unjust god and an unjust city, he cannot live with his madness and its results.

Theseus, a just man from an apparently just city, resolves Heracles' problems on a social level. He will purify the hero himself and restore Heracles to society in Athens. Euripides' characters frequently choose to minimize *miasma* (see *Hipp.* 1448–51 or *Orestes* 75–76), but we cannot tell whether Theseus' indifference to Heracles' pollution represented a larger trend in Athenian society.[29] In Athens murderers returning from exile obtained ritual purification before they took up a normal position in civic life (Demosthenes 23.72), a formality that Theseus apparently will accomplish for Heracles. Theseus emphasizes his willingness to take responsibility for Heracles' pollution and insists on Heracles' innocence; the hero has now no need to rely on the justice of the gods. Although Euripides rarely expresses social optimism about cities, he consistently presents Athens as a place that can cope, ritually and artistically, with the violence represented by the terrible heroes of myth. If Athens can accept Medea after she deliberately "sacrificed" her children, why not Heracles? The *Medea* passage about Athens (824–65) seems to hint, however, that this special capacity of Athens is associated with the greatness of her artistic traditions; wisdom dwells where Harmony gave birth to the nine Muses. The

[29]For discussions of purity and pollution in ancient society, see, among others, Adkins 1960: 86–115; Dodds 1951: chap. 2; MacDowell 1963, esp. 110–29; Moulinier 1952, criticized by Vernant 1980: 110–29; Rudhardt 1958: 21–52; and Gagarin 1981. Gagarin's de-emphasis of the role of pollution in Athenian homicide law is not convincing. Homicide trials were held in the open air, Solon's amnesty law excludes homicides; all such details seem to reflect legal concern with pollution. See also Bond 1981 on lines 1232–34.

Heracles, as we shall see, makes the hero's killing of his children a tragic sacrifice to the Muses.

Theseus establishes for the hero a relation with a community that despite his disaster values his heroism and specifically his past benefits to mankind. By arguing that both men and gods are subject to *tuchai* (misfortunes, 1314), Theseus makes Heracles' sufferings part of a universal burden of sorrow. Heracles responds with a determination to depend on other human beings for survival (1403, 1425; compare also 1337–38) rather than on Zeus or a paternal universe. Amphitryon will become his sole father (1263–65) and Theseus his "son" (1401).[30] His status in society will be defined by Theseus' friendship and his gifts. Deprived of his family, Heracles' powers will serve Athens alone. Whereas Iris earlier argued that Heracles threatened to transgress human limits, the hero here takes his place firmly on the side of man.

Heracles' final view of the gods also expresses a determination to depend on man rather than on the gods for identity and justice. Redefining man's relation to the gods, he implies that Theseus should not project man's own violence and other illegitimate human desires onto the gods (1341–46):

> I do not think the gods desire illegitimate love or to fasten chains on each other's hands. I do not think it worthy nor will I be persuaded that one god is master of another. For god needs, if he is truly god, nothing. These are the wretched *logoi* [stories] of poets.

Human beings may commit adultery, make wives jealous, create hierarchies of power, and punish each other. Gods do not or should not. This controversial passage insists that Hera could not be jealous of Heracles' birth, for Zeus could not have adulterously fathered Heracles; it denies or censors the version of events presented in the peripety.[31] Heracles' assertion is consistent with his

---

[30]For the importance of the theme of the two fathers in the play, see most recently Gregory 1977.

[31]My interpretation of this vexed passage comes closest to the views of Arrowsmith 1954: 175–83, Kroeker 1938: 99–102, Stinton 1976, esp. 83, and Pucci 1980: app. 2. Arrowsmith has an excellent summary of earlier views. We cannot

decision to treat Amphitryon as his true father. As long as he thinks of the gods as human beings, his fate, like that of Ajax, seems a divine mockery too unbearable for a man who has rationalized his entire life as a series of labors performed for his father, Zeus. Heracles cannot pray to such a repellent Hera (1307–8). Suicide becomes the only alternative (1146–52, 1247). The decision to understand the force that destroyed him as *tuchē* or the *tuchē* of Hera (1393) does preserve for Heracles a relation to the divine. (I define *tuchē* here as a sign of gods at work, and as "chance" only insofar as this divine activity is incomprehensible and arbitrary from the human perspective). But he will depend on the divine in one respect only, to rationalize his disaster. This divine *tuchē* is still responsible for Heracles' madness, and thus he can escape from an intolerable mental imprisonment in his own nature and choose to survive and accept a relation to a new community.

Hera's *tuchē*, then, does not so much reassert the old anthropomorphism as capture the inscrutability of man's relation to godhead (be it *tuchē* or Olympians). Euripides' contemporaries, after all, had no expectation that divination through sacrifice would put the divine force under their control nor always even reveal with which divinity they might be communicating or should communicate. They expected favorable omens only when their plans accorded with divine necessity, which Greek authors frequently characterized as inherently arbitrary and indifferent to men's aspirations, values, and standards of justice. In this respect ritual practice implied the recognition about divinity that Heracles reaches here. Gods who give or enforce justice must be anthropomorphic and violent. Heracles' slavery to divine *tuchē*, in contrast, seems to

---

avoid the challenging implications of this passage by insisting that Heracles' words are *only* a reply to Theseus (see Bond 1981: xxii and ad loc.). Stinton, in arguing that Heracles is not denying the existence of arbitrary divinities but finds them unacceptable and prefers the new ideal he presents here, adduces many parallel passages such as Pindar *Olympian* 9.28ff. and Eur. *Hippolytus* 120 and *Bacchae* 1348. One might add *Ion* 440–51, where Ion speculates on the consequences for mortals of divine injustice and irresponsibility. Lines such as 1243–45 do not indicate that Heracles is making a complete break with divinity as such.

imply a continued relation to divinity but no confidence in a divine justice.

Heracles' decision marks an interesting moment in the development of tragedy. The *Heracles,* like the *Oresteia,* makes aetiology the *telos* (concluding moment) of tragedy, and Athenian society the reward for mankind's transformation of suffering into knowledge. In both cases the gods as violence personified enter directly into the tragic *agōn* (Erinyes/Lyssa) but give way before strengthened mechanisms of social control. In Aeschylus, however, piety prevails only through an immeasurably larger portion of divine concern (Athena) and concession (the Eumenides), whereas Euripides' men can fall back only on *philia* (friendship), ritual, and imagination: Theseus' capacity to purify Heracles at Athens derives from his command of that city, and Heracles' restored sanity rests on his adroit denial that he has experienced what the audience has in fact seen—the vindictive human gods of the peripety. Remasking those gods in incomprehensibility, Heracles may now understand himself as the victim of an order that neither resembles man nor invites his judgments. And this too is a familiar figure: the Sophoclean hero walking through a tragic foundation myth, but with powers of redemptive self-delusion that are purely Euripidean.

In the final scenes Theseus offers Heracles both land (*temenē,* 1329) and a cult (1331–33) in Athens.[32] His new community will restore to him the honor apparently destroyed by the gods (1333), and it will accept glory in compensation for receiving the hero (1334–35). The sacrifices (*thusiai,* 1332) that he will receive suggest either a combination of divine and heroic rites or, more probably, heroic rites. In his cult at Athens, a cult that Theseus is apparently preparing to establish, Heracles was one of the few Greek heroes to receive both Olympian and chthonic sacrifice, and Athens claimed to have been the first to worship the hero in both forms.[33] Yet

[32]Tarkow 1977, in discussing the role of Athens in the play, thinks Heracles turns to the intellectual world of Athens as he becomes a spiritual rather than a physical hero in the final scenes. Theseus serves as an intellectual sounding board for the hero in his painful transition.

[33]See Woodford 1971 for the most up-to-date treatment of Heracles' cults in Attica and the ancient references to his double nature. On the cults of Theseus see

there are several reasons for interpreting Theseus' offer as one of a hero cult. Theseus offers to a very humanized hero, *after* he has gone to Hades (1331), sacrifices and raised stone monuments (*laïnoisi t' exongkōmasin*, 1332; see *exongkoun* used of raising a tomb for Clytemnestra in *Orestes* 402); and Theseus, who received exclusively heroic honors in Athens, offers to share his own *temenē* (a term often used for a divine precinct) with Heracles.

Though dead, a hero could still receive honor and offer assistance to his worshipers from the world below. Yet Heracles' claim to this special daemonic status now rests on Theseus and Athens, not on the paternity of Zeus. Indeed, Theseus' offer of a cult that is neither initiated nor supported by divine authority is as striking as his comparable offer to perform pollution rites for a hero whose appeal to the gods for purification has been rejected.[34] Leaving aside numerous other aetiologies of hero cults, we have only to compare the similar situation in Sophocles' *Oedipus at Colonus*. Here Oedipus acquires cult status in a traditional manner, as Theseus and the chorus accept the prophecies about his death offered to the hero by the oracles from Delphi. Through the city's experience of Heracles' imagination, courage, and suffering, we see that Athens will receive the advantage of the hero's divine energies in a form more human and predictable than that embodied in the forces variously called Zeus, Hera, or *tuchē*. The hero offers the city divinity with a human face, a power that can mediate positively between the city and an external reality now visualized as totally nonhuman.

Athens wins a crown for adopting Heracles (1334) and transforms a Theban and Panhellenic hero into a local Athenian deity (hero cults were always local).[35] Here the community creates its

---

Nock 1944: 144. The term *thusiai* could continue to suggest both divine and chthonic honors for the audience, if not for Heracles. For the use of *thuō* to refer to a combination of divine and chthonic honors (although the term *enagizein* is more common), see Casabona 1966: 83–85.

[34]Hero cults were generally accorded by gods and imposed on communities; see esp. Crotty 1982: xi and chap. 4, and Rohde 1925: 129–31.

[35]Nagy 1979 argues that epic texts suppress the mention of hero cults precisely because this poetry aims at being Panhellenic rather than tied to a specific location. Regional poets, in contrast, celebrate hero cults precisely because they are local. Euripides' play transforms a Panhellenic hero into an Athenian one. Just as the

own divinity and ritualizes its relation to the hero through sacrifice. Heracles will remain in Athens, but his powers will be limited by his humanity and his mortality. The gods exist simply to rationalize his disaster and to declare his innocence. For the first time in known poetic tradition Heracles finds a permanent place *within* a *polis*. (Sophocles' play, in contrast, returns the hero to a sacrifice on the margins of civilization where he lived his life.) This resolution of Heracles' sacrificial crisis restores the relations among hero, god, and community shattered in the peripety. Ritual remains necessary for the ordering of human experience, but the superstructure by which it is rationalized is transformed. In this sense the *Heracles* reflects a trend in late fifth- and fourth-century religious thinking; as the Olympian gods become less anthropomorphic, heroes and *daimones* serve to mediate between gods and men and open the way for mortals to achieve a divine status.[36]

The Restoration of Heracles' Perverted Labors (*Agōnes*)

Amphitryon finds three factors responsible for Heracles' crime: Heracles, the bow, and a god (1135). When Heracles first contemplates the terrible *agōn* in which he slew his family, he wishes to reject his past glory and painful labors and associates his famous weapons exclusively with the murder of his children (1270–78 and 1377–81). Indeed, although the chorus and characters find consolation and meaning in the labors, Heracles from his first entrance has been only too willing to abandon the labors and his glorious past for the sake of defending his family. Finally, Heracles, as he accepts responsibility for the murders precipitated by Hera, also reluctantly adopts the *koinōniai* (companionship, 1377) of the weap-

---

hero cult promised by Theseus lays exclusive claim for Athens to Heracles' heroic powers after death, Euripides seems to claim for Athens exclusive recognition of Heracles' heroism. This act defies what we know about Heracles (he was praised, worshiped, and claimed by other cities) but is not inconsistent with the chauvinistic practices of Attic tragedy.

[36]On this point, see Vernant 1980: 107–8. See Nock 1944: 165 on the greater closeness of heroes than Olympians to the ordinary man.

ons as murderers of his children. As the weapons say to Heracles (1380–81):

> Through us you murdered your wife and children. Wearing us you wear the murderers of your children.

Heracles thus attributes the blame for his crime to the *tuchē* of Hera and to the weapons as *paidoktonous* (child murderers, 1381).[37] The Greeks sometimes considered weapons to be responsible for a crime and hence polluted.[38] For example, the sacrificial knife at the Attic Bouphonia was condemned for the murder of a bull and banished.[39] Just as Theseus ignores Heracles' *miasma,* Heracles, with a magnificent gesture of self-mastery as he takes up the hated weapons, now ritualizes his relation to his weapons and hence to his own past violence. Heracles determines to keep his weapons only for self-defense, for standing up against (*hupostēnai,* 1350) and enduring possible aggression. Just as Heracles has resolved to be a slave to *tuchē,* he will now keep his weapons wretchedly (*athliōs de sōisteon,* 1385), as, clinging to his side like the children he destroyed (see 1379),[40] they endlessly remind him of his crimes. By accepting dependency on Theseus and by confining his powers within new limits (he will act only defensively; his labors are over), Heracles becomes a hero who will act within a *polis* rather than, as before, on the margins of civilization.

Theseus, in accepting Heracles into Athens, chooses to ignore, in addition to Heracles' *miasma,* the apparent perversion of the hero's labors. He insists that Heracles can offer Athens a crown of glory by coming to the city (1334–35). By establishing a cult he gives Heracles an opportunity to benefit the city with his powers. Theseus also attempts to use the hero's past glory, celebrated at length in the suppliant action, to persuade him to survive (1248 and 1250, 1410, 1414; in the apparent lacuna at 1313 he may have

[37]On this point, see Pucci 1980: 185.

[38]See Bond 1981 on line 1381.

[39]See esp. Pausanias 1.24.4 and 1.28.10 and Porphyry *De abst.* 2.29–30 on the Bouphonia.

[40]On the ironic similarity between weapons and children here, see Bond 1981 on line 1379. See also lines 79 and 986. Heracles kills the children with the very weapons, club and bow, that he had promised them.

expanded on this motif in reply to Heracles' despair). The final scenes, then, establish a new context for the labors that were earlier denigrated by Lycus, ignored by Thebes, and perverted by the mad hero.

Heracles keeps his weapons for his own defense and, by implication, for the benefit of his new city. The decision is crucial, given the lengthy debate on weaponry in the earlier part of the play. There the tyrant Lycus tries to establish the irrelevance of Heracles' labors and of his bow in contemporary warfare. Lycus attacks the truth of Heracles' parentage and relegates his beast labors to the precivilized past; Heracles' choice of weapons, bare arms and a bow, offers no proof of courage in a world in which the noblest military figure is the hoplite.[41] For Lycus, the hoplite shows superior courage as he stands in the ranks of his fellow spearsmen enduring blows directly, instead of at a distance like the bowman (157–64). Lycus' attack clearly reflects a general decline in the popularity of portrayals of Heracles' beast labors and of Heracles as bowman in the art and literature of the classical period.[42] Amphitryon, countering with a defense of the bowman, asserts that the hoplite, a slave to his weapons, can have no heroism apart from his fellow soldiers, whereas the bowman can defend his friends without taking foolish risks (190–203).

Scholars have related the debate over weaponry to the bow's prominent role in Athens' battles with the Persians and Spartans (the success of the archers at Sphacteria in 425 or the failure to employ archers in the hoplite defeat at Delium in 424).[43] Yet the text's characterization of the bowman has far more to do with

[41]Recent work on the Athenian hoplite stresses the association between the hoplite and the development of democracy. Athens was in essence a nation of equal men in arms. See Detienne 1968 and Vidal-Naquet 1968b.

[42]See Bond 1981 on line 158.

[43]Recent battles may have influenced the reaction of the audience to this passage, yet only literary *topoi* can explain the passage. Bond 1981: xxxii and on line 161 mentions *Iliad* 2.385, Soph. *Ajax* 1120, and the later Xenophon *Memorabilia* 3.9.2 and Dio Chrysostom 58.1. We might add Archilochus frag. 3 W, which also contrasts the bowman's mode of warfare with that of the swordsman and spearsman. Bond argues that the central issue in this debate is the contrast between two kinds of bravery. Heracles wielded the spear in other earlier poetry (cf. the pseudo-Hesiodic *Shield* poem), so that Euripides' decision to make Heracles exclusively a bowman is deliberate.

literary tradition and the tricky, adaptable descendants of Paris, Odysseus, and Teucer than with fifth-century battlefields. Euripides' Heracles puts to the test the heroism of the bowman as it is represented in the literary tradition. After seeing an unfavorable omen Heracles enters Thebes secretly (596–98) and agrees to ambush Lycus rather than attack the city directly in his old style (566–606). The bowman Odysseus makes a similar secret return home in the *Odyssey* and sets a comparable trap for the unjust suitors. Heracles acts alone, and his primary goal is to use his weapons for the defense of his family, to ensure the survival of the group; so too Odysseus in the *Odyssey,* though with some help from his friends. For all Heracles' success in destroying Lycus with his bow, the peripety leaves unresolved this debate on weaponry inasmuch as Heracles' powers have turned against those whom they were meant to protect. The strategy of leaving the defense of a group in the hands of a single human being, vulnerable to *tuchē,* remains questionable.

This debate over the heroism of the bowman can best be understood through a more detailed examination of its prominent role in the Homeric poems.[44] In *Iliad* 11.369–95, the bowman Paris, hiding behind a column on the gravemound of Ilus, shoots Diomedes in the foot. Diomedes laughs at the wound and the weapon. Those who feel the spearsman Diomedes' blows know instant death. Although this passage denigrates the heroism of the bowman relative to that of the spearsman, and perhaps, by setting the episode near a gravemound, associates Paris' weapon with the past and the dead, we also know that the invincible spearsman Achilles met his fate from an arrow in the foot and that the war could not be won without Philoctetes, who brought the bow of Heracles to Troy (*Iliad* 2.724–25). In short, although even in the *Iliad* Heracles is the hero of a previous generation and his style of heroism is no longer the predominant one, the epic tradition as a whole (the *Odyssey,* the *Little Iliad* of Lesches) recognized that both the direct violence of the spearsman and the strategy of the bowman were necessary to success in warfare.

[44]Galinsky 1972: 10–14 has a complementary interpretation of these *Odyssey* passages. I have confined discussion of Heracles' heroism and weapons (a large topic in the tradition) to the issues raised directly by the play.

The *Heracles*

In the *Odyssey,* Odysseus becomes a hero of the bow who was inferior even at Troy, as he says, to Philoctetes alone (*Od.* 8.219). Odysseus leaves his best bow at home for the ultimate task of protecting his own family and for surviving that defense by trickery and skill. Achilles, the spearsman, regrets his choice of glory over survival (*Od.* 11.488–91). The *Odyssey,* then, offers an implicit defense of the heroism of the bowman; yet even here the potential instability or antisocial quality of the bowman is recognized and established through comparisons and confrontations between Odysseus and Heracles. Shunning the example of Heracles and Eurytus of Oechalia, Odysseus declines to use his prowess with the bow to compete with the immortals (*Od.* 8.215–25). *Odyssey* 21 recounts the history of Odysseus' bow: the youthful Odysseus received it from Iphitus, who had in turn received it from his father, Eurytus. Odysseus and Iphitus never had the opportunity to enjoy their newly established guest friendship because Heracles, ignoring the wrath of the gods, violated the rules of hospitality by killing his host Iphitus. In each case Heracles acts as a foil for Odysseus, both by his positive example of glorious bowmanship and by the negative example of his misuse of that strength. The Odysseus of the *Iliad* is primarily a spearsman, not a bowman. In the *Odyssey,* although he still adroitly wields the spear in fighting the suitors, he is primarily a bowman. Yet Odysseus, unlike Heracles, willingly holds his heroism within human limits and seeks collaboration with the gods rather than rivalry. Most important of all, he exacts retribution for violations of hospitality rather than abusing it like Heracles. Odysseus retains the glory of the earlier generation of heroes but adapts his heroism to a more modern and ethically bound environment.

Elsewhere in the *Odyssey,* Odysseus meets his heroic predecessors Achilles and Heracles in the underworld. Achilles, despite his glory, would rather be a laborer on earth than a king of the dead. Odysseus meets Heracles' image in the underworld (11.601–27) while Heracles himself is on Olympus. The terrifying ghost of the hero, who appears about to shoot his bow at any moment, wears a belt recording his mighty deeds. The image suggests isolation and volatility. Yet in addressing Odysseus he weeps, lamenting his life of hard labors and his enslavement to a man far worse than himself. Heracles, unlike Achilles, is a figure both dead and immortal.

Yet in playing degrading social roles as a slave to his labors and to Eurytus he has suffered no loss of stature. Like Heracles, Odysseus goes on to play the role of a beggar in the interest of his family's and his own survival, but without the loss of *kleos* that would have met Achilles had he chosen to go home to his father in Phthia. Yet Odysseus' judicious planning and his final actions as part of a group allow him to escape Heracles' lonely instability. In the *Odyssey* the older form of heroism, that of the bowman, once it is subjected to new physical and ethical limits, rivals and almost surpasses that of the spearsman. Sophocles' *Ajax* provides another complementary relation between spearsman and bowman. Teucer the bowman, though denigrated by Menelaus, speaks bravely to defend the reputation of the dead spearsman Ajax and to protect his family. Yet in both the *Ajax* and the *Odyssey* the bow continues to serve best off the battlefield, where defense outweighs aggression and glory for its own sake.

The poetic tradition, then, sufficiently explains the issues raised in the debate on weaponry in the *Heracles* without recourse to recent military history. In both Homer and Euripides the bowman is associated with self-defense and survival, with the seemingly less heroic mode of waging war in disguise or at a distance, from a place where the victims cannot locate in advance the origin of the death that comes upon them. Heracles, by coming to Athens as the future recipient of a hero cult and dependent on Theseus and Athens for a place to survive, resolves the earlier debate between Lycus and Amphitryon on the heroism of the bowman. In the *Odyssey* the image of the bowman was transformed and adapted to new conditions. The heroic style of an earlier generation was found to be essential to the survival of the individual and the group and in the final scenes became a necessary complement to the heroic and direct aggression of the Iliadic spearsman. In the suppliant action of the *Heracles* Megara, using formulae traditional to an appeal to a dead hero, calls on the absent Heracles to aid his friends in the world above (490–96).[45] The living Heracles answers her call, ambushes Lycus, but then destroys the family he has just rescued. Theseus recreates this protective role for Heracles in the context of

[45]See Bond 1981: 191.

[172]

The Heracles

an Athenian hero cult. The image of the bowman surviving and
sending his unending supply of arrows from an unseen source
within the city suits that of a dead hero defending his city from the
world below. (See 196 on the bowman's endless supply of arrows,
and 200 on his hidden position.) In *Iliad* 2.369–95, Paris' hidden
position behind the tomb of his ancestor Ilus implicitly associates
the bowman with the powers of the dead. Similarly, in Aeschylus'
Libation Bearers the ghost of the hero's father and other underworld
spirits can send an avenging *belos* (almost certainly an arrow) from
the world below (see 286–87 and, more metaphorically, 380–81;
see also 161–63, 694, and 1032–33); the dead Heracles of *Odyssey*
11, too, stalks through Hades ever ready to shoot his bow (608). In
Euripides' play, Heracles' new dependence on Athens, his slavery
to *tuchē* (1357), and his willingness to stand up against death directly (*hupostēnai* 1350; *huphistatai*, 1349; *engkarterēsō thanaton*, 1351,
if the text is correct)[46] recall the characteristics of the hoplite established earlier in the play by Lycus: the hoplite's direct confrontation of death, his slavery to his weapons, and his dependence on
and subservience to a community (163–64; see also 190–91). The
heroism of the individualistic bowman no longer stands in contradiction to that of the hoplite but supports and merges with it. Here
Euripides implicitly exploits the alternative tradition of Heracles as
hoplite rather than bowman that had existed from epic onward and
was prominent in late fifth-century vase paintings, especially in
representations of Heracles' pyre on Mount Oeta.[47] Athens thus
purifies Heracles of both his *miasma* and the potential instability
associated with the isolated and sometimes deceptive or antisocial
heroism of the past. The play does not deny that Heracles' heroism
is in some sense anachronistic in the world of the hoplite, as Lycus
has argued, but finds an appropriate place for it in a new context.
The *agōnes* of Heracles are complete, yet they remain relevant in

[46]Many argue that the text should read *engkarterēsō bioton*. See Bond 1981 ad loc.
Wilamowitz 1895 ad loc., if he was correct in thinking that *paraspizont'* in 1099 was
a metaphor drawn from hoplites fighting in a phalanx, offers further strength to
my argument. Fragmenta tragica adespota 374 N characterizes Heracles as a slave
to his *aretē*.

[47]See Beazley 1947: 103ff. on representations of Heracles' pyre with greaves,
shield, and corselet. See note 43 above.

the context of the *polis,* where *agōnes* are performed in accordance with the rules of civic life and for the defense and glory of the city as well as the individual (see 1334–35).

The resolution of the conflict between spearsman and bowman has important implications for the audience and for fifth-century Athenian democracy. Hoplite warfare, as Lycus shows, entails collective action in place of the self-assertion characteristic of the archaic hero, egalitarianism in place of personal *kleos.* In the story of Aristodamus, Herodotus (9.71) associates that soldier's drive for individual excellence with the kind of madness that attacks Heracles in Euripides' play (he is described as mad, *lussonta,* a word derived from the same root as Lyssa). Yet Athens was also a supremely agonistic society, in which both the training for warfare, hunting, and athletics, and the popularity of the archaic hero in myth and cult stood in contradiction to the strictly communal ethic of political and military life.[48] The hunter and the ephebe, whose sphere of action was outside the central spaces of the city, favored trickery, survival, and the traditional Greek drive toward individual excellence and success. The bow was, of course, originally a hunter's weapon. Megara's speech of lament for her sons emphasizes the child-loving Heracles' training of his children, who were to inherit their father's weapons and to rule Greece in a Panhellenic dynasty (462–79). In Attic cult, too, Heracles served as a model for youths, who, for example, drank with Heracles and dedicated their hair to the hero in their initiation to the phratry at the Apatouria. Indeed, as Farnell emphasizes, Heracles' "higher social function" in Greek cult "does not range beyond his protection of the Epheboi and his care for their physical development. He

---

[48]For a general discussion of the contradictions and tensions posed by the agonistic nature of Greek society, see Gouldner 1965. Vidal-Naquet 1968a and 1981b and Lonis 1979: 25–40 call attention to the particular contradiction between the ethics of hoplite warfare and those of athletics and hunting. Lonis suggests that the view presented in the *Laches* may have been more widespread than other critics have thought, and he stresses the ritualized nature of Greek warfare, which incorporates in a carefully controlled form agonistic elements from other spheres of activity. Alternatively, it could be argued that Greek society has deliberately structured spheres in which the drive for individual glory can be spent, thus allowing citizens to commit themselves more fully to collective effort in areas such as warfare and politics, where the communal effort must take first place.

is not concerned with the higher political life."[49] His cults in Attica are to be found not on the acropolis but in suburbs and remote demes such as Marathon, where the Athenians apparently received the hero's protection in the famous battle against the Persians (Herodotus 6.108 and 116; the Athenians camped in his precinct).[50] At *Laches* 181e–182d Socrates argues that the ethics of single combat and hoplite warfare can be compatible. Similarly, the *Heracles* implicitly demonstrates that the ideal of the archaic hero and his individualistic heroism need not conflict with Athenian political ideals, provided that the hero submits to the city, retains self-control, and remains marginal to its higher political life.

The Poetic Crisis

The *Heracles* questions not only the relations among god, man, and community, as expressed in sacrificial ritual, or the status of Heracles' mythical labors and the form of heroism that they represent, but also the entire past poetic tradition about Heracles. The earlier scenes of the play, up through the central crisis, present in succession three different views of the hero: the epinician Heracles, the domestic Heracles, and the violent and criminal Heracles. (On the structure of the *Heracles,* see the appendix to this chapter.) Epinician poets favor Heracles, the Panhellenic hero par excellence, as a model for their aristocratic athletes and emphasize his role as superhuman culture hero. Following Indo-European tradition, all serious Greek poets make it their mission to praise what they view as socially valuable and to blame what should be rejected (for example, Pindar *Nemean* 7.61–63 or 8.39).[51] In the suppliant scene of the *Heracles,* however, the chorus adopts in its praise of

[49]Farnell 1921: 154. See also Woodford 1971 on the connections between Heracles and youth in Attic cult.

[50]Farnell 1921: 108. The ghost of Theseus also reportedly emerged from the underworld to fight with the Athenians at Marathon (Pausanias 1.15.3). Theseus' own heroic exploits were modeled on those of Heracles, yet as a whole the later hero was explicitly associated in Attic myth and cult with the democracy (Farnell 1921: 340).

[51]Comparative studies in Indo-European poetry and studies of early Greek poet-

Heracles a stance most closely analogous to epinician poetry. The Heracles who finally arrives in Thebes, however, is decidedly not the extraordinary epinician hero, but modest, pious, an ideal son and husband, and an emphatically loving father. Finally, this novel domestic Heracles lapses in the peripety into another familiar Heracles, the criminal hero of epic.

Euripides enjambs these three views of the hero, emphasizing the separateness of each and the apparent contradictions among them. For example, the criminal Heracles of the central crisis is represented in the language of the text as a perversion of the hero of encomiastic poetry, and the domestic Heracles has a stature inadequate to his grand mythical tradition. The scenes following the peripety, however, restore the relation among these three apparently contradictory interpretations and recreate a hero who is equal to the mutability of events (see 1245) and appropriate even to contemporary Athens. The Heracles whom Athens will worship in hero cult is the acknowledged if apparently blameless author of terrible deeds, as well as being human, dependent, and suffering. He retains his past glory, yet by his crime and suffering he has been reduced to equality with other men, and in this sense becomes a true participant in a democratic society. Ironically, in destroying the Heracles of earlier Greek literature, the gods confer tragic stature on him and ensure his survival as a hero in Athens. Greek tragedy, of course, often ennobles heroes by portraying their suffering. Yet the *Heracles* through its radical disjunctions in character and action makes its audience particularly conscious of the process by which a tragic poet creates a new heroism by transforming previous tradition. The Heracles who emerges from Euripides' tragedy is, unlike Sophocles' hero in the *Trachiniae,* a strikingly

---

ry have made a clear case for the role of the poet as dispenser of praise and blame. See Dumézil 1943 and Ward 1973. For archaic Greek poetry, see Detienne 1967, Nagy 1976 and 1979: 213–75, and Crotty 1982. For praise and blame vociferously exercised in the theater, see Plato *Laws* 876b. The praise poetry of the choral odes of the *Heracles* is closest to the epinician tradition in mediating between hero and city, praising the hero and defending him against detractors and traditions that might denigrate him; in its insistence on the contemporary relevance of the hero and his role as heroic model; and in its acknowledgment of human instability and the importance of the gods to human success. See my discussion later in this chapter.

novel figure who resembles in part the philosophical hero of Prodicus and the later Stoics; he determines to survive on the basis of a
deliberate decision to control and rationalize his suffering and to
view from a radically different perspective both divine reality and
his own painful experiences.

Euripides frequently translates the titanic figures of saga into the
everyday world, as if to test the mythic tradition with the touch-
stone of the ordinary. Here his goal seems unusually clear: the
creation of an Athenian hero. In an almost programmatic fashion
Euripides shows how tragedy can create from the anachronistic
and individualistic heroes of the past a hero who remains relevant
to a fifth-century Athenian *polis*. The tradition about Heracles lent
itself particularly well to Euripides' tragic experiment, both because Heracles was a problematic hero even in epic and because he
had so rarely been made the central subject of a tragedy. So far as
we know, fourteen tragedies treated Heracles and his children, but
only Sophocles' *Trachiniae* and Euripides' play made Heracles the
tragic hero. Indeed, despite Heracles' enormous popularity in cult
and the fine arts, the Heracles of literary tradition was simultaneously too superhuman (as Iris herself complains in this play)
and too pervasively anticultural in his behavior to fit readily into a
genre that specialized in domestic and civic disasters. Both Sophocles and Euripides avoid direct mention of his untragic transformation into an Olympian deity after death.

Let us now examine the way in which the play presents the three
Heracles in succession and then discredits each in turn as too limited to survive in memory with the resilience and range that they
acquire in combination.

The Epinician Hero

The Athenian audience would have brought to the *Heracles* a
poetic vision of Heracles primarily shaped not by tragedy but by
the older epic, hymnic, and lyric traditions and by contemporary
Old Comedy and satyr play. From the perspective of these earlier
traditions, the hero was frequently the subject of admiration and
praise. For his victory over the giants and his other labors, Heracles earned praise in the Homeric hymns, Hesiod, Bacchylides,

Pindar, and the visual arts. And so it is in the first stasimon of the *Heracles*, which portrays the hero as a champion of civilization over chaos, lawlessness, and barbarism. The Heracles of *Iliad* 5.637–56 and of the pseudo-Hesiodic shield poem avenges violated hospitality. In Hesiod's *Theogony*, Heracles continues Zeus' civilizing work on earth by destroying monsters born of the older generation of Titans. With his voyage to what became the Pillars of Heracles he establishes the limits to human achievement and thereby to poetic *kleos* as well (Pindar *Olympian* 3.44–45, *Nemean* 3.21). Numerous cities besides Thebes and Argos/Mycenae, in whose myths he figures most prominently, staked literary claims to the hero. As Pindar says (*Pythian* 9.87): "That man is mute who does not lend his voice to Heracles." For Pindar, Heracles is the major Panhellenic model of *aretē* (*Nem.* 1.31–34), the foil for the athletes and kings praised in his poems.

In the first, or suppliant, action of the play, Megara, Amphitryon, and the chorus hold up to the test of events a hero who essentially belongs to a pretragic, encomiastic and epinician, tradition. On a purely formal level, it is worth noting that the chorus sings three odes that all critics agree are traditional praise poems, whether hymnic or epinician.[52] Megara offers a funeral lament, another speech of praise, for Heracles' children. Amphitryon praises Heracles to counter Lycus' blame of the hero. Megara and Amphitryon try to defer the children's grief through hope in the hero (76–77, 99–100); later Megara summons the courage to die in his image. The chorus tries to find in Heracles the subject for song, dance, and celebration, and hence a way of softening the bitterness of old age. According to these powerless Theban elders, his heroism can unite them in a set of shared values, and praise of him provides potential consolation for suffering and a model for courageously accepting their lot.

Amphitryon's prologue, as is often the case in Euripides, imme-

---

[52]For an analysis of the three choral stasima and their relation to the hymnic and epinician traditions, see Wilamowitz 1895; Kranz 1933: 131 and 191; Kroeker 1938; Arrowsmith 1954, esp. 91–92; Parry 1965 and 1978: 158–63; and Bond 1981. If Euripides' epinician for Alcibiades was in fact composed around 416 and the play dates to 417–14, the event may have inspired Euripides' preoccupation with epinician poetry in this play (see Plutarch's *Life of Alcibiades* 11).

diately raises for the audience the problem of contradictory mythical traditions about the hero. Were the motives for Heracles' labors filial, based on a desire to restore Mycenae to his father? Or was Heracles driven by the goads of Hera or by necessity (17–21)? The first motive, apparently a novel one in the tradition, prepares for the later appearance of the surprisingly domesticated Heracles; the second, for the persecution of Heracles in the peripety; the third, necessity, anticipates Heracles' own final view of the forces that have shaped his fate. Amphitryon upholds Heracles' claim to Thebes on the basis of his good birth and his divine and human fathers, in contrast to the claims of Lycus, whose ancestry is obscure in the Theban tradition (31–32; see also 663, 810). Megara then voices regret for the lost glory of Heracles' family. She defers the grief of Heracles' children with stories of past myths: *ego de diapherō / logoisi mutheuousa,* "I lead them on telling fables" (76–77).⁵³ Amphitryon urges Megara to continue this deception: *pareukēlei logois / kleptousa muthois athlious klopas homōs,* "charm them with stories, / cheating them with words, wretched deceivers though words are" (99–100). He himself, however, finds a source of optimism only in the cyclical transitions offered by time; the best man relies on values of the spirit, on hope (101–6). Faced with extinction from a dictatorship established by violence in a *stasis*-ridden city and the absence or probable death of Heracles, Amphitryon essentially confesses that the glorious myths about Heracles offer only a fragile and deceptive consolation in the present. The elders enter, emphasizing their friendship for the hero and his family but lamenting their helpless old age, their lost heroic past, and the indifference of Thebes to Heracles.

Lycus abruptly intervenes and attacks Heracles' parentage and labors, although his fear of the hero's children to some extent belies his words. Lycus, replies Amphitryon, blames (*memphēi,* 189) the bow. He, Amphitryon, has nothing but words to counter Lycus' *amathia* (ignorance of correct values, injustice, 171–76), but he will defend Heracles' traditional reputation (see 205: *tōn kathestōtōn peri*).⁵⁴ His words are enemies to Lycus (204–5). Heracles has

---

⁵³See Bond 1981 ad loc.
⁵⁴On *amathia* in the play, see Bond 1981 on line 347. Note the use of the similar term *skaios* at 283 and 299.

shared a victory song with the gods (180); the centaurs are witnesses of his prowess (181–83). If Dirphys, Lycus' homeland, were
asked a comparable question, it would not praise him (*ouk an
s'epaineseien*, 186). Amphitryon reproaches Greece and Thebes for
failing to show gratitude to Heracles and hence to defend his children (217–28). Later Amphitryon extends this accusation of *amathia* (347) and lack of *philia* (341) to Zeus. The chorus makes a
point of praising Amphitryon's words (236–37), whereas Lycus
sneers at the uselessness of words in comparison to action (238–
39).

After Lycus' departure, Megara tries to use Heracles as a model
for facing disaster. She bows to the uselessness of words as a
weapon against Lycus (298). She evokes her own nobility and the
labors that she underwent in bearing children (*hamochthēsa*, 281; for
mochthoi used of Heracles' labors, see 355–56). She proposes to
imitate her husband (*emoi te mimēm' andros ouk apōsteon*, 294) by
accepting death. The children may be excluded from their an-
cestral halls, but Heracles' name at least remains (338). He was
literally a model for his three sons, for he resolved to leave his
lionskin to one, his club to another—a *pseudē dosin* (pretend gift,
471) to teach his child—and his bow to the third. He planned to
establish all three, with suitable marriages from Athens, Thebes,
and Sparta arranged by Megara, as kings in Argos, Thebes, and
Oechalia. The Panhellenic hero wished to found a Panhellenic dynasty, to create a source of Greek unity that will be lost after the
death of the children. The chorus echoes Megara's lost hopes in the
first stasimon (348–441), celebrating Heracles' Panhellenic heroism
and his use of the bow and the club. Yet for Megara Heracles has
finally been reduced here to a model for dying, not for living.

The play opens, then, with an implicit poetic crisis. Heracles is
"dead," and the world is dead to Heracles. Lycus and Thebes are
indifferent to the values of *eugeneia* (noble birth), *philia,* and the
poetic tradition about Heracles and threaten to destroy all that he
represents. The gods, centaurs, and landscapes evoked by Amphitryon as witnesses of Heracles' prowess have no voices in the
world of the play until the surprising peripety. The absent Heracles has no defense but words, whereas Lycus supports his blame
of the hero with actions.

The name Lycus (Luk-os), meaning wolf, has associations with the tradition of poetic invective, or blame poetry. Gernet has established an Indo-European model for the motif of the wolf as outlaw and outsider.[55] The root *luk*–appears in the name Lycambes (Luk-ambēs, "having the steps of a wolf"), the figure who elicited invective from Archilochus for humiliating him. The king Lycurgus (Luko-orgos) denigrated the divinity of Dionysus.[56] Hence the name Lycus itself evokes a figure ignorant of correct values and an enemy of the praise poet. This *amathēs* enemy of praise poetry questions the authenticity, nobility, or relevance of the hero or poet whom he attacks. The name Lycus, which Euripides is probably introducing into the legend for the first time (see 27–34), evokes three useful sorts of associations. First, it creates another "beast labor" for the hero (at 701 Lycus' entrance immediately follows the choral description of Heracles as beast killer). Second, it recalls the wolf's paradoxical associations with both hoplite (egalitarian and communally oriented) warfare and tyranny, demonstrated by Detienne and Svenbro.[57] Indeed, Lycus' namesake Lycaeon (compare Zeus Lukeios) is explicitly associated not only with tyranny but also with human sacrifice and cannibalism.[58] Third, it labels the dramatic opponent of praise.

Frequently proponents of ignorant invective such as Lycus deliberately *misrepresent* the actions and values of the hero. Thersites in *Iliad* 2, for example, pretends that Achilles could not really have been angry at Agamemnon, since he did not kill him. In Pindar *Nemean* 8.32–34b, the enemies of Ajax use *echthra parphasis,* hateful distortion or misrepresentation, to obscure and blacken the reputation of the hero. The praise poet must rescue the hero from such misrepresentation or *psogos* (blame), identify and praise what is praiseworthy, and bring *kleos* to a *philos* (*Nem.* 7.61–63, 8.21–25 and 39). He addresses an audience of friends who are labeled *sunetoi* or *phroneontes* (*Olym.* 2.85 and *Pyth.* 5.107; Bacchylides 3.85), wise and experienced men who can understand the true nature of

[55]Gernet 1981: 125–39.
[56]See Nagy 1976: 193–99 and West 1974: 25–28.
[57]See Detienne and Svenbro 1979. There was another Lycus in Theban tradition, who usurped the throne of Thebes during Laius' infancy.
[58]See Piccaluga 1968 on Lycaon.

human victory and failure, of friendship and divine favor. He mediates the relation between victor and community and unites his audience in festive celebration and a set of shared values; he makes men forget their mortal suffering as they confront the glorious actions of heroes and victors. Negative criticism has little place in a praise poem (*Pyth.* 2.52–65, Bacchylides 3.67–68), and both Homer and Pindar justify only the blame of an inferior or wicked person (*Nem.* 8.38–39, *Il.* 2.211–77). A jealous refusal to praise (*phthonos*) becomes in essence a form of revolt against the gods, who are in part responsible for mortal achievement.[59] The comic poet Aristophanes explicitly adopts this tradition in his parabases, where he lays claim to constructive praise and blame and appeals to the intelligence of his audience. In a similar fashion, the scenario, vocabulary, and themes traditional to earlier praise and blame poetry recur in the early scenes of the *Heracles,* where Heracles' perceptive friends, who seek to praise him fittingly and enduringly, confront the ignorant enemy, who blames, misrepresents, and denigrates him. Amphitryon appropriately reserves his scorn for those who neglect the hero, while Lycus establishes his impiety through his ignorant attack on the glorious son of Zeus. The chorus seeks in Heracles a source of consolation and forgetfulness, while Megara and her sons find a model for action.

The epinician poet also makes his audience conscious of his skill in selecting from the mythical tradition. By highlighting or rejecting certain aspects of that tradition, he restores the past to the present and heightens the present through forging links to the glorious past or a larger-than-human reality. He makes the praise of god and hero, and of the contemporary victor and his city, part of a single process (for example, Pindar *Olympian* 2.2). The poet takes care not to emphasize the possible disjunction between the heroism of the past and the realities of the present; his poetry fits the moment (*Pythian* 9.76–79). The praise poet and his *laudandi* (the people praised) enter into a reciprocal relationship: in exchange for the patron's benevolence and support, poet and community offer immortality to the hero or athlete. Yet their praise

[59]See Crotty 1980 on the refusal to praise as a form of revolt against the gods.

has no meaning without an acceptable heroic theme and a receptive context.

As the suppliant action of the *Heracles* develops, however, Euripides increasingly enlarges the gaps between hero, god, and contemporary world closed by the artistry of epinician poetry and simultaneously stresses the need of the characters to put their hope in heroic *aretē*. The chorus and characters fail to suppress the distinction between past and present. The absence of Heracles and the silence of Zeus in the face of multiple appeals to protect the interests of his son suggest a loss of divine favor. In the face of the hostility of Lycus and the indifference of Thebes, Megara and Amphitryon can use the past only as a source of deceptive consolation for the children; Megara finds in Heracles only a model for accepting death, not for life; the chorus cannot assuage the bitterness of old age in song.

Each of the three choral stasima draws on the conventions of encomiastic poetry. Yet all but the last ode suggest that the praise offered fails to fit the moment or to provide even temporary consolation. The first stasimon, sung in response to the certainty that Heracles is dead and all hope for the family lost, commemorates Heracles' glorious deeds. In closing, the elders regret the loss of their youth and of Heracles' former greatness (436–41), as well as the threatening situation at hand. They catalogue Heracles' labors at length, emphasizing his Panhellenic over his Peloponnesian labors, while suppressing the hero's more ambivalent exploits and concentrating on those that contributed to civilization.[60] Yet after making the widest possible geographic and moral claim for their hero, they add that Heracles' spoils from his victory over the Amazons remain as museum pieces at Mycenae (416–18). This detail, this need to verify the labors by reminding the audience of a last tangible relic, implicitly confirms Lycus' argument that Heracles is irrelevant to the world of the play. Heracles and his *aretē* are vulnerable to circumstance. Hence the choral song of praise for the

[60]On this point, see Bond 1981 ad loc. Barlow 1982 rightly comments on the nonviolent tone of the labors in this ode but mistakes Euripides' purpose in making them sound so remote and mythical.

absent hero combines themes appropriate to dirge, hymn, and encomium.[61]

Parry, following the lead of Wilamowitz and others, has analyzed the second stasimon as a traditional encomiastic poem, with a mixture of themes from epinician poems, paeans, and hymns.[62] The elders of the chorus establish themselves as competent *laudatores,* worthy to praise the hero through their ability to distinguish good from bad. After a gnomic opening they meditate in traditional fashion on the association of youth and *aretē,* on old age as a foil for youth, on the alliance of good birth and *aretē* (including a formal genealogy of the *laudandus*). They praise Heracles' beneficence as son of Zeus; he is as worthy of paeans as Apollo (687).[63] They celebrate the consolatory powers that song, festival, and tradition have had and will continue to have for the old: *mē zōien met' amousias,* "may I not live without the Muses" (676). In their choice of themes they perhaps hint at Heracles' future conquest of Geras (old age), his marriage to Hebe (youth), and his association in vase paintings with the Muses (see 674). Through song they recapture participation in renown for themselves (677–86) and become one with the singers and celebrators of gods throughout Greece (687–94). Heracles' miraculous return apparently reestablishes the relations among god, man, hero, and the present necessary for the kind of epinician poem that the chorus can now sing for the first time in the play.

The first antistrophe undercuts in part the festal tone appropriate to the epinician form. Heracles has in fact won a second life by his return from Hades; yet the chorus laments that the gods do not have human wisdom (*xunesis / kai sophia kat' andras,* 655–56), nor do they make a practice of rewarding the virtuous with two lives and marking the bad man with one (657–68). Instead of praising

[61]See Bond 1981 ad loc. The tone of lament, as might be expected, does not predominate. Bond notes the use of Pindaric phrases here.

[62]See note 49 above. Parry 1965 adopts the critical approach to Pindar of Bundy 1962. Bond 1981 accepts and expands upon Parry's approach. This ode offers (perhaps recalling *Agamemnon* 121) a *to eu* (694) to the first stasimon's *ailinon.* Wilamowitz 1959 (1895): III, 148 regarded the second stasimon as the equivalent of a parabasis; the present analysis should make the relation between the ode and the rest of the text more clearly integral.

[63]Wilamowitz 1895 on 694 treats the whole ode as a paean.

time's revelation of *aretē* or justice and making the traditional prayer for their patron's increase of wealth, the elders remark that time brings only a meaningless increase of wealth (671–72).[64] Although recognition of the ephemeral nature of divine favor and of the uncertainty of human existence permeates epinician poetry, the poet generally avoids questioning divine morality or casting doubt on the divine blessing manifest in the moment of success. Even in the chorus' moment of happiness, there lurks the unresolved problem that had already troubled Pindar: how to rescue human *aretē* and the celebration of human *aretē* from its vulnerability to circumstances.

The final ode before the central crisis and after the death of Lycus reaches a pitch of hysterical optimism. Recovering full confidence as praise poets, the chorus adopts common epinician motifs. Its doubts are at last swept away. Time offers hope through change, the slandered gods are just, and the heirs of these changes are new songs (*metallagai suntuchias* / ⟨*neas*⟩ *etekon aoidas*, 766–67; see 737–41, 757–60, 772–80). Heracles' success confirms the previously questionable myth of the double birth and the paternity of Zeus (798–806; 802–4 may echo Pindar *Nemean* 10.54). Recalling Amphitryon's earlier appeal to the landscape in his defense of Heracles, the chorus asks the entire landscape of Thebes to join in the song and dance that break out in the city at the tyrant's death (763–64, 781–97). Lycus' discordant death cry merges with the tune of the chorus' victory celebration (751–54). The tone is reminiscent of Alcaeus' well-known fragment on the death of the tyrant Myrsilus (332 LP).

For the epinician poet, human success derives in part from talent and effort but depends ultimately on divine benevolence. Too much praise violates *kairos* (suitability and proportion, Pindar *Pyth*. 10.4; Bacchylides 13.17; see also *Olym*. 13.48). The poet accepts what god gives and subordinates his art to fortune (*Pyth*. 3.108–15 and 10.10–24). In short, epinician poetry continually faces the problem of ensuring that the praise of human *aretē* does not become excessive and so form a dispraise of god. To be sure, the chorus of the *Heracles* piously envisions Heracles' defeat of Lycus as a confirmation of divine justice. And in the case of Hera-

---

[64]See Bond 1981 ad loc. As Bond points out, however, the rest of the ode often echoes Pindar in theme and phrasing.

cles even Pindar himself violates his own insistence on mortality, moderation, and piety (see *Nemean* 1 and frag. 169 S). Yet by the standards of epinician poetry the eagerness of the chorus to elevate Heracles to what amounts to divine status should make the audience uneasy.[65] The chorus earlier proposed to praise the son of Zeus with the paean special to Apollo (687), and Megara saw in Heracles a savior no worse than Zeus (521–22). The chorus here forgets both the hostility of Thebes to the hero and its own earlier sober appreciation of the uncertainty that informs everything human. Though their optimism is dramatically plausible, the elders implicitly justify Iris' claim that Heracles, however innocently, threatens the status of the gods.

At the moment before Heracles' actual return, Megara closes her lament for the children with a final wish that Heracles come back even as a dream (494–96) to challenge the despicable men who are about to murder their children. In *Pythian* 3, Pindar warns against such desires. Hieron is ill; yet Pindar recognizes the impropriety of wishing for Asclepius' return from the dead to heal him (1–3). One should not reach for what is far off, unreachable. Instead, Pindar offers Hieron the medicine of song; this charm alone properly gives men immortality. The suppliant plot of the *Heracles,* which demands for its happy conclusion the return of a "dead" hero, raises the same questions and tensions and offers no solution.

Praise poetry directly and repeatedly confronts the instability of the divine favor necessary to human achievement. Yet the setting for an epinician poem is festal (Pindar *Nemean* 4.1), and success, not irreversible disaster, is its appropriate theme:

> Do not reveal to strangers what misfortune is approaching us. I offer you this advice: we should show openly our portion of good and delightful things; but if some god-given, insufferable calamity falls on men, this it is appropriate to hide in darkness.
>
> (Pindar frag. 42 S)

The poet's duty is to obscure myths that denigrate gods or heroes (*Nem.* 5.14–18, *Olym.* 1.35–53): "that which is not loved by Zeus I

---

[65]Sheppard 1916: 77–78 argues that the choral praise of Heracles is here dangerously excessive. Bond 1981 argues that the optimism of the chorus is justifiable.

The *Heracles*

keep utterly silent" (Pindar frag. 81 S). Praise follows the way of justice (*Nem.* 8.35–39; Bacchylides 13.8–11).[66] In *Olympian 9*, for example, Pindar deals directly with this issue in relation to Heracles, whose life illustrates the importance of divine favor to human success (28–29). Pindar then refers to Heracles' battle with Poseidon, Apollo, and Hades at Pylos. Could Heracles have fought against the gods in any way other than *kata daimona* (in accordance with divinity)? The poet stops himself from pursuing this theme and rejects the opportunity to blame (*loidorēsai,* 37) the gods or to associate them with a war on men (40–41). Heracles' myths could pose limitless problems for the praise singer, a fact that Pindar magisterially acknowledges and dismisses in a single gesture. Because at the same time the praise poet feels free to blame the wicked or to let the vicissitudes of others heighten his own hero's glory, he runs a certain risk of contradiction.

By epinician standards, then, Heracles, stained with crime and the seemingly unjust disfavor of the gods (including a hint of *theomachia*), becomes in the peripety an altogether inappropriate subject for praise. The fall of the hero is described as the fall of a monument or statue off a pedestal (1306–7). Heracles' crime puts the function of the chorus, who have identified themselves as a group of Theban praise poets, at issue. Sophocles' chorus in the *Oedipus Rex* (895–96), wondering how it can continue to sing if irreligious outrage is not punished, uses the phrase *ti dei me choreuein,* "how should I dance?" Euripides' chorus responds to the peripety by lamenting Heracles' crime and falling silent for the final 338 lines of the play.[67] This silence eloquently expresses an inability to celebrate the criminal Heracles. Amphitryon alone survives to find a limited place in Heracles' future, and he has been the most skeptical in offering an alternative view of heroism as hope and submission to time (101–6), then dissociating himself from

[66]On this point, see Detienne 1967: 60.

[67]Bond 1981 accepts Camper's attribution of lines 1311–12 to the chorus. I do not find this emendation convincing, especially from a dramatic point of view. The chorus' silence is necessary to make Heracles' change of mind at 1341–46 even marginally convincing. The situation is comparable to that in the *Ajax,* which offers a similar choral silence in the final scene. Here the defense of the anachronistic hero, who lost Achilles' arms to the more modern hero Odysseus, passes to the bowman Teucer.

Zeus for proving a far less diligent father than he himself has been (339–47).

The "Human" and Domestic Heracles

Greek poetry prior to Attic tragedy occasionally refers to Heracles' mortality, pain, and suffering but apparently gives little or no attention to his domestic and filial side. In *Iliad* 18.115–21 the fate of the mortal Heracles is held up for the contemplation of Achilles at the moment when he is choosing his own fate. The poet here suppresses the alternative tradition, which granted Heracles immortality and divinity after death. The *Odyssey* passage discussed earlier keeps both versions: Heracles' shade is in Hades, but he himself is on Olympus. Much of the post-Homeric tradition emphasizes the painful burden of Heracles' life of continual *ponos*.

Bacchylides' fifth ode offers the first example of Heracles as a heroic figure capable of pity, learning, and mature suffering, a figure subsequently made popular by tragedy, the Sophist Prodicus, and the later Stoic tradition.[68] In this poem Bacchylides makes Heracles contemplate the pitiable fate of Meleager, the helplessness of even the most heroic man before *tuchē,* and thereby his own vulnerability to divine wrath. Meleager, like Heracles in the *Heracles,* did not deliberately murder his kin. Although Heracles' response to the vision of Meleager's shade is to suppress the tears he sheds for the first time in his life and to reject the efficacy of lament in favor of action, the poem hints at the hero's own encroaching entanglement in a comparable fate. Moved by Meleager's beauty, Heracles will soon marry his fatal bride, Meleager's sister, Deianeira (see also Bacchylides 16).

Given the rare emphasis in earlier poetic tradition on Heracles' mortality and vulnerability to ordinary human limits, the Heracles who finally appears onstage in the *Heracles* must have come as a remarkable surprise. Euripides' Heracles is pious; he immediately thinks of his duty to the gods (608–9) and emphasizes his willingness to respect human limits. He asserts that he will give up his glorious labors (575) for the private goal of protecting his children

---

[68]For a comparable interpretation of Bacchylides 5, see Lefkowitz 1969.

(578–82).[69] This Heracles, unlike any other known Heracles of
tradition, is capable of acting as the just ruler of a *polis* and of
establishing with both Theseus and his family the bond of true
philia. Tradition, which normally confines the violent Heracles to
protecting the civilized world from its margins, would have led
the audience to expect an explosive and disruptive entrance. Sophocles' hero or the larger-than-life rescuer of satyr drama or Euripides' own *Alcestis* were far more typical.[70] Instead this Heracles
is a bowman in the style of Odysseus, revising his plans to fit new
circumstances and using caution and deception where he would
once have been more direct (566–606).[71] He puts down his glorious weapons and stops his children's tears with the reassurance of
strong hands. Unlike Amphitryon, who expresses discontent at
being reduced by age to the care of children (45), Heracles will not
reject nursery service (*therapeuma teknōn*, 633). Heracles is also, in
essence, a democrat.[72] He leaves the stage with a refreshing and
modest comparison between himself and his fellow men (633–36):

> . . . All men's natures are alike. Both noble and obscure men love
> their children. They differ in wealth. Some have, others have not,
> but all men love their children.

The Heracles who enters surprises only by his mildness. He
manifestly has his wits about him, and right on his side in killing
Lycus, whom no other authority will check or punish. This Heracles mixes epic attainment (566–73) with the common touch. Since
the killing of the children seems elsewhere to have occurred at the
start of the hero's career, the audience might by now have assumed

---

[69]Bond 1981 comments on the shocking nature of line 575.

[70]The Heracles of the *Alcestis* and satyr play typically adopted the role of rescuer
that he plays here.

[71]See Arrowsmith 1954: 105 on Heracles' caution. He sees it as evidence that in
the dramatic world of the play Heracles' old heroism is not false, but no longer
applicable to the new reality in which he finds himself. Bond 1981 on line 598
defends Heracles' secrecy and caution, citing *Od.* 11.455.

[72]I am exaggerating here both to emphasize his deviation from an aristocratic
character and to show how this scene prepares for his later role as hero of a
democracy. Bond 1981 on 633–36 stresses the democratic tone of Heracles' views
here.

it as discarded. Hence it is all the less prepared for his sudden lapse into murderous lunacy.

This adaptable and domestic Heracles is nevertheless curiously disappointing. He can to some degree meet Lycus' charge of anachronism, although he is still isolated and self-dependent. By the standards of literary tradition, Euripides' heroic bowman is certainly admirable. But this character cannot fulfill the chorus' desire to sing of a figure essentially larger than human and equal to the glorious exploits he is reported to have performed. We are not surprised when Amphitryon, almost comically, tries to verify Heracles' trip to the underworld: "Did you *really* go to the halls of Hades, son?" (610). A Heracles who is so willing to turn from his public and Panhellenic labors to attend only to the concerns of his own family seems inadequate to the human need for an image to praise and for a hero who belongs only to a larger community, subject to a divinely ordained fate more extraordinary and, perhaps, more terrible than our own.

Euripides was, of course, famous for reducing mythical characters to ordinary human beings. But the arrival of a domestic Heracles in this play is made unusually surprising, both because of the delayed and seemingly miraculous entrance of the hero and because the chorus in the first stasimon has nearly embalmed him in the superhuman glories of his past. The dramatic reality of this very human Heracles does not offer much support to the chorus' ecstatic return to poetic celebration in the encomiastic tradition. As we know from Achilles' choice in the *Iliad* (although the *Odyssey* contests this view), a private life does not produce *kleos*. And no human life offers certain happiness. Hence the choral recovery of festivity and song implicitly relies less on the hero than on a radical shift of events, on *tuchē*.

The Violent or Criminal Heracles

Hera's imposition of madness and the crime of kin murder on Heracles presents the volatile criminal Heracles familiar in the epic tradition. This hero, as was suggested earlier, habitually strains the limits of civilization. Treacherous, lustful, and gluttonous, he frequently turns his powers against his family, guests, his music teacher Linus, or good centaurs such as Pholus and Cheiron. He is subject to bouts of madness and performs unjustified rapes. This is the hero found in Sophocles' *Trachiniae,* where Heracles has sacked an entire city to win Iole for himself and, in a fit of anguish, throws his faithful servant Lichas over a cliff. In comedy and satyr play (or the *Alcestis*) the hero puts extraordinary pressure on hospitality, taking advantage of all the food and/or sex that he finds available. This Heracles, occupying an unstable position between beast and god, order and disorder, is a figure belonging to one of the earliest generations of Greek myth, extraordinarily prone to violence and never quite part of civilized life. Indeed, he frequently undermines the very culture that it was his function, from its margins, to protect. As Pindar says cryptically in a fragment (169 S), "Custom, king of all, brings on with sovereign hand what is most violent and then makes it just. I infer this from the deeds of Heracles."[73] (See also frag. 81 S and Homeric *Hymn to Heracles* 6; contrast Pindar's treatment of Heracles in the epinician odes.) The least domestic of heroes, he is never allowed to rule as king and never fully integrated into the political and social life of a Greek city. Pindar shows in the passage in *Olympian* 9 discussed earlier that this Heracles never quite submitted to the pious designs of epinician poets; he equally eludes the chorus after the peripety.

Hera's intervention in the action through Iris and Lyssa perverts and interrupts the poetic themes and connections between themes on which the chorus has based its praise of Heracles. As the suppliant action concludes, the chorus has managed to sing itself into some kind of epinician harmony with god, hero, and community. The triumph of world-encircling praise rests precariously on forgetfulness and the suppression of blame. As near personifications of what has been cast out, Hera's accomplices invade to reassert the poetry of blame. Iris and, by her actions, Lyssa misrepresent the pious, modest, and human Heracles seen so far onstage and stain him with the kind of *psogos* and *parphasis* that Pindar attributes to the uncultured enemies of the praise poet. Iris, contested by Lyssa herself, argues that the hero has made the gods "nothing" (841–42)

---

[73]On the difficulties of interpreting this fragment, see most recently the discussion of Crotty 1982, with further bibliography.

and deserves his new pollution (831–32). Lyssa, or Madness, though she temporarily defends and praises the hero (849–54),[74] goes on to accomplish everything that Heracles' *amathēs* enemy and detractor, Lycus, had intended. (See my earlier discussion of the parallels between Hera and Lycus.) The name, *Luk-ia, or "female wolf," underlines her functional connection with the tyrant.[75] Her action will separate Heracles from his father, Zeus, and from Thebes; she makes his labors kin murders and turns the chorus' last song of praise, which putatively unites Thebes in a choral celebration of the hero, into a cacophony. The archaistic quality of her trochaic tetrameters markedly separates the speech from the surrounding drama. The impression remains that the gods wish to blame and destroy the pious Heracles, while Madness alone wishes to praise him. Nevertheless, the disjunction between Heracles the psychopath and Heracles the culture hero remains as marked as that between the obliging family man and the demigod of the preceding praise poetry. Euripides clearly makes no attempt to create a psychologically believable portrait of his hero, but instead deliberately juxtaposes incompatible literary traditions about the hero to create a discontinuous character.

After these two abrupt turnings in the plot, however, we are curiously close to where we began. Blame poetry, after all, shares the assumptions of praise poetry, so that Lyssa and Iris in fact restore Heracles to the world in which the chorus and his family originally located him. He reenters saga, though now as the god's victim rather than as the favorite. It is the intervening Heracles, the family man, who does not fit. An ordinary Heracles is in some sense no Heracles at all.

The Tragic Resolution

The conjunction of a tragic disaster, the appearance of gods on the machine, and lament is typical of the concluding scenes of a

[74]Bond 1981: 287 comments that Lyssa's language here is typical of the modest style of *laudationes*. Like Pindar and the chorus of the *Heracles* she stresses Heracles' civilizing missions. Iris insists that Lyssa should be true to her name and not be sane (*sōphronein*, 857).

[75]See Theocritus 4.11 for another play on the probable etymological connection

Euripidean tragedy.[76] But in this case the gods on the machine cause rather than resolve the disaster, and it is left to Theseus to help save the hero from suicide. The final scenes of the play suggest a new beginning and offer an alternative interpretation of events already completed. The symmetry between the first and last actions is underlined by the unexpected intervention of a second savior, Theseus (unexpected in part because the savior in most suppliant actions is king of the country in which the suppliant action takes place). Heracles leaves the stage following in the wake of Theseus just as his sons followed in his own wake at the conclusion of the suppliant plot (see the repeated image of the boat, used at 631–32 and 1424). The concluding scenes recombine the three Heracles on the basis of an *aretē* immune to the disaster of the peripety. The play finally recreates heroism through catastrophe, praise through blame, and disrupts ultimately to restore the reciprocity of past and present.

The peripety creates the precise balance needed for an Athenian hero who is somewhere between the human or domestic Heracles and the divine son of Zeus, the hero of the poetry of praise. For in hero cult the city worships a figure both remote and familiar, both dead and alive. The moment of violence eventually restores to Heracles a complex and permanent relation to the divine that prayers for positive aid to a paternal Zeus in the suppliant plot did not. Heracles finally synthesizes the position of Megara, who argues for submission to necessity, with that of Amphitryon, who, defending survival and reliance on human *aretē*, made the novel argument that the *anēr aristos* (noblest man) does not abandon hope (105–6). Heracles' experience of the divine leads him to accept for himself a role as mediator between god and man appropriate for

---

between *lukos* and Lyssa: *kai tōs lukōs autika lussēn*. For Homeric treatment of Lyssa, see Lincoln 1975. See Duchemin 1967 on the ancestry of Euripides' Lyssa. Aeschylus' Lycurgus may have also become maddened by Lyssa during a sacrifice.

[76]Bond 1981: 279 and 281 stresses that divine appearances are usually confined to prologues and epilogues. Exceptions are the Dionysus of the *Bacchae* (present throughout the drama, but making a divine revelation of his power in the palace scene), Euripides' *Rhesus*, Aeschylus' *Psychostasia* and *Xantriae*, and possibly Sophocles' *Niobe*. Iris' appearance is like a second prologue. Schmidt 1963: 200–201 comments that in this play Theseus takes the role of the typical Euripidean deus ex machina and offers a mythic way out of the (essentially irresolvable) dilemma created by the plot.

the Athenian cult. His disaster finally ties him irrevocably to the
glorious labors that he was about to abandon; dignity requires
both that he defend himself and that he bring with him to his new
city his heroic capacities.

Heracles' humanity, even his domesticity and openness to democratic principles, become in the Athenian context no longer incompatible with his heroism but essential to it.[77] Heracles, faced
now with an internal rather than an external Hades (1297–98),
becomes a hero of the spirit as well as of the body. His endurance,
dependence, and self-mastery create in him a spiritual unity with
the Athenian hoplite, and his adaptability, cunning, and drive for
survival make him once more the model for youth that he was for
his children and became in Athenian cult. (The resolution also
constitutes an implicit defense of Euripides' habit of populating his
tragedies with domesticated characters.)

Heracles' disaster forces him to turn from a political environment that has rejected his heroism as anachronistic to a new city
that accepts his heroism as glorious for itself. The tragedy separates the hero from his family (Theseus is now his son) and from a
rejection of his labors in favor of a private life, thereby making him
dependent on a new social order. This detachment from private
ties and individual glory in favor of a devotion to the needs of the
city was a characteristic demanded of the Athenian citizen as
well.[78] The new relation to the divine, to Athens, and to his labors
makes Heracles once more an object of worship and a potential
subject for praise. The hero of a cult became a principle of group
unity, a model for action, and a defender of his worshipers.[79] Now
Heracles can, despite his crime, be truly available, even after death,
to those who wish to celebrate him. At the same time, by becoming the hero of a cult he is a hero who belongs, not as in earlier

[77]Arrowsmith 1954 and Kitto 1939 are particularly eloquent on Heracles' hu-
manistic triumph and his shift from physical to mental courage. On the changing
concept of *aretē* in the play, see especially Arrowsmith, Chalk 1962 (with the
critical response of Adkins 1966), and Wilamowitz 1895.

[78]For a discussion of the role of the Athenian citizen in these respects, see
Connor 1971 and Humphreys 1978, esp. chap. 8.

[79]The dead hero could become angry and punish even those who worshiped
him. The hero's reception of a cult depended as often on an act of violence as on an
act of superior *aretē*. On the hero's ambivalence, see Rohde 1925, esp. 129–31 and
134–36; Harrison 1922: 334–39; Nock 1944: 158; Brelich 1958; and Nagy 1979.

poetry to all Greece, but to one specific locality. In the *Heracles* Athens confronts the heroism of this problematic and aristocratic figure of the past and finds for Heracles a permanent and active place within the limits of a democratic *polis*. As Vernant has remarked:

> But it is a surprising paradox that there is no cult of the hero in Homer and Hesiod. . . . The cult of the hero is a civic cult, instituted by the City. The City is the frame of reference in which heroes, quite diverse characters or old vegetal spirits are gathered into a simple religious category, assigned to places in their Pantheon. These heroes and heroic legends, while they are relegated to the past, condemned, called into doubt, still do not cease to stimulate certain questions, precisely insofar as they represent mental attitudes, values, patterns of behavior, a religious thought, a human ideal opposed to that of the city.
>
> Thus we have the following situation. The City is calling itself into question through dialogue with heroic characters, which continually produces a confrontation of two systems of values.[80]

The *Heracles* simultaneously confronts the difficulties posed by Heracles' heroism for an Athenian *polis* and the contradictions posed by Heracles' tradition for a tragic poet. The play makes it clear how tragedy is a descendant, as Aristotle suggested, of encomium through epic: that is, how tragedy makes heroes through sacrifice and creates a new poetry of praise.

The chorus, in response to the news that Heracles has killed his children, can find no mythical parallel to equal the horror of Heracles' deed (1016–20). But in offering consolation to Heracles it describes Procne's terrible murder of her only child as a sacrifice to the Muses (1021–22):

> μονοτέκνου Πρόκνης φόνον ἔχω λέξαι
> θυόμενον Μούσαις·

I am able to tell of the shedding of blood sacrificed to the Muses by Procne, who had only one child.[81]

---

[80]Vernant 1970: 283.
[81]On problems of text and translation in these lines, see Diggle 1974: 14–15. Wilamowitz 1895 on line 1025 saw in 1025–27 an allusion to the role of the chorus

Even in Homer, characters rationalize their present sufferings as material for future songs (*Iliad* 6.355–58). Hecuba expresses a similar view at *Troiades* 1242–45:

> If some god had not destroyed us . . . we would have been unknown. We should not have given songs to the Muses of posterity.

In the *Heracles* passage Procne, too, as she endlessly laments the son she has killed, provides a theme for poetry. The language used here by the chorus ties the sacrificial action of the *Heracles* to the poetic discourse of the play and opens the possibility of interpreting the central crisis as just such a "sacrifice" to the Muses, goddesses with whom Heracles was in fact associated in vase painting and later in cult.[82] In other words, sacrifices to the Muses, like real ones, frame and provide the community with a way of controlling acts of violence, of compensating for or remedying losses, and even of purifying murderers of their crimes. Heracles "sacrifices" to the Muses not a sacrificial animal nor his enemy Eurystheus and his sons (936–40, 982–89), but his own innocent family. Tragic sacrifices are performed offstage and reported by a messenger who surrounds his report of the violent and terrifying act with pity or a promise of poetic immortality. By these means tragedy ritualizes or provides a way of controlling our experience of violence. It achieves catharsis by substituting a fictional victim for ourselves, thereby purifying us of violence and terror. And for the protagonist, as Pucci has shown, the experience of loss immunizes the sufferer against future loss and allows him to gain some measure of control over his pain.[83]

The sacrifice of Heracles' family to the Muses is ultimately a

---

as singers and dancers. Bond 1981 ad loc. finds the usual interpretation too cynical. Yet all previous uses of this *topos* (that men are sacrificed to be an object of song) refer to disastrous events.

[82]See Bond 1981 on line 674 for Heracles' association with music in the visual arts beginning in the early fifth century and with the Muses in the Hellenistic period. The Muses appeared on Heracles' shield in the pseudo-Hesiodic *Shield of Heracles*. See Daremberg-Saglio: III.2, 2060–61 on cults of the Muses. In later Greek art Melpomene, the Muse of tragedy, is often pictured with the attributes of Heracles, the club and the lionskin (p. 2069).

[83]Pucci 1977. For further discussion of these issues in Euripidean tragedy, see Pucci 1980.

restoration of order through violence even while it intitially appears, like the failed pollution sacrifice, to be a perversion of order. Art and ritual both attenuate violence without effacing it and make divinity pertinent to human aspiration. It is ironically correct, then, for Madness to praise Heracles, for her actions in making Heracles sacrifice the children and thus blaming him ultimately lead to the establishment of a hero cult, and with it a permanent place in Athens for this potentially explosive figure of the past. Lyssa's Dionysiac and hence in essence democratic and tragic poetry, while seemingly perverting the aristocratic epinician poetry of the odes, uncovers common ground between apparent oppositions.

Yet Euripides does not attempt, like earlier Greek poets, to claim that the poetry he creates is a word received directly from the Muses and a reflection of divine truth; instead, it is a sacrifice made by the human imagination *to* the Muses, who remain outside it and in an uncertain relation to it. Heracles determines to be a slave to *tuchē*. Euripides, by allowing each part of his plot to be overturned by a chance occurrence (Heracles' return, Hera's action, and Theseus' arrival are all forms of *tuchē*), confesses that his own art, like Heracles' future survival, is subservient to fortune, to a changing social reality, and to the human capacity for generosity and mental adaptability.

Tragic praise, then, is fundamentally similar to but more inclusive than that of the traditional praise poet. As in Pindar, the hero is made relevant to the present, and the criminality of the gods is finally denied. Yet Euripides allows Heracles' denial of the gods' criminality to bypass the audience's dramatic experience of Iris and Lyssa. The tragic poet makes the decision to deny a repellant part of the tradition an act not of skillful piety, but of heroic self-delusion. Both versions of the event remain in the audience's memory; and Heracles himself becomes a greater hero. Pindar, in defending himself and his heroes against detractors, is forced to tread crooked paths, to use against his enemies the stealthy attack of the wolf (*Pythian* 2.84–85). Like Pindar, Euripides has skillfully devised a song of praise that fits its object, although he has done so by a devious route.[84] Euripides' tragedy creates heroes for Athens

[84]See Plato *Cratylus* 408c on the tragic as of the order of *pseudos*. On the deceptiveness of tragic truth, see Rosenmeyer 1955.

and establishes praise through illegitimate violence—not through the violence of war, which can be legitimate and external to society, but through an act intolerable to the internal structure of a culture. As a hero of cult the dead Heracles can help and be meaningful to Athens without physically returning to earth. The tragic poet finds a way to control the hero's violence imaginatively but not, as in most epinician poetry, through purging the hero of his terrible myths and denying reality to the criminality of the hero.

More generally, tragedies such as Euripides' *Heracles* or Sophocles' *Oedipus at Colonus* follow and surpass Simonides' famous scolion composed for the Scopadae, preserved mainly by Plato in the *Protagoras* (339b–c, 344c–346e).[85] Here the poet, observing the epinician dictum that success makes a man *agathos* (noble), whereas irresistible disaster (*amēchanos sumphora*) makes him *kakos,* insists that he will continue to "praise all who do nothing shameful willingly" as long as the offending party is not "excessively resourceless and knows city-supporting justice, a healthy man." For "not even the gods fight with necessity." By distinguishing deliberate crime from failure due to accident and necessity, Simonides is often said to have marked a turning point in the evolution of Greek encomiastic poetry, culminating, by way of tragedy, in Aristotle's insistence in the *Nichomachean Ethics* (1101b10–1102a4 and 1114a23–29) that praise and blame are appropriate only for voluntary actions. But whereas Simonides modifies and humanizes the heroic ideal offered in encomiastic poetry, tragedy emphasizes the achievement of value for a community through rather than in despite of the taint of violence and suffering.

In sum, then, the hero Heracles begins the play in the underworld, or putatively dead. The central crisis puts him into a social and psychological underworld where, as a sinner like Ixion (1298), he finds no release from pain nor any relation to a human community.[86] He receives not the second life the gods seem to have given him at the end of the suppliant plot, but a second death, and then, through Theseus' mediation, a second life once more. The final

[85]See Crotty 1982: 33–40 for discussion of and recent bibliography on this Simonides fragment.
[86]Ixion shed the first human blood; Pindar *Pythian* 2.31–32.

scenes put Heracles back into the underworld where he began the play, but retain as well a relation for the hero to the future. While seemingly perverting the premises upon which Greek society controlled internal violence, whether through sacrificial ritual, through *agōn,* or through song, the final scenes once more make possible the relations among god, hero, community, and the present shattered in the peripety. Through exposing the fictions upon which ritual is based and establishing the ritualizing function of poetry, the play cleanses Heracles of his violence and retains an important place for ritual in the community; without denying the existence of that violence, the play deflects it sufficiently, as in ritual, from the human actor.[87]

The *Heracles* brings its problematic hero into a permanent relation to Athens, yet it does so without denying its own contradictory argument. The remaining contradictions are both structural and psychological. The programmatic nature of the play, its forceful implicit argument for the role of tragedy in integrating seemingly anachronistic myths and poetic traditions into the ideology of the city, offers a rather cold and abstract counterbalance to Heracles' vivid and terrible suffering. Theseus' promises and his ability to make an imaginative break from the past that binds Heracles to suicide give Heracles a context in which he can survive death. But only Heracles can treat his own suffering. Theseus' offers are interludes in or subsidiary to his grief (1340: *oimoi. parerga . . . tad' est' emōn kakōn*).[88] He must establish his own boundaries for that suffering in a mental act that echoes his earlier boundary-establishing physical labors; now he "wrestles" with Theseus in words (1255).[89] When in the future Heracles becomes a dead cult hero and the stone that in his grief he wishes to be (1397; see also 1332 for

---

[87]Girard 1977 argues that tragedy decomposes and demystifies ritual, and then replaces ritual itself. This may in essence be true, but the fact that Euripides' plays often end with the establishment of a cult seems to suggest that he sees his play as acting in conjunction with ritual and along parallel lines. On this point, see also Whitman 1974: 118–19.

[88]It is not clear whether the *tad'* in 1340 refers to Theseus' offers or to his arguments about the gods.

[89]See also 1205–10, where Amphitryon "wrestles" with Heracles while supplicating him. See Gorgias 11.13 DK on the wrestling metaphor used of rhetorical exercises. For other passages in Euripides, see Bond 1981 on line 1255.

the stone monument that Heracles will receive as a cult hero), perhaps his suffering will be healed. Heracles' heroism now depends on his suffering and he leaves the stage in unbearable anguish.

Euripides' insistence on imposing on his domestic Heracles the violent lunatic of the epic tradition draws attention away from the man to the problems posed by his myth. It frankly suggests that the resolution of this programmatically structured play is fictional and counter to our intuitive sense that madness must be in some sense integral to a character, not simply imposed on it from without. Similarly, Heracles, who did not in his madness consciously experience Iris and Lyssa, determines to survive through a denial or partial denial of the divine intervention that the audience has witnessed onstage. The *logoi* of the poets attacked by Heracles are Euripides' own *logoi;* but the silent chorus, witness to the central crisis, does not intervene to deny Heracles.[90] The final moment echoes the close of the suppliant action; the savior Theseus now draws Heracles in his wake as a boat just as Heracles did his sons. The repetition, given the sudden shift of *tuchē* that followed the first action, does not entirely inspire confidence. Indeed, lines 1386–88, in which Heracles requests Theseus' help with Cerberus, have been interpreted as an expression of the hero's concern for his own stability, of his fear of another attack of madness or impulse to suicide produced by grief over his children. Yet Heracles' act of imagination allows the audience to understand precisely the limits of the sacrifice and the irony of the healing poetic deception that Euripides' tragedy offers to the Muses. As Gorgias said: "Tragedy, by means of legends and emotions, creates a deception in which the deceiver is more honest than the non-deceiver and the deceived is wiser than the non-deceived" (frag. 23 DK).[91]

Appendix: The Structure of the *Heracles*

Critics of the *Heracles* have been universally disturbed and puzzled by the structure of the play. Scholars disagree on how the play is divided (into two or three separate actions) and on its

[90]On this point, see Pucci 1980: 178. See also note 67 above.
[91]Freeman 1971, trans.

unifying principle or principles. Unless one accepts the play as a drama of divine punishment, in which Heracles is destroyed for daring to become more than human,[92] or unless one assumes that Heracles enters the stage already potentially unstable or megalomaniac to the point that his sudden madness arises necessarily and probably from his own disturbed internal state,[93] one must explain, as even these critics are aware, a dramatic structure in which causal connections between the parts are clearly problematic. I have divided the play into the first, or suppliant, action; the central episode of madness, or the peripety; and the final action, in which Heracles regains sanity, is distracted from suicide, and chooses to live in Athens.

Scholars have searched for thematic connections between the parts or some principle on which to rationalize the deliberate disjunction between these separate actions. Some find structural cohesion in the ethical themes of *aretē* as opposed to *bia* (violence), of *philia* (friendship), wealth, hope, gratitude, *sōtēria* (salvation), pity, *amathia* (ignorant insensitivity and injustice), or *authadia* (self-willed stubbornness). The place of these principles in the universe and the contrast between human and divine responses to them form the central tension of the drama.[94] Others find a principle of unity in the theme of self-sacrifice[95] or in the double parentage of Heracles.[96] Strohm and Schwinge stress the repeated need for a savior to rescue different protagonists from a decision to die.[97] Some critics look to the characters, emphasizing the continual presence of Amphitryon onstage or the changing perspective on Heracles and the humanization of the hero.[98] In Bond's view, the play is unified through being a meditation on mistaken human views of the gods.[99] The gods first appear unjust, then just; the

[92]See esp. Burnett 1971 and Grube 1941.
[93]Wilamowitz 1895.
[94]Interpretations in this group, aside from the earlier work of Wilamowitz, include esp. Sheppard 1916, Chalk 1962 (criticized by Adkins 1966), Conacher 1967a: 78–90, and Garzya 1962: 26–40.
[95]Strohm 1957.
[96]Gregory 1977.
[97]Strohm 1957 and Schwinge 1972: 193ff.
[98]See esp. Kitto 1954 and Greenwood 1953: 82–83.
[99]Bond 1981 enlarges on the views of Kroeker 1938: 110–24 and Petersen 1915: 36–50.

peripety changes the audience's views once more. After Heracles determines on a new view of the gods, the play finally stresses the value of friendship and the hero's decision to endure.

The most recent extensive and ambitious interpretations of the play are those of Rohdich and Arrowsmith.[100] I shall summarize briefly their arguments, since neither work is readily available (Bond mentions neither) and both have influenced my own.

Rohdich sees the central crisis as the introduction of the tragic or mythic world view into the play. For him the unity of the play consists in the tensions, which he finds throughout Euripides' work, between a sophistic and a mythical interpretation of events. The first and last parts of the play stand to each other as thesis and antithesis. The Heracles of the first action is a sophistic hero, an autarchic bowman who offers a salvation that in essence rejects the rule of supreme beings in favor of a strictly human power to make the world better. The sophistic view cannot accommodate Heracles' madness, the form in which the tragic intervenes in the dramatic action. Only the tragic view can comprehend suffering as part of an ordered world concept. Heracles ends by adopting the sophistic viewpoint, but the tragic contradictions between his attitude and "reality," what he has experienced in the play, remain.

Although Rohdich's interpretation essentially complements my own, I see the issues raised by the crisis of the first action in the context of a broader, presophistic poetic tradition. The sophistic insistence on human self-sufficiency in the final scenes arises from a crisis in the presophistic world view, represented in the traditional praise poetry sung by the chorus, which insists on the instability of man without god and on the dependence of human *aretē* on the gods. The tragic response developed in the resolution includes, through the mediation of both human imagination and cult, a recognition of both the tragic elements in the Heracles tradition and a place for his earlier heroism.

Arrowsmith explains the relation between the parts of the *Heracles* with a theory of tragic "conversion." He assumes that there is no necessary or probable causal relation between the first and last

[100]Rohdich 1968: 71–104 and Arrowsmith 1954.

actions.[101] The first action, traditional and melodramatic, dramatizes the "given" of the myths and legends about Heracles and an
outworn theology, "the world as it is said to be" (*logos*). The
second action, with its "sharply anachronized contemporary reality," presents the world of "things as they are" or "things as they
must be" (*ergon*).[102] The hero's suffering tests the beliefs and values of the first action and converts them under dramatic pressure
to another level of reality.[103] Part one is created to be replaced by
part two. The Pindaric hero of physical courage, with the *aretē* of
aristocratic *eugeneia,* learns through suffering the internalized courage of a moral *aristos* demanded by fifth-century reality. By the end
of the play the characters, motives, and values have been "pushed
forward to the very frontiers of reality and morality."[104] For example, Amphitryon's ideas about the mutability of human life
(though gnomic and trite in part one) and his heroic affirmation of
hope prepare for Heracles' final acceptance of his subservience to
tuchē in part two; yet hope has become not so much real solace as
an acceptance of the human instinct for survival.[105] The play, by
allowing such contradictions to survive, makes it clear that "conversion" involves transforming, not simply rejecting, the values
and myths of the first action.[106] Finally, the peripety emphasizes
the dislocation between the parts and expresses "the furious disorder of experience."[107] The structure of the play thus mirrors and
expresses the tragic idea.[108]

Though rich and complex, this interpretation of the play seems
to underestimate the complexity of the first action, with its plot
and characters (for example, Lycus) invented, not drawn from the
logos of mythical tradition; with its equally anachronistic setting;
and with its already very human Heracles. The last action is in
many ways more idealized than the first. This theory neglects the

[101]Arrowsmith 1954: 8.
[102]Ibid., 10–11 and 42.
[103]Ibid., 42.
[104]Ibid., 46.
[105]Ibid., 66–73.
[106]Ibid., 195.
[107]Ibid., 40.
[108]Ibid., 37 and 68–69.

symmetrical and complex relation between part one and the central crisis. Finally, notwithstanding Arrowsmith's admirable discussion of the magnificence of Heracles' heroic humanism in the face of the disorder of experience, I see Heracles as moving as much toward the impersonality of a cult and a new *logos* or myth as toward humanity and "reality" (*ergon*).

]5[

The *Bacchae*

Euripides' *Bacchae* demands interpretation on many levels. Most critics have read the play primarily as a religious statement. The poet either offers a defense of Dionysus in a drama of justified divine retribution or attacks Dionysiac religion and, by implication, other similar contemporary Athenian mystery cults. Others emphasize the play's demonstration of an inescapable human irrationality that finds an outlet both in religious cult and in the mob violence of Athenian democratic politics.[1] The text undeniably

The interpretation of the *Bacchae* offered in this chapter was first presented to the Princeton Department of Classics in 1973. The chapter is drawn from my 1975 Harvard dissertation, "Ritual Irony in the *Bacchae* and Other Later Euripidean Plays." An abbreviated version of some of the material here was published as Foley 1980. Segal 1982, which deals with some of the ideas discussed here, especially that of metatheater, was published nearly ten years after the consolidation of my own views on the play and after the completion of this chapter. Hence I have not attempted to annotate the areas in which Segal's stimulating and generally complementary views overlap with or expand on my own.

[1]For excellent surveys of the central critical problems presented by the *Bacchae*, and especially its treatment of theological issues, see the introduction to Dodds 1960, Winnington-Ingram 1948: 6–13, Diller 1955, and Rohdich 1968: 162–68. Dodds and Winnington-Ingram view the play as an eclectic demonstration of Dionysiac religion that ultimately takes no firm moral position, but emphasizes the overpowering reality and amorality of the divinity and the forces that the god represents in human existence. On the relation of the play to contemporary thought, morality, and politics, see esp. Nilhard 1912, Deichgräber 1935, Arthur 1972, Diller, and Rohdich. My interpretation of the play is meant to enrich and not to exclude the standard interpretations of Dionysus in the *Bacchae* as a nature god or a god of religious ecstasy. The prototheatrical form of Dionysus' appearance in the play is yet another aspect of a complex and multifaceted divinity.

raises questions about the nature of divinity and reflects the precariousness of social and political life in late fifth-century Athens. Yet for the contemporary Athenian, Dionysus was associated not only with ritualized release of self-control and with madness, with women and the natural world outside the *polis,* with Apollo at Delphi, and with the civilizing if ambivalent gifts of wine and festival, but also with theater itself; for the tragedies, comedies, and satyr plays of Athens were presented in his honor. Our earliest evidence suggests that Greeks always worshiped Dionysus in a theatrical form: through masks, costumes, miracle plays, music, and dance. Euripides wrote the *Bacchae* at a time when his contemporaries were becoming increasingly self-conscious about the nature of their theater god.[2] In Aristophanes' *Frogs,* Dionysus, as spectator, actor, and judge in his own festival, seeks to save the city by rejuvenating its dramatic art.[3] Contemporary visual artists were just beginning to popularize the theatrical Dionysus, seated among actors who display the masks and costumes of plays performed in honor of a young and often effeminate god.[4] The *Bacchae,* too, since its subject is the introduction of a cult into a city-state, specifically the rituals of the god of tragic festival, becomes as well a play about the ritual aspects of tragedy itself.

In the *Bacchae,* in a manner similar to the *Heracles* and the *Electra,* Pentheus' tragic disaster is represented as a perverted sacrifice and *agōn* that form part of a corrupted Dionysiac festival. As in all the other plays examined in this book, the ritual crisis reflects a fundamental disruption in the relation between man and god and among men in the community. Pentheus and his city have rejected the worship of Dionysus, and the god promises in the prologue to

[2]The controversy over the relation between the origins of Greek tragedy and the worship of Dionysus is irrelevant to my argument, since we know that Euripides' contemporaries thought of Dionysus as a theater god.

[3]See Aristophanes' *Clouds* 518–19 for another reference to Dionysus as patron of comic poetry. It is not clear whether Cratinus' *Dionysalexandros* and *Archilochoi* or Eupolis' *Taxiarchoi* exploited Dionysus' role as god of theater, although he certainly played the role of arbiter in the underworld in the first two of these plays.

[4]The earliest known artistic treatments of Dionysus in a theatrical context are the Pronomos vase (*ARV2* 1336), the Peiraeus relief (fig. 51 in Pickard-Cambridge 1968), and possibly the fragments of a vase from Taranto now in Wurzburg (*ARV2* 1338). These works date from the end of the fifth to the early fourth century.

enact the full revenge necessary to assert his divinity. The unity of Thebes is destroyed: the maddened women have departed for the wilds to experience a communion with their god and nature itself; within the city Pentheus is opposed by his elders, Cadmus and Tiresias, as well as by a growing number of the population, represented by the *therapōn* and first messenger. In this atmosphere of "sacrificial crisis" the boundaries between god and man and beast, between sacred and profane violence, have collapsed. Pentheus, insisting on his differences from others, becomes entangled in "mimetic rivalry" with the divine stranger; he inevitably becomes the object of the proliferating violence and loss of differentiation. As in the *Heracles,* Euripides uses the ritual crisis to explore simultaneously god, man, society, and his own tragic art.

What Dionysus brings to Thebes and to Hellenic culture in the *Bacchae* is festival, and in particular a form of embryonic theater. Pentheus is sacrificed because he cannot understand and incorporate truth in the symbolic form that festival and theater offer to the adherent, the spectator, and the *polis*. In the *Bacchae* Euripides closed a career of increasingly manipulative and illusion-breaking treatment of dramatic conventions[5] by presenting yet another fin-de-siècle "theatrical" Dionysus. The poet used the god to investigate the complex relation between ritual and theater, festival and society. By taking festival back to its origins, he examined the role of festival and theater in establishing, enforcing, or threatening the social order, and the way that art interprets human and divine experience for the city.

In the *IA* and the *Phoenissae* the poetry of the choral odes and the discontinuities of the action remain in counterpoint, and ritual creates a fragile link between the two realms. In the *Heracles* Lyssa's inversion of the traditional praise poetry of the choral odes and Heracles' tragic sacrifice of his children ultimately create from an anachronistic epic hero a humanized hero for the Athenian democratic *polis*. Past myths retain a transformed authority as Heracles' crime becomes a sacrifice to the Muses. In the *Bacchae* myth and action, odes and iambic scenes, are intertwined from the start, as is appropriate in a plot that represents a penetration of the secular

[5]See, among others, Segal 1971 and Winnington-Ingram 1969.

world by a divine power. The action of the play gradually becomes, until the final scenes, fully ritualized and mythical, and Dionysiac poetry transforms reality as the chorus becomes one with and even predicts the action. Here poetry becomes performance. As the barbarian chorus serves equally to represent a populist Greek ethics familiar in most tragic choruses and to introduce a radical foreign cult, it both reflects on the political and social aspects of ritual, on the capacity of ritual and drama for danger, violence, and salvation for society, and opens new questions about its own role in drama. Only in the final scenes, when Dionysus has left the level of human action, does the audience experience fully the distance between secular reality and the order and vision created through myth and ritual so characteristic of Euripides' late drama. The mysterious pronouncements of the god from above the stage offer mythical truths incomprehensible to Cadmus and Agave lamenting below, and neither Tiresias nor the chorus nor the stranger speaks to decode them. In the *Bacchae*, then, tragedy emerges from a sacrificial disaster, but it is ultimately defined by the gap that develops between the Dionysiac vision and the strictly human and sane imagination.

Ritual and the Death of Pentheus

The action surrounding Pentheus' sacrificial death, beginning with Dionysus' transformation of Pentheus into a maenad and ending with the return of Agave with the head of her son, suggests affinities with a ritual sequence in Greek festival, that of *pompē, agōn, kōmos*.[6] Hence the sacrifice of the king must be considered in relation to this larger festal context. After Pentheus has shown himself obdurate against all other demonstrations of Dionysus' divinity, the god charms him with the possibility of actually seeing or being a spectator (*theatēs*, 829) to the behavior of the maenads on

[6]On the eclecticism of the presentation of Dionysiac ritual in the play, see esp. Dodds 1960: xxvii–xxviii. See Bather 1894 and Coche de la Ferté 1980 on possible primitive and archaic elements in the death of Pentheus. On Pentheus' sacrificial death, see Girard 1977, Seidensticker 1979, and Darkaki 1980. See my later discussion of Thomson 1946 and Winnington-Ingram 1948 on *pompē, agōn, kōmos*.

the mountain. He maddens the king, dresses him in the robes, fawnskin, *thursos,* and long hair of a female follower of the god, and instructs him in the movements of maenadic dance. Each detail of apparel is dwelt upon in sequence. Dionysus adjusts Pentheus' costume, touching his head, hands, and feet, thereby "consecrating" his victim, setting him apart from the profane world. Pentheus' words at 934 acknowledge the context:

> Go ahead, arrange it. For we are in fact ritually dedicated [*anakeimestha*] to you.

Once he is costumed, Pentheus experiences a change of sight. He sees double, two Thebes and two suns, and the stranger appears to be a bull. The god offers to escort Pentheus by an obscure route to the contests, *agōnes,* in which he himself secretly plans to be the victor (964–65, 974–76):

> Thus the appropriate contests await you. Follow and I will go as your protective escort [*pompos . . . sōtērios*].
> . . . .
> . . . I am leading the young man into this great contest [*agōn*] in which I and Bromios will come out the victors. The event itself will show the rest.

Later the messenger describes Dionysus as *pompos:* "and the stranger who was escort in our embassy" (*theōrias,* 1047). The god has led Pentheus from the city to experience a *theōria* (embassy, the experience of being spectator, or spectacle) where he encounters the god's chorus (*chorous kruphaious,* 1109) of maenads on the mountain. Pentheus, in order to see the maenads better (1058, 1060, 1062), mounts a tree with supernatural aid. Since trees were sacred to Dionysus, the god severs the earthborn Pentheus from his origins and places him symbolically in his power.

The maenads now see him, although he can barely see the maenads (1075). A new light appears; silence falls. The maenads' eyes turn in their heads, and at the god's command they pelt Pentheus with stones, branches, and *thursoi,* tear up the tree on which he is perched, and throw him to the ground. Thinking he is a beast, they rip him apart. His mother, Agave, acts as priestess of

the ritual (*hierea phonou*, priestess of murder or death, 1114), which
Cadmus later explicitly calls a sacrifice (1246–47): "A fine sacrifice
[*to thuma*] you have struck down for the gods and to the feast invite
Thebes here and myself." (See also *mainadas thuoskoous*, 224, and
thuousin, 473, of participants in a Dionysiac rite.) Pentheus, once
eager to make a "sacrifice" of the women (796) or to sever the
stranger's head (241), becomes a decapitated sacrificial victim himself. (See the similar reversal of Pentheus' plans to sacrifice—
sphazōn, 631—the stranger, which results instead in his own demise—*katasphageis*, 858.) Tearing off his *mitra* (headband), he returns to sanity at the last moment, recognizes his errors (*hamartiaisi*, 1121), but fails to communicate his identity to his mother.
His mother, imagining herself a hunter, returns home with the
head of Pentheus to celebrate a feast or revel (*kōmos*) with the city,
the chorus, and her family in honor of her own and the god's
victory on the mountain. She congratulates Dionysus for being
kallinikos (victorious, 1147; see also the chorus on the Cadmean
bacchants in 1161). The chorus commends Agave for her part in
the *agōn* (1163–64: "a brilliant contest, to cast on your child a hand
dripping with blood") and invites her to share in a triumphal
celebration (*kōmon*, 1167, *sungkōmon*, fellow reveler, 1172). Agave
pronounces herself *makaira* and *eudaimōn* (happy and blessed, 1180
and 1258) for her victories over the "beast." Yet the play closes
with Agave wishing to dissociate herself from the memory of the
thursos (1386) and departing on a new *pompē* (*ō pompoi*, 1381, if the
lines are not interpolated) into lonely exile.

Pentheus' death shares with normal sacrificial procedure the
dedication of a chosen victim to the god through special adorn-
ment, ordinarily with a wreath or gilded horns, but here with a
change of clothing; the pelting of the beast, here with branches,
generally with grain; the moment of ritual silence; the luring of the
victim to make a religious error and to "consent" to its demise; the
scream of the women; and the implication of all participants in the
sacrificial death.[7] Similar but by no means identical preliminary

[7]For procedure in sacrificial ritual, see Chapter 1. See esp. Seidensticker 1979 on
the parallels between the sacrificial death of Pentheus and the procedures of the
normal ritual; Seidensticker fails to come to terms with the aberrant and horri-
fyingly perverted nature of this human sacrifice of the king. On the relation of

procedures were used in various Greek rituals involving the expulsion of a *pharmakos* or scapegoat.[8] In other respects, however, though called a sacrifice after the event, the ritual is an aberration, a perversion of the controlled civic norm. In a wild rather than civic context the unwilling victim is torn apart by the hands of maddened women rather than despatched with due ceremony and a sacrificial knife by men. A stranger presides over the event. Boundaries between sacred and profane, pure and impure, collapse. Spattered with blood and pollution (*Christus Patiens* 1694), Agave returns to nail her son's head on the palace (animal skulls were sometimes dedicated in this fashion) and to invite Thebes to an unholy feast. The benefits of the ritual clearly fail to accrue to the sacrificers,[9] and Pentheus does not serve as a *pharmakos* to save his city. The king's body is pitifully reconstructed, then apparently left unburied onstage by his family without a hint of future regeneration and rebirth for the city. Thebes is notably absent in the final scene, and the future promises exile for the shattered royal house and new and hostile Dionysiac incursions into Greece from Asia. Agave is repelled by the god's rites, and even the vengeful chorus seems shaken by the fate of Cadmus and his daughter. (See the pity expressed for Cadmus in 1327, and perhaps by implication in the use of *talaina* for Agave, 1200, and *tlamon* at 1184).

When they appear in conjunction the three terms *pompē, agōn, kōmos* mean respectively a procession before a religious festival, the contest(s) celebrated at such a festival, and the festive revelry that follows such contests. Each word, taken alone, also has additional connotations applicable to the dramatic context here. *Pompos* is used of Hermes escorting souls into the underworld as well as generally of the protective escort of a god; both meanings have an ironic applicability here (see *pompos . . . sōtērios* at 965). The verb *pompeuō*

Dionysiac sacrifice to the civic norm, see esp. Detienne 1979a: chaps. 5 and 6, Guépin 1968, and Darkaki 1980.

[8]For Pentheus as *pharmakos*, see esp. Dodds 1960 on line 963. For a discussion of Greek rituals involving a *pharmakos* and their relation to the *Oedipus Rex*, see Vernant in Vernant and Vidal-Naquet 1981: 87–119.

[9]Vickers 1973: 318: "Agave thought that she was the sacrifier, but she discovers she was only the sacrificer; and whereas the interests of those two persons are usually identical, in the dénouement of this play they are violently opposed. To Dionysus accrue the benefits."

is specifically associated with the ribald jests and abuse that occurred during the processions at Dionysiac festivals (Demosthenes 18.124). If the associations of *pompeuō* can apply to *pompos* and *pompē*, the god here predictably uses the *pompē* to mock his rival (842, 854). In a society in which contest in any form played such a central role, it is difficult to specify the meaning of *agōn*, which can refer to a debate, a trial, an athletic or theatrical contest, a labor of Heracles, and a struggle. Pentheus' *agōn* concludes a struggle with the god that concerns power and justice (vengeance), words, perception, and transformation through costume and movement. The word *kōmos* is used of revelry, often accompanied by feasting and dancing, of the procession celebrating a victor in the games, of a band of revelers generally (such bands were said by some to explain the etymology of *kōmōidia*),[10] and of a revel in honor of gods or heroes (*Helen* 1469 of Hyacinthus, and Demosthenes 21.10, *tois en astei Dionusiois hē pompē . . . kai ho kōmos*). The *kōmos* of this play is both a victory song for the god and a revel/potential feast for Agave and the chorus. The term *kallinikos* is used originally of athletic or military victors, and later of the victorious dramatic poet or comic hero. The words used for spectacle here, *theatēs, theama,* and *theōria,* resonate both with the theme of festival in the play (in Aristophanes' *Peace* Theoria is festival personified, redolent of games, sex, food, and sacrifice) and with the wordplay on sight and insight present throughout the *Bacchae.* Pentheus, representing his city, goes to the mountain intending to be a spectator. Instead, his sight changes, and he becomes a spectacle and participant, while the god alone remains a spectator.

The pattern *pompē, agōn, kōmos* used here brings to mind a *typical* festival pattern. But the dramatic context allows us to be more specific. Winnington-Ingram notes that the pattern *pompē, agōn kōmos (kallinikos)* must be meant to refer to the Olympic games.[11] The pattern does fit what ancient sources tell of the games, both in the sequence and in the naming of the proceedings: the *pompikē hodos* at Olympia, the athletic *agōnes,* and the triumphant, near godlike welcome given the victorious athlete, including a feast at

---

[10]On the origin and etymology of *kōmōidia,* see Pickard-Cambridge 1962: 132–62.

[11]Winnington-Ingram 1948: 24 n. 3 and 128 n. 2.

the Prytaneion. Such a reference would provide an apt conclusion for the contest of power between man and god throughout the action, sometimes pictured in athletic terms (491, 800), sometimes portrayed as a struggle between hunter and hunted. The ironies of this hopeless physical contest are patent. The role of contestant is split between Pentheus, who will compete with women (and the god), and his mother, who competes against her son. The audience for these contests consists of women; yet women were not allowed to participate in the games and were probably even excluded as spectators at Olympia. Dionysus persuades Pentheus, as the champion of the state, to exit to death from his city not openly in armor, but secretly by back streets, while looking forward on his return to a luxurious embrace from his mother (965–70):

D. Follow, and I shall go as your protective escort.
    From there another will bring you back . . .
P. Yes, my mother.
D. . . . a sight remarkable to all.
P. For this purpose I come.
D. You will come back carried . . .
P. What luxury you speak.
D. . . . in your mother's arms.
P. . . . and you will drive me to self-indulgence.
D. Yes, indulgence—of a sort.
P. I am achieving what I deserve.

This passage very possibly makes an ironic allusion to epinician themes expressed, for example, in Pindar *Pythian* 8.83–87, which also refers to the return of athletes, this time losing athletes, from athletic contests:

> Yet at the Pythian festival their homecoming was not ordained to be happy. Nor, as they returned to their mothers, did sweet laughter stir delight about them. But apart from their enemies, stung by mischance, they slink along through back streets.

Pentheus' secret departure anticipates his "athletic" failure; he skulks out of the city like Pindar's defeated athletes, while the ironies of his triumphal return into, or in, his mother's arms are grimly obvious. Pentheus dies as the failed champion of a male population of Thebes, which barely makes a dramatic appearance. Like Hector's last running race with Achilles, this is a contest not for a prize, but for the life of a man (*Iliad* 22.159–61). The *agōn*, designed to control competitive violence within a society and to promote its glory, collapses into intrasocietal violence and disaster for its participants. To equate theomachy with a contest of strength so thoroughly perverted not only travesties a norm but also implicitly recalls the repeated epinician warning to the athlete to attribute victory to the gods and not to overstep human limits in the pride of success.

Thomson reads the pattern *pompē, agōn, kōmos* in several ways, but first in terms of Greek and especially the Spartan adolescent initiation ritual.[12] His interpretation is highly speculative, given our tenuous knowledge of Greek initiation rituals, and especially of Attic initiation. Yet aspects of Pentheus' downfall do suggest a kind of perverted initiation into the god's mysteries and/or a regression from hoplite to ephebe initiate and even to a helpless infancy, as Pentheus imagines the luxury of returning home in his mother's arms. The choice to abandon hoplite's arms and to adopt the tactics of deception, the movement to the wild, the involvement with hunting, and the cross-sexual dressing belong in Greek myth and practice to the period of prehoplite initiation.[13] The dressing of youths in female costume in certain Attic festivals (Oschophoria, Anthesteria), Achilles' female disguise as a youth, and the deceptive tactics used by Orestes to carry out the commands of the oracle in the *Libation Bearers* are examples from literature and practice that grow out of such initiatory traditions. Dionysus and the women retain the order, authority, and steadfastness characteristic of the hoplite, and the god, not Pentheus, achieves a full masculine identity in the play. The god proves himself the Olympian son of Zeus, reborn as son of the father from the male thigh,

[12]Thomson 1946: 130–33, 156–62, and 97–119.

[13]On the role of hunting and adolescent initiation in Athens, see esp. Vidal-Naquet 1968a and 1981b; on the use of such imagery of hunting in tragedy, see Vidal-Naquet 1981a. On cross-sexual dressing in adolescent initiation rituals, see Dodds 1960 on lines 831–33 and 854–55, Gallini 1963 on the play, and more generally Vernant 1980: 22–25 and Brelich 1969a. On the Oschophoria, see Parke 1977: 77–81.

while Pentheus regresses to the world of women, his head gro-
tesquely embraced in his mother's arms (1277). Both the obvious
psychological implications of Pentheus' regression and his destruction by a competitive and enveloping mother have been well discussed by a number of critics.[14]

As in the *Heracles* and the *Electra*, Euripides uses the imagery of
sacrifice, *agōn*, and festival in the *Bacchae* to make multiple ritual
allusions. But here the festival, or protofestival, introduced by
Dionysus can also be read as a primitive version of his own theatrical festival in Athens. The specifically *poetic* inspiration behind
the costuming of Pentheus that inaugurates the festal pattern is
emphasized by the use of the verb *ekmousoō* in 825: *Dionusos hēmas
exemousōsen tade*, "Dionysus has inspired these actions in us." Dionysus' effect on the landscape is also presented throughout the
play as comparable to that of a poet such as Orpheus or Amphion,
whose poetry is so powerful that it can move nature (114, 561–64,
726–27). And, if the tradition that Thespis produced a *Pentheus* as
one of the earliest Greek dramas was current in Euripides' time,
the choice of subject for Dionysus' introduction of a primitive
drama into Thebes would be particularly appropriate.[15] Thomson
also notes the similarities between the pattern *pompē*, *agōn*, *kōmos*
and the official language used to describe the first day of the City
Dionysia. The *pompē* followed an *eisagōgē*, in which the statue of
Dionysus was brought from Eleutherae by ephebes with accompanying festivities and sacrifice to rest in the theater precinct, and
culminated in the sacrifice of a bull to Dionysus in his sacred
precinct. The *phalloi* carried in the *pompē* commemorated the myth
in which the Athenians at first resisted Dionysus' entrance into the
city but were smitten by a disease from which they freed themselves by manufacturing *phalloi* in honor of the god (Schol. Aristophanes *Acharnians* 243). Both the festal pattern of the Dionysia and
the play commemorate the prehistoric introduction of the worship

[14]For psychoanalytic interpretations of Pentheus, see esp. Sale: 1972, Green
1979: 172–75, La Rue 1968, and Segal 1978a. Vian 1963: 178 stresses that in Hesiod
and the *Melampodia* Cadmus does not lack a male heir. Hence Euripides must have
altered the myth or chosen a variation that makes Pentheus' psychology more
believable.
[15]For Thespis' *Pentheus*, see the *Suda* on Thespis.

of Dionysus into a city, disastrously at Thebes but finally successfully at Athens; both *eisagōgē* and *pompē* included an important role
for the ephebic initiates and sacrifice.

The theatrical festival as a whole, with its day of processions
followed by the dramatic *agōnes,* and concluding with celebrations
in honor of the victorious poets, could equally well be understood
as reflecting the pattern *pompē, agōn, kōmos.* The festival included a
sacrifice performed at the altar of the god in the center of the
orchestra, a ritual that was often repeated and perhaps visually
recalled in the metaphorical sacrifices of the tragic victim(s) in the
plays that followed.[16] Finally, this same festal pattern is inherent,
as Cornford has argued, in the language and structure of Old
Comedy, which centers on the formally structured *agōn* or debate
and concludes with a celebration of victory (sometimes including
or preceded by sacrifice) by the comic hero or heroes and often also
by the poet himself.[17] The dramatic poets themselves describe
tragic and comic debates or contests as *agōnes,* and their victors as
kallinikoi. (See Aristophanes *Acharnians* 392, *Frogs* 785 and 867, for
agōn used for debates occurring in the plays, and *Acharn.* 504 of the
theatrical contests at the Lenaia; see also Euripides *Heracleidae* 116,
Suppliants 427, *Phoenissae* 588 and 930, and *Antiope* frag. 189 N.
For *kallinikos* applied to victors in comic debates or contests, see
Aristophanes *Acharn.* 1227–28, 1231, 1233; *Birds* 1764; and *Knights*
1254.)

The order of events at the City Dionysia poses some difficulty
for this reading, for the law of Euegoros, quoted by Demosthenes,
refers not only to a *pompē* but also to a *kōmos* that may well have
occurred on the first day *before* the dramatic *agōnes* but after a series
of performances in honor of various gods at their shrines and a
sacrifice to Dionysus.[18] Yet what Dionysus seems to be introducing to Thebes in the *Bacchae* is in any case a protofestival. Hence
the audience could recognize in this emerging "theatrical" festival
a conflation of the initial day of the City Dionysia, with its intro-

[16]On this point, see Burkert 1966a and the discussion of Burkert's theories in
Chapter 1.

[17]Cornford 1934.

[18]On the problem of the order of events at the City Dionysia, see Pickard-
Cambridge 1968: 63–66 and Deubner 1932: 138–42.

duction of the god and his worship; the festival as a whole, with its dramatic *agōnes* followed by the celebration of victory by the poets; and comedy, with its comparable structural pattern. This would, of course, be the case only if the audience experienced Dionysus' introduction of his worship as a "play" or as an emerging form of drama that could be interpreted as either "comedy" or "tragedy."

In the protodrama of the *Bacchae* Dionysus uses "festival" or "comedy" to make the city of Thebes "see" his divinity and to establish his worship. Up to the death of Pentheus, when the god withdraws from the level of human action, Euripides has Dionysus assert increasingly greater control over the play and make it an expression of his divinity. In his triumphant play within a play he costumes Pentheus and brings him to a prearranged setting on the mountain as both spectator and participant in an *agōn*. Both the maenads on the mountain, the doubles of their sisters in the chorus (see 1109), and Pentheus begin as spectators dressed by the god, and then, at the god's command, become unwitting participants in a drama in which Pentheus is both mocked and "sacrificed." At the heart of the *agōn* become sacrifice Pentheus undergoes a literal *peripeteia* (tragic fall, 1111–13) from high to low and a vain and momentary *anagnōrisis* (tragic recognition, 1113–19) of his situation and his own disastrous errors of perception (*hamartiaisi,* 1121, Aristotle's own term for tragic error).[19] The episode closes with a *kōmos* or celebration of the god's victorious action shared by an "audience" (Agave and the chorus) whose minds are under the control of or dedicated to the god. From this perspective Dionysus' revenge takes the form of a crude and terrifying "theater," a horrible conflation of "tragedy" and "comedy," in which the king's death is, for the god and his followers, a divine joke and a cause for the kind of triumphant celebration that traditionally closed Old Comedy, but for Pentheus the fulfillment of a tragic *penthos* in which he does not survive to come to terms with his *hamartiai,* in which he fails to communicate his tragic recognition to his mother, and in which Pentheus the would-be spectator and a "chorus" of Theban women have become actors in a spectacle that

---

[19]See Dodds 1960 on 1117–21.

they cannot evaluate or control. In his own "drama" the god who fuses and blurs all the antithetical distinctions by which Greek culture defined itself (man and god, man and woman) also blurs the distinction between tragic and comic genres. Euripides, in contrast, offers the audience in the final scene an answer to Dionysus' play and a firmly tragic perspective on the same events.

Dionysus' Theater

In the *Bacchae* Dionysus reveals himself to Thebes primarily through the means common to theater and the larger Dionysiac tradition: voice, costume, music, dance, and song. It is precisely for this reason that the *Bacchae* is one of the few Greek plays whose text permits reliable inferences about the stage production. We know what musical instruments the chorus carried and the major features of the costumes of all the principal characters except the messengers. We know that the mask of Dionysus was smiling (439, 1021). We can reconstruct much of the stage business concerning costumes and musical instruments. The language of the play refers with remarkable frequency to the visual and musical experience onstage and emphasizes that both honoring and comprehending the god are essentially theatrical acts, an exploration of the nature of illusion, transformation, and symbol. If the Thebans are to receive the god without disaster, they must, like Cadmus and Tiresias, accept a transformation of the ordinary self through costume and respond to the music, dance, and emotional release that Dionysus offers. Compare, for example, the effect on Pentheus of Tiresias' speech about the god with Tiresias' and Cadmus' gesture of dressing and dancing as his followers. The physical transformation communicates to the king as the rationalizing speech does not. As both the god and his chorus emphasize, ritual, sound, gesture, and symbol express the god as effectively as or even more effectively than language. The god's defenders use riddling and ambiguous words, and it is only after the stranger leaves the stage at 976, having completed his plans for revenge, that there is a renewed emphasis on effective verbal communication. Pentheus, the ruler of Thebes, is destroyed through his inability to

The *Bacchae*

understand truth in the symbolic form that Dionysiac festival and theater offer to the adherent or spectator. Hence unlike Dionysus, Tiresias, or Cadmus, he finally cannot play a role but surrenders to it. The *opsis* or theatrical spectacle (Aristotle *Poetics* 1450b28) of the *Bacchae* is not simply a *hēdusma* or additional "seasoning." The plot or arrangement of events, the action or *praxis,* and the spectacle become for large parts of this play one and the same thing.

Dionysus begins the play by sending his followers into Thebes to beat their drums about the palace of Pentheus "so that the city of Cadmus may *see*" (58–61):

Raise up the drums native to the *polis* of the Phrygians and invented by mother Rhea and myself, and, surrounding the royal palace of Pentheus, beat them, so that the city of Cadmus may see [hōs horai Kadmou polis].

He will make himself manifest (*emphanēs,* 22) to Thebes through dance (21). He will fasten on fawnskins and hand the *thursos* to the citizens (24–25). He has forced the female population of Thebes to adopt his costume (*skeuēn,* 34). In short, Dionysus, himself in human disguise, will reveal his divinity to Thebes primarily through spectacle, costume, and sound as he controls and stage-directs the play.

The language and action of the play allow Dionysus, until the return of the second messenger, to make the play and the manifestation of his divinity an indivisible process. His role as stage director/actor corresponds with his role in the plot—to demonstrate and then to avenge his divinity; his role as *chorodidaskalos* (see 58–61) is inseparable from his roles as leader and god of his worshipers; his role as producer of stage illusions matches his ability to inspire a change of mental state in his followers; and, as we shall see, his presentation of his smiling mask, his "comic" performance in a tragic *agōn,* communicates to the audience his religious ambiguity. Dionysus makes his chorus his players and the destruction of Pentheus a "play," replete with set, costume, and spectators. Until the final messenger speech there is no action in the play (the chorus', Cadmus', Tiresias', the *therapōn*'s, the first messenger's) that is not controlled by or voluntarily supportive of the god

[219]

except, for a brief period, Pentheus'. The play itself becomes the net in which the increasingly isolated Pentheus is trapped. Euripides' characters, especially his gods, sometimes seem to control the staging of a play. In the *Medea,* for example, Medea perhaps expresses her transformation to something more than human through her power to stage her final encounter with Jason from the chariot of the sun.[20] The bodies of the children are not displayed at the human level on the *ekkuklēma* as expected; nor does Medea pay physically for her crimes. Mother and children are magically wafted offstage. But in the *Bacchae* Dionysus' control over the stage action becomes a pervasive expression both of the god's own nature and of his control over theater as its patron. Yet Dionysus' play within a play does not, like many modern plays within plays or like the comic parodies of ancient tragedy, function primarily to distance the audience from the drama and call attention to and question its own reality as art; instead, it implicates the audience in the drama and calls attention to its own art as reality. That is, theatrical illusion demonstrates the reality of the god, and illusion and symbol are the only modes of access to a god who can take whatever form he wishes (*hopoios ēthel'*, 478).

Dionysus begins the play by directing the entrance (55–56) of a chorus consisting of his followers from Asia, not the citizens of Thebes. They make his music and use his instruments, sing imitations of his ritual songs to cult meters, dance his dances, tell his myths, and, in the palace scene, respond to a divinity that Pentheus can neither see nor control. They are in effect his players: each ode reflects or anticipates the shifting demonstration of divinity promised in the prologue.[21] In the parodos they display the god's costume, music, and dance and invite Thebes to join in their worship (see especially 105–6). In the first stasimon (370–432), taking their cue from Tiresias' speech in defense of the god, the women present in lyric form a similarly anachronistic view of the god as a fifth-century patron of symposia, poetry (410), and festivals. They endorse the opinion of the ordinary man (*plēthos*, 430), which is

[20]On Medea's probable transformation to goddess at the conclusion of the *Medea,* see Knox 1977.
[21]Here I disagree with many critics in my sense of the relation of the chorus to the action. See esp. Parry 1978: 146.

The *Bacchae*

immediately voiced onstage by the *therapōn*.[22] The second stasimon (519–75) marks the transition in Dionysus' position from powerlessness to power, moving from despair at Dionysus' imprisonment to a recognition of his divinity when it is manifested in the destruction of the palace and in the sound of the god's voice offstage (576–603). Whatever we conclude occurs in the palace scene, whether nothing at all or a major or minor change in the stage building, no stage business at this point could adequately imitate the apocalyptic destruction of the palace, including lightning and earthquake, which the chorus sees while Pentheus does not.[23] The miracle must become for the audience more symbolic and prophetic than realistic. The audience sees not a miracle, but a chorus enacting the experience of a miracle, or presenting a theatrical illusion. The third stasimon (862–911) takes up the god's words in the previous scene—he will avenge the god who is *deinotatos* (most terrible / wonderful) and *ēpiōtatos* (kindest) to men— by moving from release to vengeance, using the same metrical patterns in the strophe and antistrophe to express joy and anger; it is immediately followed by the scene in which Pentheus sees double, and sees for the first time the bestial as well as the gentle aspect of the stranger. In the fourth stasimon (977–1023) the chorus prophetically imagines Pentheus' destruction on the mountain, soon to be reported by the messenger; the messenger speech is immediately followed by a choral celebration of the god's victory over Pentheus (1153–64).

In the *Bacchae*, then, the chorus reenacts or enacts beforehand through partially ritualized song, dance, and music what Dionysus and his converts enact largely with language and gesture. By these ritualized and mythical means, the chorus demonstrates how the

[22]See Dodds 1960: 117 and 131 on the relation among the first stasimon, the Tiresias scene, and the appearance of the *therapōn*. The movement noted by Dodds in the third and fourth stasimon from particular to universal, which is contrary to Euripides' usual practice, may arise from the exceptional responsiveness of the women of the chorus to shifts in the fate of their cause in each preceding scene.

[23]For discussion and bibliography on the palace scene, see esp. Dale 1969: 124–25, Grube 1935: 44–47, Roux 1961: 30–42, and Castellani 1976. I am inclined to agree with Dodds 1960: xxxvii that Euripides has put "a psychological miracle at the center of the action." Theatrical (or psychological) illusion is the only avenue by which the god can be worshiped and understood.

god can be "seen," worshiped, and interpreted. The Asian women, however, do not occupy the same position, emotionally, intellectually, or perceptually, between the royal family and the audience as the chorus in other tragedies. Though voicing uncannily familiar Greek ethical sentiments, they are ultimately a voice alien to the community and use the language of *sōphrosunē* (self-control and moderation) and *hēsuchia* (apolitical quiet) to serve their passionate desire for revenge. The presence of this unruly chorus of barbarian women not subject to civic authority, together with the absence of any male citizens who are not converted to the god, has the effect of isolating Pentheus from his city and putting the action on the plane of myth and ritual. History reasserts itself only with the prophecies of Dionysus in the final scene. Unlike the foreign chorus of the *Phoenissae,* for example, the women of this chorus express no sympathy for the king or the *polis,* and their attitude, because of their exclusive allegiance to the god, comes to seem pitiless and inhumane. Instead of performing the function of relatively reliable ethical and political mediation typical of the Greek chorus, they move gradually toward the more extreme perspective of the maddened spectators to Pentheus' tragedy on the mountain. This creation of multiple audiences to the god's theatrical demonstration of his divinity makes the spectators conscious that they are viewing and interpreting the god's actions through a series of subjective and unreliable perspectives and performances. Access to the god is indirect and symbolic; how spectators interpret what they see is a product of their own degree of involvement in and assent to the events before them.

Dionysus confronts Pentheus through speech, music, costume, dance, and stage illusion. Euripides represents Pentheus' inability to understand and control Dionysus not only through the king's failure to interpret his words but also through his failure to discern the god within the theatrical forms that express him. Just as Dionysus is god of wine and the wine itself (278–79, 284), so Dionysus is god of theater and the theatrical forms that manifest him. Every scene in the *Bacchae* up to the final messenger speech makes an issue of Dionysiac costume and movement as a visible representation of the elusive god. Large sections of the two long messenger speeches, as well as the parodos, communicate his divinity through descriptions of the costumes, songs, and movement of the maenads. In the early scenes Pentheus' response to Dionysiac dress, a mixture of incomprehension, fear, and attraction, precipitates his downfall; he rejects the god by rejecting the visible and aural signs of his worship. He reacts to his grandfather's offer of an ivy crown as if he were threatened with mental contamination (344). After a detailed examination of Dionysus' dress and appearance in their first meeting, Pentheus wishes to strip off parts of the stranger's costume onstage (493–96). His response to dance and music is equally violent. He tries to send the stranger to dance in the darkness of imprisonment in the stables (511). He also tries to stop the god's followers from making music, to suppress the insistent beating of their drums (513–14).

It is with theatrical weapons, also, that Dionysus destroys Pentheus. He entraps the king in a series of spectacles directed by himself. Twice, both in the stable scene, which the god reports as a "messenger" (616–37), and in the final disaster on the mountain, Dionysus calmly sets the scene—in the second case replete with costume, actors, and set—and then stands back or disappears into a position of heavenly observation, an unmoved spectator of human struggle. The god's control extends to predicting the content of the first messenger speech before the messenger speaks (657) and to directing Agave, offstage on the mountain, to stretch out her hands in readiness to receive her prey (973). The servant of the king not only reports the events on the mountain but also advocates acknowledgment of the god's divinity (769–70); Agave and her sisters respond unanimously to the god's voice. The stable scene, in which Dionysus teases Pentheus with a bull that the king imagines is the stranger, and then with his own false image, is a sort of offstage rehearsal for Pentheus' mad scene, in which Pentheus inverts the illusion, seeing the stranger as a bull. The report of these events in the god's own unusual messenger speech teases the audience with its pretense of uncertainty. (See especially 629, *kaith' ho Bromios, hōs emoige phainetai, doxan legō,* and 638.) What the audience knows to be true, since it knows that the stranger is a god, is presented as speculation to the chorus onstage. The choice of the more "primitive," satyric, and less characteristically tragic (*Poetics* 1449a19–28) trochaic tetrameters rather than the iambic trimeters normal in most messenger speeches seems appropriate to the irony here: the mocking god appropriates the role of human messenger to his own inhuman and deceptive ends.[24] The chorus' visual experience of the palace miracle comes to seem a less ambiguous acknowledgment of the divine presence than Dionysus' speech.

Dionysus goes on to lure Pentheus, in a manner unique in extant tragedy, to change his costume and become his player/worshiper.[25] By playing on his internal conflicts, through costume he separates Pentheus from his role as king and hoplite (see especially 809–46). In the scene in which Pentheus begins to succumb to the god's power, Dionysus clinches his victory through a detailed description of the costume he is to wear: long hair, a female *peplos,* a fawnskin, and a *thursos* (830–35). Pentheus wavers between donning the dress of the god's worshiper and putting on his armor and proceeding against the women with force (845–46). He believes he will gain through his disguise the enticing perspective of a mere spectator (956–59, 1058–62, also 829). Instead, once he has dressed as a woman, he rehearses his part and adjusts his costume like an actor before a play (925–44); he relishes his resemblance to his mother or her sisters and imagines that his dress will endow him with the powers of a maenad (945–46), little realizing that his change of costume has committed him to becoming instead part of an "unhappy spectacle" (1232, of Agave with the head of Pentheus) beyond his control. In the stable scene Pentheus has contended with beast and stranger as separate images. Now he sees Dionysus as a beast, and in sensing that the stranger represents more than the man he has been playing onstage, he "sees" the god and his inhumanness for the first time. Costume, costume change,

[24]See *POxy* 2, no. 221, for a fragment, possibly from a messenger speech in trochaic tetrameters from Phrynichus' *Phoenissae,* and compare the striking lyric messenger speech by the Phrygian slave in Euripides' *Orestes.*

[25]See my later discussion of a possible toilet scene in Aeschylus' *Edonoi.* Pentheus' adoption of another costume / role has many implications. Ritual and theater share a devotion to dressing and cross-sexual role-playing. The psychological aspect has been much discussed. By becoming a maenad Pentheus moves into a space characteristic of the god, where the differences between male and female, human and divine, man and beast, spectator and participant, are lost. For further discussion of these issues, see esp. Gallini 1963 and Segal 1978a.

and acting thus become a central dramatic image for understanding and worshiping the god.

Only occasionally in Greek tragedy does the meaning of a scene depend primarily on role-playing and on the costume changes that a character makes onstage. The reverse is true for Old Comedy. Comic and tragic (or satyric) costume change serve similar functions only when the change of costume is intended to manipulate and deceive or to effect an escape, rejuvenation, or restoration to heroic status; and it can be argued that all such changes are essentially more characteristic of comedy than of tragedy. In the *Helen*, for example, Menelaus is transformed from a shipwrecked and almost comic nobody into a Homeric hero; simultaneously, Helen changes to mourning garb, a deception that leads to a symbolic remarriage between the two long-estranged spouses. In contrast, when Heracles' children put on mourning garments in the *Heracles*, when Cassandra throws off her signs of priestly authority in Aeschylus' *Agamemnon*, or when Eteocles (probably) arms himself to meet his brother in the *Seven against Thebes*, the change of costume entraps the characters in a tragic pattern of action beyond their control. Such costume change is relatively rare in Greek tragedy and is generally reserved for climactic moments. In the *Bacchae*, however, costume change serves as a sign of conversion to Dionysiac worship, and what are largely comic techniques with costume and props are used for the first time in a play that has a disastrous outcome.

Indeed, Dionysus' theater deliberately unsettles the audience with its striking merging of comic and tragic stage business with costume and props. Cadmus and Tiresias gracelessly but strategically accept the worship of the god by donning his fawnskin and *thursos* and adopting a hobbling dance. The "comedy" of this scene (see 250, 322) centers on their fussy concern to play their new roles correctly. As often in comedy, the theatrical point lies in the lack of correspondence between the internal and the external, between the state of mind on the one hand, and body and costume and movement on the other. The dramatic juxtaposition between the identical movements of the graceful and authentic chorus and the decrepit playacting old men as worshipers of the god is comparable, from the point of view of theatrical effect, to a scene such as that in the *Thesmophoriazusae* between Agathon, Euripides, and Euripides' kinsman. The kinsman is too crude and masculine to adopt comfortably the female dress that the effeminate Agathon wears very naturally as an inspiration to his dramatic poetry; this inability to play the role is prophetic of his failure to maintain his disguise in the women's assembly and exposes Euripides' "weakness" as a dramatist. It also serves to remind the audience of the male actor's traditional role in impersonating women. Aristophanes' own disguised heroes, like Dionysus in the *Bacchae*, have no trouble duping their victims. In contrast, Cadmus in the final scene ultimately finds himself facing the tragic rather than the comic implications of his opportunistic (333–36) role-playing and conversion. If he returned to the stage still wearing the god's emblems, the changed and now pitiful effect of the costume must have strikingly underlined this point.

The same ludicrous fussing over Dionysiac costume is repeated in the terrible scene in which Pentheus tries awkwardly to rearrange his costume with the help of Dionysus. The king parodies the god. The visual effect is comparable to the confrontation between Heracles and Dionysus at the beginning of the *Frogs*. The ludicrous god, dressed in an effeminate saffron robe, tragic buskins, and a lionskin, comes face to face with the original he is trying to impersonate and whose powers he is trying to acquire, Heracles. God absurdly imitates man (or former man) to acquire extraordinary strength. Also laughable is the inability of a divinity to carry off the kind of role change that Aristophanes' comic heroes usually accomplish without difficulty. The Dionysus of the *Frogs* thinks that the costume gives him courage; instead it exposes his pretenses to true divinity and his all too human cowardice. In contrast, the smiling god of the *Bacchae* expresses his divine authority by his control over role change and his ability to make those onstage believe whatever he intends. Dionysus can change with sinister ease from divine to human and back, in all probability without even a change of costume.[26] Pentheus' change of costume reveals his human limits; in imitating the god he does not acquire,

[26]See the section on the mask of Dionysus.

as he expects, extraordinary powers over his environment, but the cerements of death (see 857–59 and 1156–57)[27] and the exposure of a divided self. Again, change of role / costume simultaneously effects comic exposure of self-ignorance and tragic entrapment.

In Aristophanes' *Wasps* Bdelycleon tries to remake his father into a leisured elderly aristocrat by persuading him to reject his juryman's rags for refined and pretentious garments. But the intransigent Philocleon finally retains a kind of fierce, if childish and absurd, integrity more generally characteristic of the tragic hero. The effeminate and luxurious robes fail at the process of reform even more fully than Bdelycleon's rhetorical victory in the *agōn,* which has merely confined his father's obsession to the privacy of the household. Pentheus' consent to a change of role brings him a "comic" exposure inappropriate for a tragic hero, whereas Philocleon's heroic invulnerability to comic correction through costume gives a surprising twist to the comic denouement of the *Wasps.* Comedy, as Bergson and others have pointed out, reduces the spiritual to the physical and divides mind and body so that the latter ludicrously mirrors the hidden rigidities or unconscious desires of the former.[28] When Philocleon's sexuality and aggression burst incorrigibly through the trappings of culture, or the relative's masculinity cannot be masked by feminine dress in the *Thesmophoriazusae,* the exposure is appropriately comic. But the use of costume and gesture—that is, of the body—to make a comparable exposure on the tragic stage moves the action uneasily close, in style if not fully in tone, to the comic. The terrifying and mythic *verbal* exposure of Hippolytus' denied sexuality in his destruction by a bull and his own mares is replaced in the *Bacchae* with the revelation of Pentheus' ambivalent sexuality through the physical cloaking of the masculine body by crudely adopted feminine dress and movement, and with the attempt by Cadmus and Tiresias to mask old age with the supple movements of youth. Aristophanes' *Thesmophoriazusae* at 136 borrows a line from Aeschylus' *Edonoi* in

---

[27]But see Dodds 1960 on *piston Haidan* at 1157.

[28]See Bergson 1956: 61–190, esp. 93–94. *Tractatus Coislinianus* 8, which may reflect the contents of Aristotle's lost book of the *Poetics* on comedy, takes a similar view of comedy's treatment of soul and body: *ho skoptōn elengchein thelei hamartēmata tēs psuchēs kai tou sōmatos.*

which Lycurgus mocks Dionysus for his feminine dress and appearance: *podapos ho gunnis; tis patra; tis hē stolē;* "From where comes this 'woman'? What is his fatherland? What is this female dress?" (Aesch. frag. 61 N). Since the allusion to Aeschylus is followed by the dressing of Euripides' relative as a woman, we can speculate either that Euripides adopted the dressing of Pentheus as a woman from Aeschylus' Dionysiac drama (in art Pentheus is portrayed in armor or in masculine garments as he spies on the maenads or is attacked by them), or that Euripides was inspired by Aristophanes to invent the toilet scene of the *Bacchae,* going beyond Aeschylus' emphasis on the sexual ambiguity of the god's identity to borrow Old Comedy's ludicrous transformations of the body to express an equivalent ambiguity in the human soul. Euripides' gesture is in any case outrageous, since Aristophanes' parody seems clearly directed at addressing the limits that tragedy must respect in relation to costume.

In the case of the comic hero, the voluntary transformation of self through costume is a form of temporary control over circumstances not subject in reality to the force of the individual's desires or actions. Cadmus and Tiresias try to make such a "comic" accommodation to phenomena beyond rational control; by being willing to "act" they can accept the god while retaining their identities. They are simultaneously actors / worshipers and spectators. The mad Pentheus retains no such comic distance from his role. To worship Dionysus, or to be a comic hero, is to accept or adopt a temporary change of role, and to receive in exchange participation in a boundary-transcending experience. Euripides, by adopting techniques from Old Comedy, can evoke in the audience expectations about comic role-playing: the ways in which costume change can be used to expose the hidden desires, ignorance, or pretension of the hero's enemies or to express the power, however temporary, of the hero's imagination over reality. In comedy this exposure of desire or ignorance or manipulation of reality is laughable because the characters are grotesque and the consequences minimal and temporary—certainly not deadly. In the *Bacchae* the same theatrical techniques expose with accelerating horror the tragic inadequacy of man to understand and control himself or his

The *Bacchae*

environment. Dionysiac madness becomes the dark double of comic befuddlement.

Myths about Dionysus' introduction of his worship to new cities can end happily or disastrously.[29] Those who accept the god are blessed with *eudaimonia;* those who reject him are punished with madness and a deadly metamorphosis. In the Homeric *Hymn to Dionysus,* for example, the sailors who fail to recognize the god suffer metamorphosis, whereas the steersman, who does, receives *eudaimonia.* Euripides retains or at least appears to retain this possibility of a "comic" or "tragic" outcome in the early scenes of the *Bacchae.* (Much of what I say below seems also to fit satyr play as well as comedy. Satyr play often included the imprisonment and escape of a chorus of satyrs dedicated to Dionysus and the worsting of an *amathēs* enemy to the god. See Euripides' *Cyclops* 173 and *Bacchae* 480 and 490.[30]) Dionysus will punish Pentheus only if he insists on resisting the god (50–63); he and his adherents argue that accepting the god means wine, festival, and release from care (see Thucydides 2.38 on festival as a release from care and a suppressant of grief). In the final scene the god repeats this argument when he tells Cadmus that if he and Agave had known how to exercise wisdom (*sōphronein,* 1341), they would have been happy and blessed (*eudaimoneit',* 1343). The similarities between the language of the early choral odes of the *Bacchae* and that of the comic chorus of Eleusinian initiates in the *Frogs* are for this reason not surprising. (See *Frogs* 326–29 and *Bacchae* 80 and 106–7; *Frogs* 345–50 and the Cadmus-Tiresias scene; *Frogs* 332–34, 376, 394, and 410 and *Bacchae* 160–61; *Frogs* 346 and *Bacchae* 380–81.)

[29]Burnett 1970: 26–27 gives examples of Attic Dionysiac myths in which the god comes to be accepted with considerably less difficulty and with happy results. She stresses that Dionysus offers to Thebes a civilized public cult that reverts to primitivism only when the women are attacked. Up to line 810, the god gives Pentheus a fair chance—unique in tragedies of divine revenge—to recognize the god's divinity and receive his blessings. For a more extensive treatment of Dionysiac myths, see Massenzio 1969. As his analysis shows, even the acceptance of the god usually leads to the sacrifice of the figure who introduces his viticulture (as in the case of Icarius or Staphylus).

[30]On satyric elements in the *Bacchae,* see Sansone 1978 and Seaford 1981. Seaford remarks (274) that the blinding of the Cyclops hints at the sacrificial moment when the burning torch is dipped into the sacrificial water.

[229]

As in comedy, the god offers to Thebes the possibility of temporary regeneration through a festive reversal of normal social and political categories. An apparently powerless outsider, he confronts an opponent who is in some sense his powerful double, and destroys the enemy of festive pleasure with mockery. By being granted temporary control over reality the comic or "trickster" hero, like the god in this play, uses his ability to transform his and others' identity and his ability to manipulate language, costume, and theatrical illusion to bring the world into harmony with his aspirations.[31] Dionysus also possesses the *ponēria* (amoral outrageousness) and deceptiveness of the trickster hero. The *Bacchae* chorus welcomes the return of the mad Agave, now a successful hunter rather than a mere woman (*dechesthe kōmon euiou theou,* 1167). In comedy the same gesture might well have resulted in a shared celebration between the city and the rejuvenated protagonist. But here the smiling god alone successfully completes a "comic" action as he celebrates through the returning Agave and the alien chorus a triumphant *kōmos*. Again as in comedy, even those who join in the hero's fantasies can be deceived and fail to share in his festive victory. Cadmus and Tiresias make what at first appears to be the "comic" adjustment to Dionysiac festival, shrugging off old age in dance; yet Cadmus finally pays a penalty for the god's success. Pentheus, however, by resisting the god, inverts a potentially comic outcome. He is destroyed while enacting what might be termed a parody of the comic plot actually achieved by Dionysus. The comic hero often radically transforms himself to succeed in his desires and to save his city heroically. Pentheus abandons his plans to don armor and fight for his city in favor of satisfying his personal curiosity; at the same time he interprets his dressing as a woman as heroic (962–63) and deserving of honor and celebration on his return (see 967–70). Once certain of his ability to mock the god or his converts (286, 322, 1081, 1293),

---

[31]For discussions of the comic or trickster hero in Old Comedy and elsewhere, see Whitman 1964 and Salingar 1974. See *Tractatus Coislinianus* 6 on the importance of *apatē* in comedy. Revenge and rescue plots overlap in their common concern with plotting and deception.

Pentheus becomes not a hero but the object of divine *gelōs,* laughter and scorn (250, through Cadmus, and 503, 842, 854).[32]

In the *Bacchae* the same pattern of events is to the smiling god and his chorus a "comic" celebration of Pentheus' exposure and defeat as an enemy to festival, and to the appalled second messenger and to Pentheus' family an occasion for tragic pity and lament. In sum, the god has enacted a comic plot pattern and, wearing a smiling mask, defeats his enemy in an *agōn* and concludes his victory with a festive *kōmos.* But once Dionysus' play is concluded, Pentheus' perverted sacrificial death and fruitless *peripeteia* and *anagnōrisis (kakou gar engus ōn emanthanen,* 1113; 1115–19), accompanied by the inability of the maddened participants to pity their victim, can be read as an abortive tragic action. Agave reaches and survives the full tragic *anagnōrisis* of her *peripeteia* and her error in failing to recognize the god denied to Pentheus (*Dionusos hēmas ōles', arti manthanō,* 1296; see also Cadmus at 1297, 1344, and 1346). She accepts her fate, although she wishes never to see a *thursos* again (1381–86). She now sees the mask of Pentheus as human—the representation of her son and a cause for *penthos,* not bestial and a cause for triumph. Cadmus now calls the *phonos* (slaughter, 1114) of Pentheus a *thuma* (sacrifice, 1246), hence reestablishing a sacrificial perspective on the king's death. Lamenting Pentheus, he sadly recalls the overzealous youth's past kindnesses to him (1311–22). The second messenger is Pentheus' first sympathetic defender in the play (1032–33, 1039–40), and the first besides Pentheus to champion the men of the city (1036, if the text is correct), who have hitherto been silent or converted to the god. He mourns the collapse of the royal house (1024–28). The adjective *perissos* (extraordinary, excessive), formerly used of men like Pentheus (429), is now applied to Agave's revenge (1197). The implication of these final scenes seems to be that the gods may impose patterns of action on men, but that tragedy emerges from a

---

[32]Sacrificial and tragic victims may also be mocked, but here the combination of vocabulary (*gelōs* and *kōmos*), the god's smiling mask, and the god's dramatic strategies suggest the idea if not the tone of Old Comedy, as well as the traditional disgrace of being ridiculed by one's enemies. I share a sense of the tone of these comic scenes with Seidensticker 1978. See also Dodds 1960, esp. 192.

strictly human (and sane) perspective; the human and humane experience and vision of Pentheus' family and of the second messenger invent tragedy from the divine "comedy."

Dionysus, then, does not merely borrow from the plot structure and stage business of comedy to make his theatrical demonstration of divinity. As the god who presides over both comedy and tragedy in the dramatic festivals, he dissolves and transcends the boundaries between the comic and tragic genres. Dionysus makes his victims see with pleasure what the sane mind would experience as painful. Pentheus would like to see what causes him distress (815); the mad Agave will think herself free from misfortune when she is actually supremely unfortunate (1259–62; see also the contrast between 1232 and 1258). Plato in the *Philebus* (48c–49c5) suggests in a very complex passage that tragedy and comedy are united by a concern with self-knowledge. Comic delusion is accompanied by weakness; ignorance in those who have the ability to retaliate is hateful and ugly. Pentheus' situation, as he moves from a supposed position of strength to one of weakness, falls uncomfortably between the hateful and the ridiculous; the god's apparent "comic weakness" at first obscures a hateful strength. Similarly, the audience, trapped through comic / tragic irony and a partial identification with the god's cause (for it knows that Pentheus is wrong), is torn between fear and horrified laughter at the king's delusions. Until the final scenes the god thus denies clear access either to the comic laughter or to the tragic pity by which the spectators control their theatrical experience. They neither maintain the intellectuality, the emotional alienation, and the sense of collective understanding by which comedy attempts to exclude and thereby correct the rigid and misguided member of society with mockery in the manner eloquently described by Bergson;[33] nor can they feel full pity and fear for Pentheus as a being better than but dangerously similar to themselves.

In Plato's *Symposium* (223d3–9) Socrates argues with Aristophanes and Agathon that tragedy and comedy could be written by the same man. Socrates is presumably championing an unlikely cause. Or he might equally be alluding with characteristic irony to a fin-

[33]Bergson 1956.

de-siècle consciousness about the two genres. Aristophanes, famous throughout his career for his parodies of Euripides (Cratinus frag. 307 K mocks Aristophanes for this habit), suggests in the *Frogs* that the health and nature of both theatrical genres are inextricably linked. A good comedy should contain, as the Eleusinian initiates say of their rites, a judicious mixture of seriousness and mockery (391–95). Aristophanes, in this unusually serious comedy, uses a theatrical Dionysus to make statements about the complex relation between the genres and to defend the value of dramatic poetry to the city (*Frogs* 1419, 1500–1503). Euripides, too, by allowing the god of theater to make his own theatrical demonstrations of divinity, reveals the shared ground between apparently opposing genres, the common preoccupation with human ignorance and pretension, with relief from suffering, with *agōn* and the exposure of human violence and aggression, and with demonstrating the gap between man's godlike desires and his ability to achieve them. In the *Bacchae* Dionysus brings "drama" to birth in Thebes as an experience and a form in which boundaries are transgressed and cultural categories and oppositions temporarily reversed and collapsed. Comedy allows its heroes to cross the boundaries separating man and god, the socially encumbered individual and his heroic desires; its audiences revel harmlessly in mockery, revenge, a delight in exposure, and a free identification with the initially underdog protagonist. The god's "comedy," with its Dionysian audience, the chorus, is revealed to be in many ways a more terrifying form of the genre. Yet when the god has withdrawn from the level of human action to the machine or *theologeion*, Euripides' tragedy frames and changes the audience's emotional response to the divine drama. The final scenes restore (or, from the historical perspective, create) the traditional boundaries between genres, drawing a sharp and specifically tragic line between man and god, the individual and his heroic aspirations, audience and protagonist, and between laughter and tragic pity. Nevertheless, the failure of the chorus to move fully toward a tragic perspective (to feel pity and fear over the fate of Pentheus); the lack of closure resulting from Dionysus' final puzzling prophecies of future punishments, pronounced from the machine; and the patent and possibly avoidable folly of the ever-combative Pentheus (he has expressed even his filial piety in the willingness to take revenge) cast in the final moments the lingering shadow of the divine comedy over the recovery of tragic vision.

Festival and Theater

In festival the distinctions that normally define a society are temporarily transformed or suppressed.[34] Most Greek festivals, for example, permitted the participation of women, who had no place in the political and military life of the city, and sometimes of strangers, metics, and even slaves. Hierarchy may give way to a world in which each individual in a community is more closely the"equal" of others, allowed to "be himself," to release psycho-biological urges in submission to ritual rather than to control them in submission to secular authority. Old Comedy's stress on obscenity and aggression is but one of many Attic examples. Status, name, property, and kin position may no longer carry the same weight; nor do distinctions of age or sex. The weak, the inferiors in the community hierarchy, may rule and have the power to restore fertility to society. Women's festivals in Athens could invert the normal procedures of civic life; political business was suspended during the Thesmophoria, which occupied civic space for rituals concerning fertility. Rulers or other scapegoat figures may be humiliated or punished (as in the Attic Thargelia). What Turner calls *communitas* emerges where structure is not.[35] Spontaneous energy is released; the forces that bind a community together with warmth and feeling and loyalty but are not formally or fully built into the organization of the community are celebrated. Both Thucydides (2.38) and Plato (*Laws* 653d) testify to the powers of festival to restore communal energy. A new lan-

[34]Many of the theoretical points made here were formulated in cross-cultural studies of festival in ritual cultures. Although I am certain that it could be done (the fictional example presented in the *Bacchae* itself conforms explicitly to this scenario), to support every detail with examples of festivals from attested Greek contexts would be too ambitious an undertaking here. For the element of the carnivalesque at the City Dionysia, especially in relation to Aristophanes, see Brelich 1969b and Carrière 1979.
[35]Turner 1969: chaps. 4 and 5, esp. 138, 167, 177.

guage and vision may temporarily hold sway. As in the Eleusinian and other mysteries, ideas are expressed in symbol, myth, and metaphor; actions are ritualized. In this state, as Turner says, regular social structure is simplified, inverted, or distanced, and Levi-Straussian "structures" are amplified, permitting scrutiny of the culture as a whole.[36] But this state of *communitas* is not simply a return to "nature." It is "nature in dialogue with structure."[37] In its controlled form festival is a reconstructive phase of society, operating according to strict ritual logic, in which the culture is modified through a confrontation of individuals as equals and an opportunity to observe social structures from another perspective. Douglas stresses that "cults . . . invite their initiates to turn round and confront the categories on which their whole surrounding culture has been built up and to recognize them for the fictive, man-made, arbitrary creations that they are."[38] The return to normalcy from the festal state ideally brings, then, a renewed sense of the arbitrariness yet necessity of the existing cultural order. Ritual cultures depend on successive phases of structure and *communitas*, and each ultimately contributes to maintaining the vitality of that culture. Again, to quote Douglas:

> Order implies restriction; . . . This is why, though we seek to create order, we do not simply condemn disorder. We recognize that it is destructive to existing patterns; also that it has potentiality. It symbolizes both danger and power.
>
> Ritual recognizes the potency of disorder. In the disorder of the mind, in dreams, faints and frenzies, ritual expects to find powers and truths which cannot be reached by conscious effort. Energy to command and special powers of healing come to those who can abandon rational control for a time.[39]

Cadmus founded Thebes with the help of the purely military Spartoi; Pentheus is the second ruler, and, true to his heritage, he

---

[36]Ibid., 133 and 167.

[37]Ibid., 140.

[38]Douglas 1966: 200.

[39]Ibid., 114; see also Turner 1969: 177 and 203. Turner stresses the equality of individuals as human beings in festival even though they may be unequal in terms of social status or in other respects.

relies exclusively on force and his hoplites to maintain order. Thebes has apparently not yet experienced the full benefits of festival. The religion that Dionysus brings to the militarized bastion of early Thebes offers the festal benefits described above and makes similar claims to being essential to the proper functioning of culture. The old can be temporarily rejuvenated; women can leave the confined internal space of the home and move about unhampered by marriage and children; pain can be released in wine, song, and dance; peace reigns.[40] As Green puts it: "Ritual is, we know, one of the manifestations that elucidate the subordination of desire to the universe of rules. It is a return of the repressed that enables us to witness, through certain ritual practices, the disguised expressions of desires whose prohibition would be absolute if they were expressed outside the limits of the ritual."[41] By adopting new garments and new movements the participant can take on another role. In accepting the god's myths and symbols he may see the world differently and express this change of state with a special ritual vocabulary. The god's costume suggests that of a structural inferior, woman; his *thursoi* and fawnskins are emblems of a ritual power that can overcome manmade metal weapons. As the chorus emphasizes, the wisdom of Dionysus is the wisdom of the masses, of the whole community: his followers speak with one voice (725). The god argues that if the city accepts his worship and the inversions it brings it could enter into a special state of bliss and atemporality (see especially 1341–43).

The world into which Dionysus brings Pentheus is both an inversion of ordinary society and a celebration of "nature in dialogue with structure." As Green puts it: "The Dionysiac ritual, then, is not a natural ritual; on the contrary, it is the culturation of

---

[40]Dionysiac rites claimed therapeutic effect in many contexts. Cybele's drums purified Dionysus of the madness imposed on him by Hera (Apollodorus 3.5.1). At *Laws* 790d–791b, Plato compares lullabies and Bacchic music: mothers sing their children to sleep, and Bacchic followers are brought to a sane state of mind by music (but see 851c for the undesirable effects of frenzied Bacchic modes). For *katharsis* in Aristotle, with extensive bibliography on the issue, see Else 1957: 224–32 and 423–47. Given the therapeutic effects of music, it is not surprising that Euripides makes analogies between music and sacrifice, especially purificatory sacrifice.
[41]Green 1979: 170; see also 171.

the natural. If the cultural excludes it, the punishment of the god will fall."[42] Outside the city is a world in which the ecstatic women are in control; they reject the marriage, agriculture, technology, and sacrifice of the city. Their symbols are taken from the wild world, not from the domestic one. They have powers not available to them in ordinary life. Yet this world of antistructure is by no means disordered or totally undifferentiated, but is organized according to a different set of meaningful ritual rules. The maenads are divided into three groups each with a leader, comparable to the actual structure of maenadic *thiasoi*. Their sacrifice resembles, though it perverts, the civic norm; it symbolizes the unity of their group and separates outsiders from insiders. Agave, as priestess, gets the choice sacrificial portion (she tears off Pentheus' arm first, 1125–27). Both messengers observe and emphasize that the women behave with tremendous order (see especially 693). Certainly, the environment on Cithairon is vulnerable to a movement to uncontrolled violence. As Girard has argued (see Chapter 1), Euripides in the *Bacchae* takes festival back to its violent origins.[43] In contrast to the women on the mountain, the chorus, when it presents the worship of Dionysus to the city, offers the experience of festival in a benign and controlled form. The Asian women sing, dance, and present new myths and symbols to the city; their violence is exclusively verbal. As in the *Bacchae,* ritual experience generally has the potential to combine constructively the comic and the tragic. As Turner puts it:

> status reversal does not mean "anomie" but simply a new perspective from which to observe structure. Its topsyturviness may give a humorous warmth to this ritual viewpoint. If the liminality of life-crisis rites may be, perhaps audaciously, compared to tragedy—for both imply humbling, stripping, and pain—the liminality of status reversal may be compared to comedy, for both involve mockery and inversion, but not destruction, of structural rules and overzealous adherents to them.[44]

[42]Ibid., 171.
[43]Girard 1977.
[44]Turner 1969: 201.

It is Pentheus who, by rejecting festival in the more civilized form in which Dionysus offers it to the city, is punished by being taken outside the city to experience the same phenomenon in an uncontrolled and violent form.

According to Girard, the *Bacchae* presents the creation of a divinity through the displacement of the mass violence used in the sacrifice of a scapegoat onto Dionysus himself. The play opens with a "sacrificial crisis," an effacement of social differences and of the difference between human and divine, which Pentheus diagnoses as a disease; following the destruction of the scapegoat it closes with the affirmation of divinity. For Girard, however, the play remains problematic because it takes an ambivalent stance, neither fully displacing violence onto the god nor restoring it to men. The play stops short of a full demystification of the secret of primitive religion, of the "double illusion of a violent divinity and an innocent community."[45] Thus Euripides does not conclude the play by emphasizing the logical restoration of peace through the unanimous lynching of the king. Instead, the final scenes create pity for the protagonists, raise questions about the nature of Dionysus' divinity, and leave the audience confused about how to judge its dramatic experience. The language and structure of the ritual arouse the expectation of ritual's solidifying effects, but the overall structure and perspective of the play systematically frustrate them.

In part, as Girard sees, the play creates its ambivalent effect by making what is essentially a diachronic process (the dramatic presentation of the historical creation of a divinity through violence) a synchronic one. Dionysus, the chorus, and Tiresias present to Pentheus the benefits of his religion in an anachronistically positive form. The promise of the civilized future precedes or merges inextricably with the violence of the mythical past, so that cause and result are permanently confused. The anachronistic choral odes stand at the center of this ambiguity. On the one hand, the language and movement of the choral odes maintain a continuous relation to the plot. The Asian women, as worshipers of the god, present the god's religion to the city, suffer his trials, perceive his

[45]Girard 1977: 136.

miracles, share his release, and finally, in the fourth stasimon, identify directly with and anticipate the destructive act of their mad counterparts on the mountain. On the other hand, these Asian bacchants also press the audience to make complex connections and comparisons between the ritualized spectacle of Pentheus' failure to accept the god and the festivities and excesses of contemporary Attic democracy. The role of the chorus raises many of the same issues raised in the three earlier plays considered in this book. In the *IA* and the *Phoenissae* the choral odes created a world of myth and ritual in tangent to the corrupt political world of the action, but intersecting with it at a crucial point where idealistic youth takes ritual as a model for action. In the *Heracles* past myths at first seem irrelevant to the life of the *polis*. Following an explosive contact between the world of myth and reality, Theseus intervenes to incorporate Heracles and his myths into the Athenian *polis*. The *Bacchae* again asks what it means to absorb myth and ritual, this time Dionysiac myth and ritual, into the life of a *polis*. As Arthur puts it: "Euripides has focused in the play not on the Dionysiac element itself, but rather on how the *polis* incorporates elements (such as the Dionysiac) which are hostile to it and on how it sustains (or does not sustain) itself against its own contradictions."[46] By the final scenes the actions of the god and the attitude and vision presented by the chorus, who do integrate myth, ritual, and reality, come to seem utterly suspect. How does the participant in and spectator of myth and festival draw boundaries between himself and these events?

The chorus, as Arthur in particular has argued, presents an apology for traditional Greek morality, for the philosophy of *to sophon* (wisdom) and *mēden agan* (nothing in excess).[47] The early choral odes describe the blessings of a Hellenized Dionysus already incorporated by the *polis*. The later stasima show how easily the language and ideals of establishment morality "can be accommodated to an opposite system of values."[48] Revenge becomes identified

---

[46]Arthur 1972: 148.

[47]Arthur 1972. See also Deichgräber 1935 for a treatment of the odes that emphasizes their relation to contemporary sophistic thought and politics.

[48]Arthur 1972: 165. See also de Romilly 1963 and Winnington-Ingram 1948 on the ambiguous language of the god and his chorus.

with loveliness, wisdom, freedom, escape, the god's smile, and values expressive earlier in the play of a society at peace. Through the chorus we see that in a city under control Dionysus emerges in symposia and in civic festivals as a celebration of the democracy's freedom from political hierarchy and rigid control of personal behavior, and as an appropriate release from care. Dionysiac rite and myth can complement the political aims of a democracy and guard against the institution of tyranny. The chorus repeatedly emphasizes that Dionysus is the god of the many and not of the *perissoi phōtes* (extraordinary men, 429). The many know how to live the "life of apolitical quiet" (*ho de tas hēsuchias / biotos,* 389–90) and how to be sensible (*to phronein,* 390). Yet in a city under pressure, pushed to excess, he appears behind the corrosive pressure of the democratic majority for revenge and for the destruction of outstanding men. Thucydides, too, in his famous analysis of the Corcyrean revolt (3.82–84), treats the thirst for revenge as the most important manifestation of a disintegrating democracy. He, too, remarks on the radical redefinition, in such circumstances, of traditionally positive ethical language to justify unethical causes. On the other hand, his Pericles in the funeral oration celebrates the need for festive release in a well-functioning democracy (2.38). The *Bacchae* seems to hover between exposing the violence inherent in Greek social life, divinity, and festival and the celebration of festival as a reconstructive phase of society necessary to its health and well-being.

Similarly, the claim of drama (explicit in comedy and by implication in tragedy) to release or expose sexuality and aggression, to attack society by showing it in a state of inversion, yet to do so without harm, and indeed with positive therapeutic benefit, is intimately tied to an exploration of the relation of festival to society. To defend or attack the inversions of festival and the social harmony created through the violence of sacrifice is ultimately to defend or attack tragedy, a poetic form that grew out of these rituals and remains a part of them by borrowing from ritual in its structure, language, and imagery and in its ability to restore and reunite society through the experience of the ritualized violence presented in its myths. The parabases of comedy claim to teach men how properly to praise and blame, but they also playfully defend sexuality and aggressive political satire in the plays. Aristophanes' drama wittily and unregretfully undercuts his claim in the parabases to be cleaner and more constructive than his fellow comic playwrights. The tragic poets from Aeschylus onward (*Prometheus* 631–34), aware in advance of the kind of critical debate they were to evoke in the philosophers, call attention to the pleasurable or therapeutic effects of experiencing what is painful.[49]

Pentheus' attempt to exclude festival and its benefits from his recently formed and crudely hierarchical city is expressed primarily as a failure of sight, or a failure to benefit from *theōria*.[50] He insists that to believe in Dionysus he must see the god directly and at first hand, not indirectly and symbolically (the god shows himself to Pentheus in disguised form): "You say that you really *saw* the god? What sort of being was he?" he asks at 477. Or, in lines 501–2:

P.   And where is he? He is not manifest to my eyes at least.
D.   Here by me; but you, being impious yourself, cannot look on him.

Pentheus seems repeatedly unable to see or hear the implications of the speeches, sounds, or images presented to him. At the same time he responds unconsciously to the god's message as he is lured to the mountain by a desire to see or spy upon the god's forbidden rites (811–16, 829, 838, 916, 956, 1060–62), although in fact he is never allowed to see the sacred activities of the maenads on the mountain (1060, 1075) until the moment of his recognition and death.

When Pentheus is finally costumed and maddened by Dionysus he comes onstage with a new and double vision. He sees two Thebes, two suns; he sees, as the god says, what he ought to see (924):

You seem to lead on ahead of us as a bull and to have grown horns on your head. (920–21)

[49]See Pucci 1980 for the therapeutic effects of pain in Euripides.
[50]For an excellent treatment of the language of sight in the play, see Massenzio 1969: 82–91. Among other points, he contrasts Dionysiac sight with Pentheus' narrower and more superficial desire to *spy*.

Pentheus' ability to see only one level of reality continues in his state of madness; he simply substitutes the beast for the smiling mask (although he continues to be aware of the stranger's non-bestial side, just as Agave is later unconsciously aware that the head of the "beast" she carries is also human, 1185–87).[51] His sight changes and he has access to a vision of divine power unavailable to him before, but it brings no insight. He is unaware of the implication that this bestial image has for himself. He cannot, like the god or the comic hero, "see" and control his transformation at the same time. In contrast, the chorus of believers caps this scene by evoking a *double* image of the god, impossible to normal vision, as a beast with a smiling face or mask (*prosōpon*) (1018–23):

> Appear to our sight as a bull or a many-headed snake or a fire-blazing lion. Go, O Bacchus. With a smiling face cast your noose about the hunter of the Bacchants as he falls under the deadly herd of the maenads.

The language and action of the play demonstrate the god's divinity indirectly and symbolically and deny that humans can adequately "see" Dionysus. The god can take any shape he wants (478) but is not fully visible to the human eye. Seeing the god, as the contrast between the vision of Pentheus and of the chorus shows, is a matter of "double sight." In fact, even the chorus and the maenads on the mountain only hear, but do not see, their god directly. (A light also symbolizing the god's presence appears at 1082–83.) He is a being who can successively or simultaneously appear as divine, animal, and human.

Pentheus defines the world through the hierarchical and rigidly antithetical structures of his society, not through the nonstructures or antistructures of ritual and festival. For him man and woman, for example, are rigidly separate categories (822); each sex has its own sphere (217); one is subordinate to the other (786). Dionysus as festival god can simultaneously invert and subvert these cultural categories: language, the role of the sexes, classes, and political hierarchy. To understand Dionysus is to understand that the order

[51]It is unclear precisely what Pentheus sees at 920–21—the stranger and his double with horns (Dodds 1960: 193); a stranger who is part man, part bull; or a bull who he realizes is also the stranger. On 1185–87, see Dodds 1960: 224.

imposed upon the world by human culture is created by that culture, and that the permanent potential exists for a reversal or collapse of this order. To accept him is to understand that festival and ritual can offer this knowledge in a form that ultimately supports rather than destroys the existing social structure.

In the *Bacchae* the same words or symbols can have two apparently incompatible connotations in the minds of supporters or opponents of the god, or at two different dramatic moments. *Sophia, sophos,* and *to sophon,* for example, mean something entirely different to Tiresias or the chorus as defenders of the god, and to Pentheus as a defender of the existing cultural order; the chorus uses these terms in so many seemingly incompatible contexts that the audience loses any certainty of what they mean to the god's worshipers (see especially 480, 655–56; 203, 824, 1190; 395, 877-97, 1005). A *thursos* may at one point be a magic wand providing food and sustenance, at another point a weapon; at a third point this symbol of Dionysus' power loses its force and must be regarlanded (1054–55) before it becomes once more something other than a mere branch. Pentheus not only fails to see and interpret symbols; he also remains unaware of, or fatally resistant to, the fact that visual or linguistic signs can refer to more than one valid level of meaning at once. Unlike Dionysus (and the audience) he has no sense of irony or metaphor.

Pentheus' terrifying transformation from spectator to spectacle shows in an extraordinarily theatrical form what it means to act or imitate without full knowledge. The god, unlike the tragic hero, never confuses representation with reality; instead he controls reality through representation. Contrast, for example, Pentheus' reactions in the stable scene and the god's open declaration, in the prologue and elsewhere, about how he will use disguise, madness, and illusion to achieve his ends. By using language on multiple levels and exploiting the physical accoutrements of theater and/or Dionysiac cult, he can manipulate and transform the world to create an upside-down festal experience.[52] Whereas the audience

---

[52]All these aspects of the play seem to be characteristic of Greek mystery cults; Eleusinian mysteries also used riddling language, symbols, and some kind of dramatic performance. Seaford 1981 suggests that the *Bacchae* makes references to the Dionysiac mysteries comparable to those made to the Eleusinian mysteries in Aeschylus' *Oresteia.*

can distinguish visual illusion from reality in the palace scene, the tragic hero, or, from the divine perspective, the "comic victim," is destroyed through his confinement to one level of language and sight and to the cultural context in which he exists. In short, most Greek tragedy unfolds as a kind of initiation into the mysteries of the divine and the mysteries of the self, which can include a kind of symbolic or actual sacrificial death (sacrificial in part because sacrifice defines a point of intersection in the relations between man and god, man and society). Yet the audience's experience of tragic irony in the *Bacchae* expands to encompass a confrontation not only with individual identity or the nature of the divine but also with the whole contradictory structure of human social existence.

Dionysus and the chorus present to Thebes the possibility that his festivals can express this potential for a reversal of the cultural order in a controlled and revitalizing form; the early scenes offer multiple demonstrations that the spectator who can understand reality (and especially divinity) through representation retains distance and identity and may return without disaster to ordinary life. The "play" or festival on the mountain perverts the drama as it has been observed up to this point. The benign (*ēpiōtatos*) god of theater can by implication present drama and myths as a constructive part of the social and political life of the city; the terrible (*deinotatos*) god presides over comparable festive reversals of normality and identity outside the limits of the city and of civilized control. Thus, while Pentheus merely *imagines* that he "suffers terribly" (*pepontha deina*, 642) in his duel with the image created by the god, he is still safe; but on the mountain he is utterly destroyed. The first messenger speech gives Pentheus the precise scenario for his own death and a chance, by learning through presentation, to avoid it; here animals, not humans, are torn apart; the myth of Actaeon serves to warn the king of his fall in advance; and the maenads, if left undisturbed, can act in an orderly and peaceful fashion.[53] Here the messenger learns from his experience to accept Dionysus' divinity, although the king cannot. The initial debates (*agōnes*) between man and god become Pentheus' hopeless struggles (*agōnes*) on the

---

[53]Dodds 1960: 167–68 suggests that the traditional story of the herdsman and the maenads would have been celebrated in ritual and dance.

mountain. The maenads literally see the king as a beast and tear him apart; unlike the chorus, they become with Pentheus actors in the play, not spectators of the action. In contrast, the chorus, as spectators, simply *imagine* Pentheus as a beast; in the fourth stasimon, where they envisage Pentheus' death, they participate, but indirectly and hence without harm, in the god's revenge on Pentheus. Finally, the chorus' single-minded and pitiless identification with the god's "play" is not that of Euripides' play, for the audience has access in the final scenes to a double reading of the god's drama that encompasses both a divine ("comic") and a humane ("tragic") reading of the same events. The audience sees, then, all levels of participation in and experience of the same events, from the complete failure to retain control, represented by madness, and the chorus' overidentification, to Tiresias' controlled participation as spectator with sufficient understanding (like that of an audience experiencing tragic irony) to survive his experience without negative consequences.

The play, by emphasizing the possibility that Dionysus may be safely incorporated into civilized life or that the mere spectator of rather than the actor in Dionysiac theater may benefit from tragic experience, offers an implicit justification for the seemingly subversive role of festival and tragedy in civilized life. The sacrifices made by art and ritual substitute for actual violence. At the same time, Euripides seems to subvert this claim. The chorus, as spectators who identify too closely with the divine revenge and who travesty the language of ethical moderation, are clear reminders of continuing contemporary excesses in the Athenian political scene. Furthermore, although the play thoroughly debunks the traditional anthropomorphic assumptions about Greek divinity, Cadmus, by insisting to the god that his revenge was just but excessive—gods should not be like mortals in their wrath (1348)—shows how little he, as well as the chorus, has learned from Pentheus' tragic disaster. In the final scene Agave and Cadmus turn away from ritual and myth, which are left to Dionysus and the chorus, in favor of rational speech. Yet no form of speech—the cynical opportunism of Cadmus, the sophistry of Tiresias, the literalism of Pentheus, the riddling language of the initiated offered by the disguised god, the ritualized and mythical language of the chorus—earlier offered a means to capture fully or to control the experience inspired by the elusive god.[54] Is the spectator forced to conclude that the god's nonverbal communication of his divinity is equally ambivalent and inadequate? An examination of the theatrical effect created by the god's own mask provides further insight into these larger contradictions offered by the play as a whole.

Dionysus' Mask

In the prologue Dionysus announces that he will manifest himself to Thebes in human disguise and reveal himself as a god to the city. To do so he has put on a human *morphē* (shape) or *phusis* (nature). He redundantly emphasizes (4–5 and 53–54) his donning of this human disguise.[55] Why does Euripides make Dionysus draw attention to this point? Presumably he must clarify for the audience some visual confusion about the god and his costume. Using the aorist participle (*ameipsas*, 4), the god says he has "put on" mortal shape. The use of the aorist followed by a main verb in the present tense (*pareimi*, 5) suggests that he appears onstage already disguised as mortal, although the audience is required to accept this figure as a god (1–2):

[54]Pentheus' inability to comprehend Tiresias, Dionysus, the *therapōn*, and the first messenger reflects not only his *amathia* but also the impossibility of communicating the Dionysiac phenomenon verbally. The god's violence and the final scene make clear that even the audience, with the benefit of hindsight, cannot accept the words of the god and his chorus as fully adequate to the experience represented in the play. The juxtaposition of the chorus' and Tiresias' explanation of Dionysus' birth also raises questions about both views. On Tiresias' speech, which I view as deliberately inadequate, see esp. Deichgräber 1935, Rohdich 1968, esp. 143–47, Winnington-Ingram 1948: 48–58, Conacher 1967a: 62–64.

[55]No scholar has in my view convincingly explained away this redundancy on textual grounds. Willink 1966: 30–31 admits that there are no strong linguistic grounds for condemnation. "To defend 53–54 is to believe that Euripides spoilt his own elaborate structure" in the prologue, "and that, too, with a doubly tautologous couplet (repeating [line] 4), introduced by a repetitive conjunction, following a clause which it could not logically follow." My point here is that the repetition is meant to be functional and emphatic. See also line 914, where the god reminds the audience that the feminine figure seen entering is indeed the disguised Pentheus.

I have come, the child of Zeus, to the Theban land, Dionysus.

Yet does this figure with the smiling mask (as we know from lines 439 and 1021) look mortal? Although we know little of tragic masking conventions in the fifth century B.C., we can safely assume that most masks representing human beings in tragedy were not smiling.[56] Moreover, although gods regularly appear in prologues and epiphanies, they rarely dominate the *praxis* of tragedies.[57] This is apparently not true of tragedies about Dionysus, in which the god is presenting his divinity to those who have not yet recognized him. Yet the continual presence onstage of this divine smile was not so commonplace as to have lost its capacity to express the gulf between god and man.[58] The masks of other gods in Greek tragedies are never described in the text as smiling. Yet if, as seems probable, the smiling mask was a convention for deities, or for Dionysus alone, rather than an Euripidean innovation, no earlier poet, so far as we know, called attention to it so emphatically and developed it so explicitly.

Dodds explains the textual redundancy here as the poet's means "of making it quite clear to the audience that the speaker, whom

[56]For the scanty evidence concerning fifth-century as opposed to later tragic masks, see Pickard-Cambridge 1968: chap. 4. Even in the fourth century the more stylized masks of the principal tragic or even upper-class comic characters are never described or pictured in art as smiling. There are no other direct references to masks in classical tragedy, and even in comedy it is difficult to abstract precise information on the nature of masks from the texts. I am assuming that masks and costumes could be seen by the audience; even if the spectators in the last rows of the theater in fifth-century Athens had a very distant view of the actors, theatrical productions are not designed for those in the back row. Scholars have made far too much of this point. For an audience that knows what to expect—such as those in a modern football or baseball stadium—small details can be apprehended even if they are not clearly seen. And in this case the text serves to clarify the visual experience by calling attention to it.

[57]Divine appearances were usually confined to prologues and epilogues. Dionysus took part in the action of Aeschylus' *Lycurgeia*, and this participation may have been typical in tragedies about Dionysus. Other divine interventions in the action of tragedies occur in Euripides' *Rhesus*, Aeschylus' *Psychostasia* and *Xantriae*, Euripides' *Heracles*, and possibly Sophocles' *Niobe*. Aeschylus' *Eumenides* and *Prometheus Bound* have divine protagonists.

[58]For further helpful comments on the god's smiling mask, see esp. Rosenmeyer 1963: 106–10 and Dodds 1960 on line 439. See also Méautis 1923: 181–82 on the contrast between the masks of Pentheus and Dionysus.

they accept as a god, will be accepted as a man by the people on the stage."[59] Dionysus thus enters the play poorly disguised as human, in the fashion of Homeric gods or the testing god of folktale.[60] His mask (and perhaps also his costume) is not, by the conventions of Greek tragedy, human. Therefore, simply by his costume he manifests his godhead, his unhumanness to the audience. The tragic irony for which the play is justly famous has a visual level. That is, the audience sees by his mask that the stranger is a god, but Pentheus has no such theatrical cues by which to recognize him. The audience is being asked to be conscious of a costume and a theatrical convention. Thus, for the audience Dionysus' mask represents smiling divinity in human disguise; for the characters, a man. One mask represents two meanings in a manner that captures the central irony of the dramatic action.

Jones has eloquently argued in *On Aristotle and Greek Tragedy* that the ancient mask was meant to be a fully adequate means of representing character: unlike the modern mask, ancient tragic masks "did not owe their interest to the further realities lying behind them, because they declared the whole man."[61] In accordance with this convention, the Greek tragic audience should not be required to "peer behind the mask and demand of the actor that he shall cease merely to support the action, and shall begin instead to exploit the mask in the service of inwardness." When "the mind's construction" cannot be found in the face, masking becomes pointless. Jones's argument concerning the identity between mask and character for the ancient poet is confirmed not only by most of the known tragedies of Aeschylus and Sophocles (such characters as Aeschylus' Clytemnestra are possible exceptions) but also by post-fifth-century visual representations of poets, who are shown composing while looking at masks.[62] Jones argues that

[59]Dodds 1960 in his note on 53–54 also includes the views of previous commentaries.

[60]See Rose 1956 on divine disguisings in Homer, and Burnett 1970: 24–25 on the theme in the *Bacchae*.

[61]Jones 1962: 45. The following paragraph summarizes aspects of the argument made by Jones on 45–46 and 270.

[62]For an excellent treatment of this issue with examples from art, see Webster 1965. Aristophanes also suggests that costumes can be a comparable form of inspiration for poetic composition (*Acharnians* 411–16 and *Thesmophoriazusae* 148–52).

The *Bacchae*

Euripides' career is uniquely marked by a whole range of "mask-piercing" and "mask-exploiting" effects that challenge the ancient masking convention. Euripides "pierces" masks by creating conflicts between a character's internal state and his role in the action of the drama. Thus, Hippolytus' tongue swears, but his mind remains unsworn (*Hipp.* 612). The mad Pentheus' willingness to dress as a woman reveals an unkingly temperament. Agave, by envisioning Pentheus' mask as a lion, apprehends, like the chorus, the bestial side of her son, the inner self that is at odds with his outer role; yet her sane vision restores his humanity. In these cases, then, "the mind's construction" is no longer fully perceptible in the face or mask that the actor presents onstage.

In the case of Dionysus in the *Bacchae,* however, the poet moves away from the "mask-piercing" effects characteristic of his earlier work—that is, the exploitation of the action in the "service of inwardness" that comes close to undermining the tragic masking convention—to make the most original "mask-exploiting" gesture of his career. By convention a tragic mask represents one character and one meaning; yet Euripides has called attention to the fact that the smiling mask of the god represents different identities to characters and audience. In addition, as the action of the play continues, the precise nature of what the mask represents to the audience becomes increasingly ambiguous. Certainly it continues to represent divinity to the audience. Yet the visual effect of the smiling mask has the same doubleness as the language of the play itself. The *eudaimonia* promised by the chorus to the adherents of Dionysiac religion is horribly ironic when the same term is applied to Agave on her return from the mountain after the destruction of her son (1258). Similarly, the god's mask remains smiling, but the visual effect of this smile does not remain consistent. The smile of the "gentle" stranger seems, from the human vantage point, to become by the end of the play a divine sneer, a ghoulish expression of inappropriate glee at a vengeance too easily executed. In short, Dionysus' mask, by becoming ambiguous, comes to owe its interest not simply to what it formally represents in accordance with the normal tragic masking convention, but also to "the further realities lying behind," the invisible forces that unite the benign and destructive aspects represented by the single sign of the god's smiling mask. The mask, then, represents the god to the audience, misrepresents him to the characters, and, as we shall see, in the final scene must be interpreted as an artifact or symbol representing the god, or as much as the audience or the characters can ever visually and directly experience of him.

Pentheus in his final mad scene with Dionysus sees double, two suns and two Thebes. The audience also sees double in this scene, though in a different way. Onstage are two feminine or feminized figures wearing long robes and fawnskins, two figures carrying the same Dionysiac paraphernalia. Each has long hair, although Pentheus' is poorly confined in a *mitra*. In Aristophanes' *Frogs* (46) and in Pollux (4.116–17) Dionysus wears the *krokōtos,* a garment emphasizing his feminine side and, to the audience, his divinity. If both Dionysus' and Pentheus' costumes were saffron, the audience as well as Pentheus would see "two suns," two brilliant yellow costumes moving side by side. The sacrificial victim of the god, here his contemporary and cousin, has visually become almost the ritual double he often seems to have been in religious and literary tradition.[63] The god wears his costume and his ambivalent sexuality with sinuous grace and authenticity. The human figure pathetically parodies the divine in costume and movement; as often in comedy, the feminine image is imperfectly imposed on the masculine. Pentheus finds it awkward to assimilate what he has so long resisted. Only the masks of the two figures remain for the audience markedly different: one smiling and hence inhuman, the other presumably unsmiling and, by tragic convention, human. At this pivotal moment in the play the divine smile of the god Dionysus is set against the mask of Pentheus the man. The presentation of the two masks isolated side by side against the similarity of the costumes visually anticipates in its significance the staging of the final scene, the total split between man and god, which becomes so poignant when in typically Euripidean fashion (for example, the *Hippolytus*) the characters are left to mourn with newly clarified vision while the god looks down from above. The smiling

---

[63]The god and his victim are mythological doubles for each other; the victim dies in place of the god, and the god thus appears to escape death. See Hubert and Mauss 1964 (1898): 77–94. For further examples in Greek myth of such doubling, see Guépin 1968; and for a discussion of its possible anthropological significance, see Girard 1977: chaps. 5 and 6.

mask of the god suddenly retains no aspect of benignity, if indeed it had any before, beside the mask of the doomed and mortal Pentheus. Euripides has brilliantly exploited a poetic device known from Homer onward—Homer with his two worlds, one of inviolable and often comic gods, the other of struggling and mortal men. *Iliad* 1, for example, deliberately juxtaposes the two gatherings of men and gods, one dissolving into anger and disaster, the other into laughter; similarly, in *Iliad* 21 the comic battle between the gods contrasts with the deadly battle between men. The visual juxtaposition of the masks here also becomes a precise theatrical expression of the division between divine and human nature that lies at the heart of the play.

The mortal Pentheus survives in the *Bacchae* solely as the mask that represents the character in Greek theatrical convention. For the audience the mask remains Pentheus' own despite his transformation by Dionysus in other respects, and finally it returns to the stage with Agave, fully recognizable even if, as some think, it was spattered with blood.[64] (Tragic masks in the fifth century were apparently whole head masks with hair attached.[65]) Only to the mad Agave does Pentheus' mask temporarily appear that of a lion, the victim of the glorious god and herself. Indeed, the text emphasizes this issue of the temporary distortion of what the mask represents by the use of the word *prosōpon* (face or mask, 1277). The conventional identification between the tragic figure and his mask formally corresponds to his dramatic situation. He cannot completely step outside of or internally withdraw from and control his character or his fate; he is strictly human. As Euripides' staging brilliantly demonstrates, the tragic character *is* his mask, and is ultimately limited in the action to what his mask represents. In contrast, gods are not limited to representing one character, one role, one place in the family, society, and universe. They manipulate roles with a freedom found only in comedy, where the character's mask may, as here, represent contradictory identities to the audience and the characters. This tragic convention is mocked in

---

[64]Cult masks of Dionysus were hung on trees or pillars and sometimes daubed with red marks, probably indicating blood. See Pausanias 2.2.6 and Farnell 1909: V, 242–43.

[65]See note 56.

Aristophanes' *Acharnians* when Dicaeopolis plays on it in a manner
comparable to that of Dionysus in the *Bacchae,* as he says to the
audience, parodying Euripides' *Telephus:*

> It is necessary for me to appear as a beggar today, to be as I am, but
> not appear to be so. The spectators know who I am but the chorus
> will be fools enough not to, so that I may jeer at them with my
> clever phrases.
>
> (*Acharn.* 440–44)

By reducing Pentheus to his tragic mask and by allowing Dionysus to exploit his mask in an extraordinary way, Euripides
demonstrates through theatrical convention the nature of the division between god and man.

Dionysus appears in his final epiphany no longer disguised as the
stranger. He could, for example, have changed his mask and costume for the familiar and uneffeminate Zeus-like divinity shown
on all but the most recent vase paintings. Yet given the rarity of
costume change in Greek tragedy, I assume here (although my
argument does not depend on this point) that the god has no need
to change his mask or even his costume for his appearance on the
theologeion, since both already represent his divinity to the audience.[66] By now the audience has lost the superior position it had,

[66]We cannot prove that mask change ever occurred in Greek tragedy. Critics
have speculated, for example, on Dionysus' appearance in the scene where Pentheus sees the god as a bull, on the mask of Oedipus after his blinding in Sophocles' *Oedipus Rex,* on the mask of Helen in the final scene of Euripides' *Helen,* and
on the possible changing of masks by the Erinyes when they become Eumenides in
Aeschylus' *Eumenides.* Yet mask change without a highly stylized system of masks
would probably be confusing to an audience, and fifth-century evidence suggests
that masks were naturalistic and not, as later, stylized; see note 56 above. Hence it
is safe, and probably safer, to assume that it did not occur here or elsewhere in
fifth-century tragedy. Even in comedy disguised characters appear to change costume, not masks; Euripides' relative in the *Thesmophoriazusae* could have changed
to a beardless mask when adopting a female disguise, but more probably he
removed a beard from the mask he already wore. Certainly if the smiling mask
was the (or a) conventional one for Dionysus, there would be no need for him to
change masks when he appeared as a god. Costume change did occur in tragedy,
as in the case of Pentheus in this play. On the other hand, the costume worn by the
stranger probably appeared, like the mask, to be a typical costume for Dionysus,
so that no costume change would have been necessary.

in the form we call tragic irony, over Pentheus. The smiling mask now represents a divinity to both characters and audience. By suggesting throughout the action of the play that human beings have access to the god by theatrical means, through mask, costume, voice, and music, or through illusion, symbol, and transformation, Euripides seems to make a strong claim for art's ability to represent a reality inaccessible to ordinary human sight. Thus, by means of the theatrical convention of a smiling mask (which is not human) the audience "sees" Dionysus' divinity as the characters at first cannot. Yet finally, when it has become clear that Dionysus can be "seen" or apprehended only symbolically and indirectly by the theatrical means common to Dionysiac religion and Greek theater, he simply appears to the spectators, and to a city that has returned to sanity, in his divine form in the epiphany. By theatrical convention, the audience must accept the deus ex machina as an adequate and direct visual representation of the god. And, in fact, it has never ceased to see the god's mask as divine. Yet the message of the action of the play is in tension with this final representation of the god. For if one mask represents different identities to characters and audience, if the smile that marks the mask means both benignity and destruction, and finally, if the mask in the epiphany can be understood only as a sign that represents forces that are in fact not directly accessible to the eye, then the audience can make sense of its theatrical experience only by becoming conscious of the god's mask as a mask in the modern rather than in the ancient tragic theatrical mode. Euripides thus achieves in the audience a sense of the mask as transcending both its previous functions as the deceptive image of the illusory god and possibly alludes to the attested use of masks of Dionysus as actual cult objects. Here the poet reflects simultaneously his own ideas about tragic art and illuminates the mysteries of a ritual practice.[67] Dionysus' divinity

[67]Evidence for the worship of Dionysus as a mask in Attic cult is substantial. Among many examples, the *kalpis* from Vulci signed by Hypsis, c. 510 B.C. (*ARV2* 30,2), is particularly appropriate for the *Bacchae* in that it portrays the worship of the mask of Dionysus in both his benign and bestial incarnations. See also Pickard-Cambridge 1968: 30–34 on the so-called Lenaia vases, or Athens National Museum 11749 for an example of vases illustrating Dionysus masks on a pillar.

in the *Bacchae* and in cult can be understood through his power to control representation. Euripides makes his anomalous untragic mask become the central mocking image of what human beings understand about divinity.

The poet heightens the inscrutable effect of the god's epiphany by making his final appearance so gratuitous to an already finished plot and so puzzling in respect to the prophecies he makes to Thebes.[68] Although the audience may "understand" that Dionysus is a god, and has come to realize with the protagonists a good deal more about the nature of this divinity than it had at the outset and a good deal more as well about how he must be grasped, it does not finally fully control this knowledge. As already noted, Cadmus, who from the beginning accepted the god more as a relative than as a divinity, cannot transcend his anthropomorphic vision of the god. The house of Cadmus, although it now accepts the god's divinity, faces yet further inhuman punishments. The play is in a sense unfinished for both Thebes and the audience. The god makes clear that the repercussions of the events at Thebes will continue to be felt throughout Greece in the form of further barbarian incursions, perhaps even (given allusions to contemporary life in the choral odes) in fifth-century Athens.

Ritual in the *Bacchae*

In the *Bacchae*, the sacrificial death of Pentheus is located even more explicitly than in the *Heracles* and *Electra* within the larger civic context that includes festival, athletic *agōn*, and very probably rites of initiation as well. The play capitalizes on and/or exposes the parallel structures and aims of these rituals; each aims at a symbolic control of violence and competitive energy, a limitation

---

[68]On this point, see Winnington-Ingram 1948: 144–47: the deus ex machina is "spectacular but empty." Perhaps Cadmus' unenthusiastic reaction (1360–62) to Dionysus' promise of the land of the blessed (*makarōn t' es aian,* 1339) for himself and Harmonia is a further ironic comment on Dionysiac promises of bliss. The association of Dionysiac worship with bliss, peace, love, poetry, and escape from toil made repeatedly by the chorus is certainly not borne out either in the play or in contemporary Athens. See Dodds 1960 on 1330–39 for a discussion of Dionysus' prophecies.

in the relation between god and man and between man and man inside the city. Tragic sacrifice makes the participant come face to face with death and with the violence that is required to maintain his social and physical existence; it strips away the veneer of civilization maintained in the civic rite with its animal victim and turns the exploding violence of the participants onto a human victim. In the *Bacchae* the sacrificers experience the god (and ultimately their own violence) directly. The similarly controlled experience of divine power and success temporarily allowed to the athlete is here perverted as the boundaries between god and man and between the participants in the contest collapse. Behind Dionysus' triumph lurk the pitiful inequality of god and man and the human inability to achieve more than temporary power and immortality. The experience of adolescent initiation, in which the individual departs from the city to confront it from the outside, through the experience of nature (and, through nature, a renewed confrontation and harmony with the mother), parallels that of festival, in which the individual temporarily steps out of his place in the social hierarchy and in history to confront the basic equality of all human beings, including men and women, masked by the structures and divisions of everyday life. As Turner argues, it is the dangerous experience of this unity and equality that allows the social system to function, and ultimately to take on a sense of necessity and order.

Sacrifice, *agōn,* and festival are ritual experiences that help to define a society from both within and without: who is a legitimate participant in the society, and how power, privilege, and prestige will be allotted within it. In their sacrificial and agonistic crises the *Heracles,* the *Bacchae,* and the *Electra* deal with the entry of an outsider, Orestes or Heracles or Dionysus, into a potentially explosive social situation or with the relation between a king, a *perissos phōs,* and the people, including women, who are members of the society but not full participants in it. Contemporary Athenian democracy confronted these same issues: the contradictions between its aim for political equality among citizens and the exclusion of members of the society from full participation, the demands of the private sphere, the need for leadership, and the inevitable competitive pressure for power and prestige that was encouraged by the agonistically oriented heritage of Greek literature.

Tragedy, as public and traditional literature, confronts these contradictions. Euripides places multiple explosions of rituals with parallel functions at the heart of his dramas. Through ritual he can bridge the gap between public and private, past and present, and between myth and contemporary democracy. Since all members of the society participate in ritual, if not in political life, through ritual he can raise issues that touch the society as a whole, not simply the narrow political sphere. He can draw on the structure and meaning of these rites as a timeless model of social order toward which his struggling plots and characters can aspire, and through which they can learn. Ritual provides both a model for social transition and a way of experiencing the society from outside its political organization. When successful, it either helps the participant adjust to the status quo (as in the *IT* or *IA*), finds a new place for an outsider within it (as in the *Heracles*), or expels those who cannot safely be incorporated. Finally, ritual becomes a structure that the poet's own art can imitate, question, and occasionally strive to surpass.

In the *Iphigenia in Aulis,* ritual (marriage and sacrifice) offers to the imagination of the innocent Iphigenia a way to find meaning in her terrible experience and to offer unity to an agonistic (eristic and erotic), uncontrolled, and changeable public world. In the *Phoenissae,* the poet allows the mythical tradition about Thebes to disintegrate under the pressure of sophistry and the corrupted competition and individualism of contemporary society; and then, through the sacrifice of Menoeceus and the perspective of the choral poetry, the plot recovers, at least in part, the tradition and the movement toward myth and ritual that it has nearly abandoned. In the *Heracles* Euripides exploits the preoccupation with *agōn* of the poetic and mythical tradition of epic and epinician that preceded tragedy. Euripides' Dionysiac (as the imagery of the peripety stresses) tragedy inverts the festive poetry of this tradition, and by destroying the hero of traditional myth through a monstrous sacrifice and *agōn* creates a hero for a democratic *polis*. In the *Bacchae,* Euripides takes tragedy back to its hypothetical origins in Dionysiac festival, sacrifice, and *agōn*. The festal experience introduced by the god is presented as a protodrama. The *agōn* of words between Pentheus and Dionysus degenerates into uncontrolled aggression, and only after the event does the contest of words between god and man resume in the despairing and rational dialogue of Cadmus and Dionysus in the final scene. The "comedy" of divine vengeance contains a momentary tragic *anagnōrisis* of *hamartia,* a movement toward self-knowledge, that is completed only in Agave's recovery of her civilized identity as wife of Echion and destroyer of her son. The experience has the order and components of a ritual, but only after the event is the priestess of the *phonos* said to have performed a *thuma.* The Dionysiac *phonos* seems to become a *thuma* in part because tragedy, like the sacrificial ritual, controls access to violence, by presenting the slaughter offstage and interpreted through the pity and fear of a human sympathizer.

In all but one of these four tragedies (the *Heracles*) the choruses are not, like so many choruses of earlier tragedies, involved citizens. They are outsiders, spectators of the action who provide, through their knowledge and experience of myth and ritual, links to the past and future of the mythical tradition. In the final scenes they may subside into silence and hand their lyric burden to the protagonists, as in the *IA* and the *Phoenissae,* where there is a tentative convergence in the plot between ritual and political reality, between iambic discourse and lyric. Or, as in the *Bacchae,* they remain foreigners, barbaric outsiders to the final tragic lament. Here Euripides' tragedy emerges from the Dionysiac protodrama simultaneously recognizing its origins in this experience and declaring its separation from it. As Green has said of the *Bacchae:* "The tragedy combines in itself the ecstasy of the festival, the ordering of ritual and the power of speech. Each of these aspects reveals a different origin, whose mode transcends the particular and constitutes a new form."[69]

After the sacrifice / *agōn* that destroys Pentheus, the protagonists, though not the chorus, put aside the ecstasy of festival and turn from the god to lament and the consolation and questioning offered by rational speech. The characters become spectators of their own experience who have left festival, if not the memory of it, behind. The tragedy follows the pattern of festival, closing with

[69] Green 1979: 182.

a return to normalcy after a period of inversion. But its return to normalcy, its control of its own violence, is not made without question. In the *IA* and the *Phoenissae* we remain uncertain as to the effect of the tragic sacrifice on the "real world" of the drama. In the *Heracles* we are left with intimations of a possible return of the hero's madness and his almost unbearable burden of sorrow. In the *Bacchae* we are left uncertain whether the *polis* will ever absorb and domesticate Dionysus or control the proliferating and dangerous repercussions of his entry into civilized life; or that we can ever be, like Dionysus, simultaneously actors in and spectators of human existence. Euripides can find no order outside ritual and myth and rational speech, yet in the end the order provided by art, ritual, and speech remains in an uncertain relation to the reality of the contemporary world.

Bibliography

Adams, S. M. 1935. "Two Plays of Euripides." *CR* 49: 118–22.

Adkins, A. W. H. 1960. *Merit and Responsibility*. Oxford.

———. 1966. "Basic Greek Values in Euripides' *Hecuba* and *Hercules Furens*." *CQ* 16: 193–219.

Arnott, Geoffrey. 1973. "Euripides and the Unexpected." *Greece and Rome* 20: 49–64.

Arrowsmith, William. 1954. "The Conversion of Herakles: An Essay in Euripidean Tragic Structure." Diss. Princeton University.

Arthur, Marylin B. 1972. "The Choral Odes of the *Bacchae* of Euripides." *YCS* 22: 145–79.

———. 1975. "Euripides' *Phoenissae* and the Politics of Justice." Diss. Yale University.

———. 1977. "The Curse of Civilization: The Choral Odes of the *Phoenissae*." *HSCP* 81: 163–85.

Austin, Colin, ed. 1968. *Nova Fragmenta Euripidea in Papyris Reperta*. Berlin.

Bacon, Helen. 1964. "The Shield of Eteocles." *Arion* 3(3): 27–38.

Bain, David. 1977. "The Prologues of Euripides' *Iphigeneia in Aulis*." *CQ* 27: 10–26.

Barlow, Shirley. 1971. *The Imagery of Euripides*. London.

———. 1982. "Structure and Dramatic Realism in Euripides' *Heracles*." *Greece and Rome* 29: 115–25.

Bataille, Georges. 1962. *Eroticism*. Trans. Mary Dalwood. Basildon, Essex. First published as *Erotisme*, Paris 1957.

Bather, A. G. 1894. "The Problem of Euripides' *Bacchae*." *JHS* 14: 244–63.

Bibliography

Beazley, J. D. 1947. *Etruscan Vase Painting*. Oxford.

Beidelman, T. O. 1974. *W. Robertson Smith and the Sociological Study of Religion*. Chicago.

Benardete, Seth. 1967. "Two Notes on Aeschylus' *Septem*." Part 1. *WS* 80: 22–30.

Bergson, Henri. 1956. "Laughter." In *Comedy: An Essay on Comedy by George Meredith and Laughter by Henri Bergson*. Trans. Wylie Sypher, 61–190. New York.

Bilinski, Bronsilaw. 1979. *Agoni ginnici: Componenti artistiche ed intellettuali nell' antica agonistica greca*. Accademia polacca delle scienze, Biblioteca e centro di studi a Roma, Conferenze 75.

Blaiklock, E. M. 1952. *The Male Characters of Euripides: A Study in Realism*. Wellington, N.Z.

Bogaert, Raymond. 1965. "Le revirement des Ménélas." *LEC* 33: 3–11.

Bond, Godfrey W., ed. 1981. *Euripides' Heracles*. Oxford.

Bonnard, André. 1945. *"Iphigénie à Aulis*. Tragique et poésie." *MH* 2: 87–107.

Brelich, Angelo. 1958. *Gli eroi greci*. Rome.

———. 1969a. *Paides e Parthenoi*. Incunabula Graeca 36. Rome.

———. 1969b. "Aristofane. Commedie e religione." *Acta Classica Universitatis Scientiarum Debreceniensis* 5: 21–30.

Bundy, Elroy. 1962. *Studia Pindarica*. Berkeley.

Burian, Peter and Swann, Brian, trans. 1981. *Euripides. The Phoenician Women*. New York and Oxford.

Burkert, Walter. 1966a. "Greek Tragedy and Sacrificial Ritual." *GRBS* 7: 87–121.

———. 1966b. "Kekropidensage und Arrhephoria." *Hermes* 94: 1–25.

———. 1972. *Homo Necans: Interpretationen altgriechischer Opferriten und Mythen*. Berlin and New York.

———. 1979. *Structure and History in Greek Mythology and Ritual*. Sather Classical Lectures 47. Berkeley and Los Angeles.

———. 1981. "Glaube und Verhalten: Zeichengehalt und Wirkungsmacht von Opferritualen." In *Le sacrifice dans l'antiquité, Entretiens sur l'antiquité classique* 27, ed. Jean Rudhardt and Olivier Reverdin, 91–125. Geneva.

Burnett, Anne Pippin. 1970. "Pentheus and Dionysus: Host and Guest." *CP* 65: 15–29.

———. 1971. *Catastrophe Survived: Euripides' Plays of Mixed Reversal*. Oxford.

Calame, Claude. 1977. *Les choeurs de jeunes filles en Grèce archaïque*. 2 vols. Rome.

Bibliography

Caldwell, Richard. 1974. "Tragedy Romanticized: The *Iphigenia Taurica*." *CJ* 70: 23–40.

Carrière, Jean Claude. 1979. *Le carnaval et la politique*. Paris.

Casabona, Jean. 1966. *Recherches sur le vocabulaire des sacrifices en grec des origines à la fin de l'époque classique*. Aix-en-Provence.

Castellani, Victor. 1976. "That Troubled House of Pentheus in Euripides' *Bacchae*." *TAPA* 106: 61–88.

Cavander, Kenneth, trans. 1973. *Iphigeneia at Aulis by Euripides*. Englewood Cliffs, N.J.

Cecchi, Sergio. 1960. "L'esodo dell' *Ifigenia in Aulide* di Euripide." *RSC* 8: 69–87.

Chalk, H. H. O. 1962. "*Aretē* and *Bia* in Euripides' *Herakles*." *JHS* 82: 7–18.

Coche de la Ferté, Etienne. 1980. "Penthée et Dionysos: Nouvel essai d'interprétation des 'Bacchantes' d'Euripide." In *Recherches sur les religions de l'antiquité classique*, ed. Raymond Bloch, 105–257. Geneva and Paris.

Collignon, Max. 1904. "Matrimonium: Cérémonies du mariage." In Daremberg-Saglio-Pottier, eds., *Dictionnaire des antiquités grecques et romaines* 3: 1647–54. Paris.

Conacher, D. J. 1967a. *Euripidean Drama: Myth, Theme, and Structure*. Toronto.

———. 1967b. "Themes in the *Exodus* of Euripides' *Phoenissae*." *Phoenix* 21: 92–101.

Connor, W. Robert. 1971. *The New Politicians of Fifth-Century Athens*. Princeton.

Cornford, Francis. 1934. *The Origin of Attic Comedy*. Cambridge.

Crotty, Kevin. 1980. "Pythian 2 and Conventional Language in the Epinicians." *Hermes* 108: 1–12.

———. 1982. *Song and Action: The Victory Odes of Pindar*. Baltimore and London.

Dale, A. M. 1969. "Seen and Unseen on the Greek Stage." In *Collected Papers*, 119–29. Cambridge.

Darkaki, Maria. 1980. "Aspects du sacrifice dionysiaque." *Revue de l'Histoire des Religions* 197: 131–57.

Deichgräber, Karl. 1935. "Die Kadmos-Tiresiasszene in Euripides Bakchen." *Hermes* 70: 322–49.

Detienne, Marcel. 1967. *Les maîtres de vérité dans la Grèce archaïque*. Paris. Rep. 1973.

———. 1968. "La phalange. Problèmes et controverses." In *Problèmes de la guerre*, 119–42. See Vernant 1968.

———. 1977. *The Gardens of Adonis.* Trans. Janet Lloyd. Brighton. First published as *Les jardins d'Adonis,* Paris 1972.

———. 1979a. *Dionysus Slain.* Trans. M. Muellner and L. Muellner. Baltimore and London. First published as *Dionysos mis à mort,* Paris 1977.

———. 1979b. "Pratiques culinaires et esprit de sacrifice." In *La cuisine du sacrifice,* 7–35. See Detienne and Vernant 1979.

———. 1979c. "Violentes 'eugénies.' En pleines Thesmophories: des femmes couvertes de sang." In *La cuisine du sacrifice,* 183–214. See Detienne and Vernant 1979.

Detienne, Marcel, and Svenbro, Jesper. 1979. "Les loups au festin ou la Cité impossible." In *La cuisine du sacrifice,* 215–37. See Detienne and Vernant 1979.

Detienne, Marcel, and Vernant, Jean-Pierre, eds. 1979. *La cuisine du sacrifice en pays grec.* Paris.

Deubner, Ludwig. 1932. *Attische Feste.* Berlin. Rep. Hildesheim 1966.

Dewald, Carolyn J. 1981. "Women and Culture in Herodotus' *Histories.*" *Women's Studies* 8: 93–127. Rep. in *Reflections of Women in Antiquity,* ed. Helene P. Foley, 91–125. New York, Paris, and London 1981.

Diggle, James. 1971. "Iphigenia at Aulis." *CR,* n.s. 21: 178–80.

———. 1974. "On the *Heracles* and *Ion* of Euripides." *PCPhS,* n.s. 20: 3–26.

Dihle, Albrecht. 1981. *Der Prolog der Bacchen und die antike Überlieferungsphase des Euripides- Textes.* Sitzungsberichte der Heidelberger Akademie der Wissenschaften, Phil.-hist. Klasse, Bericht 2. Heidelberg.

Diller, Hans. 1955. "Die Bakchen und ihre Stellung im Spätwerk des Euripides." *Akademie der Wissenschaften und der Literatur in Mainz, Abhandlungen der Geistes- und Sozialwissenschaftl. Klasse.* 5: 453–71. Rep. in Schwinge 1968, 469–92.

———. 1964. Review of Fraenkel 1963. *Gnomon* 36: 641–50.

Dodds, E. R. 1951. *The Greeks and the Irrational.* Sather Classical Lectures 25. Berkeley and Los Angeles.

———, ed. 1960. *Euripides' Bacchae.* 2d ed. Oxford.

Douglas, Mary. 1966. *Purity and Danger.* London.

Duchemin, Jacqueline. 1967. "Le personnage de Lyssa dans l'*Héraklès furieux* d'Euripide." *REG* 80: 130–39.

Dumézil, G. 1943. *Servius et la Fortune: Essai sur la fonction sociale de louange et de blâme et sur les éléments indo-européens du cens romain.* Paris.

———. 1969. *Heur et malheur du guerrier.* Paris.

Durand, Jean-Louis. 1973. "Le rituel du meurtre du boeuf laboureur et les mythes du premier sacrifice animal en attique." In *Il mito greco,* ed. Bruno Gentili and Guiseppe Paioni, 121–132. Urbino.

Bibliography

————. 1979. "Bêtes grecques: Propositions pour une topologie des corps à manger." In *La cuisine du sacrifice*, 133–63. *See* Detienne and Vernant 1979.

Durkheim, Emile. 1965. *The Elementary Forms of Religious Life*. Trans. J. W. Swain. New York.

Dyer, Robert R. 1969. "The Evidence for Apollo Purification Rituals at Delphi and Athens." *JHS* 89: 38–56.

Ebener, Dieter. 1964. "Die Phönizierinnen des Euripides als Spiegelbild geschichtlicher Wirklichkeit." *Eirene* 2: 71–79.

Else, Gerald. 1957. *Aristotle's Poetics: The Argument*. Cambridge, Mass.

————. 1967. *The Origin and Early Form of Greek Tragedy*. Cambridge, Mass.

England, E. B., ed. 1891. *The Iphigeneia at Aulis of Euripides*. London.

Erbse, Hartmut. 1966. "Beiträge zum Verständnis der euripideischen 'Phoinissen.'" *Philologus* 110: 1–34.

Erdmann, Walter. 1934. *Die Ehe im alten Griechenland*. Munich.

Evans-Pritchard, E. E. 1956. *Nuer Religion*. Oxford.

————. 1965. *Theories of Primitive Religion*. Oxford.

Farnell, Lewis R. 1895–1909. *The Cults of the Greek States*. 5 vols. Oxford.

————. 1921. *Greek Hero Cults and Ideas of Immortality*. Oxford. Rep. 1970.

Ferguson, John. 1968. "Iphigeneia at Aulis." *TAPA* 99: 157–64.

Foley, Helene P. 1978. "'Reverse Similes' and Sex Roles in the *Odyssey*." *Arethusa* 11: 7–26.

————. 1980. "The Masque of Dionysus." *TAPA* 110: 107–33.

————. 1982a. "'The Female Intruder' Reconsidered: Women in Aristophanes' *Lysistrata* and *Ecclesiazusae*." *CP* 77: 1–21.

————. 1982b. "Marriage and Sacrifice in Euripides' *Iphigeneia in Aulis*." *Arethusa* 15: 159–80.

Fontenrose, Joseph. 1968. "The Hero as Athlete." *CSCA* 1: 73–104.

Fraenkel, Eduard. 1955. "Ein Motiv aus Euripides in einer Szene der Neuen Komödie." *Studi in onore di Ugo Enrico Paoli*, 293–304. Florence.

————. 1963. *Zu den Phoenissen des Euripides*. SBAW. Munich.

Freeman, Kathleen. 1971. *Ancilla to the Pre-Socratic Philosophers*. Oxford.

Frey, Viktor. 1947. "Betrachtungen zu Euripides aulischer Iphigenie." *MH* 4: 39–51.

Friedrich, Wolf H. 1935. "Zur aulischen Iphigenie." *Hermes* 70: 73–100.

————. 1939. "Prolegomena zu den Phönissen." *Hermes* 74: 265–300.

Fritz, Karl von. 1962. *Antike und moderne Tragödie*. Berlin.

Funke, Hermann. 1964. "Aristoteles zu Euripides Iphigeneia in Aulis." *Hermes* 92: 284–99.

Bibliography

Gagarin, Michael. 1981. *Drakon and Early Athenian Homicide Law*. New Haven.

Galinsky, G. Karl. 1972. *The Herakles Theme*. Totowa, N.J.

Gallini, Clara. 1963. "Il travestimo rituale di Penteo." *SMSR* 34: 211–28.

Garlan, Yvon. 1966. "De la poliorcétique dans les 'Phéniciennes' d'Euripide." *REA* 68: 264–77.

Garzya, Antonio. 1962. *Pensiero e technica drammatica in Euripide*. Naples.

Gennep, Arnold van. 1960. *The Rites of Passage*. Trans. Monika B. Vizedom and Gabrielle L. Caffee. London. First published as *Les rites de passage,* Paris 1909.

Gernet, Louis. 1955. *Droit et société dans la Grèce ancienne*. Paris.

———. 1981. *The Anthropology of Ancient Greece*. Trans. J. Hamilton, S. J., and Blaise Nagy. Baltimore and London. First published as *Anthropologie de la Grèce antique,* Paris 1976.

Girard, René. 1977. *Violence and the Sacred*. Trans. Patrick Gregory. Baltimore and London. First published as *La violence et le sacré,* Paris 1972.

———. 1978a. *To Double Business Bound: Essays on Literature, Mimesis, and Anthropology*. Baltimore and London.

———. 1978b. *Des choses cachées depuis la fondation du monde*. Paris.

Goffmann, Ervin. 1974. *Frame Analysis*. Cambridge.

Goossens, Roger. 1962. *Euripide et Athènes*. Académie royale des sciences, des lettres, et des beaux arts. Vol. 55, fasc. 4. Brussels.

Gouldner, Alvin. 1965. *Enter Plato: Classical Greece and the Origins of Social Theory*. New York.

Green, André. 1979. *The Tragic Effect: The Oedipus Complex in Greek Tragedy*. Trans. A. Sheridan. Cambridge. First published as *Un oeil en trop: Le complexe d'Oedipe dans la tragédie,* Paris 1969.

Greenwood, L. H. G. 1953. *Aspects of Euripidean Tragedy*. Cambridge.

Gregory, Justina. 1977. "Euripides' *Heracles*." *YCS* 25: 259–75.

Griffiths, Frederick T. 1979. "Girard on the Greeks/ The Greeks on Girard." *Berkshire Review* 14: 20–36.

Grube, G. M. A. 1935. "Dionysus in the *Bacchae*." *TAPA* 66: 37–54.

———. 1941. *The Drama of Euripides*. London. Rep. 1961.

Guépin, Jean-Pierre. 1968. *The Tragic Paradox: Myth and Ritual in Greek Tragedy*. Amsterdam.

Hardin, Richard F. 1983. " 'Ritual' in Recent Criticism: The Elusive Sense of Community." *PMLA* 98: 846–62.

Harrison, Jane. 1922. *Prolegomena to the Study of Greek Religion*. 3d ed. Cambridge.

———. 1927. *Themis*. Rev. ed. Cambridge. First published 1912.

Bibliography

Hartung, Johann A. 1843. *Euripides Restitutus*. Hamburg.

Haslam, Michael W. 1975. "The Authenticity of Euripides, *Phoenissae* 1–2 and Sophocles, *Electra* 1." *GRBS* 16: 149–74.

———. 1976. "Interpolations in the *Phoenissae*: Papyrus Evidence." *CQ* 26: 4–10.

Hendrickson, G. L. 1929. "The Heracles Myth and Its Treatments by Euripides." In *Classical Studies in Honor of Charles Forster Smith*, 11–29. Madison.

Henrichs, Albert. 1981. "Human Sacrifice in Greek Religion: Three Case Studies." In *Le sacrifice dans l'antiquité, Entretiens sur l'antiquité classique* 27, ed. Jean Rudhardt and Olivier Reverdin, 195–242. Geneva.

Howe, Thalia Phillies. 1962. "Taboo in the Oedipus Theme." *TAPA* 93: 124–43.

Hubert, Henri, and Mauss, Marcel. 1964. *Sacrifice: Its Nature and Function*. Trans. W. D. Halls. Chicago. First published as "Essai sur la nature et la fonction de sacrifice," *L'année sociologique*, 29–138, Paris 1898.

Humphreys, S. C. 1978. *Anthropology and the Greeks*. London.

James, E. O. 1937. *Origins of Sacrifice*. London.

Jeanmaire, Henri. 1951. *Dionysos, histoire du culte de Bacchus*. Paris.

Jones, John. 1962. *On Aristotle and Greek Tragedy*. London.

Kamerbeek, J. C. 1958. "Mythe et réalité dans l'oeuvre d'Euripide." In *Euripide, Entretiens sur l'antiquité classique* 6, ed. Olivier Reverdin, 1–41. Geneva.

———. 1966. "Unity and Meaning of Euripides' *Heracles*." *Mnemosyne* 19: 1–16.

Kirk, Geoffrey S., trans. 1970. *The Bacchae by Euripides: A Translation with Commentary*. Englewood Cliffs, N.J.

Kirk, Geoffrey S. 1981. "Some Methodological Pitfalls in the Study of Ancient Greek Sacrifice (in particular)." In *Le sacrifice dans l'antiquité, Entretiens sur l'antiquité classique* 27, ed. Jean Rudhardt and Olivier Reverdin, 41–80. Geneva.

Kitto, H. D. F. 1939. "The Final Scenes of the *Phoenissae*." *CR* 53: 104–11.

———. 1954. *Greek Tragedy*. New York.

Knox, B. M. W. 1966. "Second Thoughts in Greek Tragedy." *GRBS* 7: 213–32.

———. 1972. "Euripides' *Iphigenia in Aulide* 1–163 (in that order)." *YCS* 22: 239–61.

———. 1977. "The *Medea* of Euripides." *YCS* 25: 193–225.

Kranz, Walther. 1933. *Stasimon: Untersuchungen zu Form und Gehalt der griechischen Tragödie*. Berlin.

Bibliography

Kroeker, Ernst. 1938. *Der Herakles des Euripides: Analyse des Dramas*. Diss. Leipzig.

Kubo, Masaaki. 1966. "The Norm of Myth. Euripides' *Electra*." *HSCP* 71: 14–31.

La Rue, Jene. 1968. "Prurience Uncovered: The Psychology of Euripides' Pentheus." *CJ* 63: 209–14.

Lebeck, Anne. 1971. *The Oresteia: A Study in Language and Structure*. Cambridge.

Lefkowitz, Mary. 1969. "Bacchylides' Ode 5: Imitation and Originality." *HSCP* 73: 45–96.

Lincoln, Bruce. 1975. "Homeric λύσσα, "Wolfish Rage.'" *Indogermanische Forschungen* 80: 98–105.

Lonis, Raoul. 1979. *Guerre et religion en Grèce à l'époque classique. Recherche sur les rites, les dieux, l'idéologie de la victoire*. Annales littéraires de l'Université de Besançon 238. Paris.

Lowenstam, Steven. 1981. *The Death of Patroklos: A Study in Typology*. Konigstein.

Ludwig, Walther. 1954. *Sapheneia: Ein Beitrag zur Formkunst im Spätwerk des Euripides*. Tübingen.

MacDowell, D. M. 1963. *Athenian Homicide Law in the Age of the Orators*. Manchester.

Magnien, V. 1936. "Le mariage chez les grecs anciens. L'initiation nuptiale." *AC* 5: 115–38.

Massenzio, Marcello. 1969. "Cultura e crisi permanente: La 'xenia' dionisiaca." *SMSR* 40: 27–113.

Mastronarde, Donald. 1974. "Studies in Euripides' *Phoinissai*." Diss. University of Toronto.

———. 1978. "Are Euripides' *Phoinissai* 1104–1140 Interpolated?" *Phoenix* 32: 105–28.

Méautis, Georges. 1923. "L'expression des masques dans quelques tragédies d'Euripide," *REG* 36: 172–82.

Mellert-Hoffmann, Gudrun. 1969. *Untersuchungen zur 'Iphigenie in Aulis' des Euripides*. Heidelberg.

Mellon, Peter. 1974. "The Ending of Aeschylus' *Seven against Thebes* and Its Relation to Sophocles' *Antigone* and Euripides' *Phoenissae*." Diss. Stanford University.

Meredith, H. O. 1937. "The End of the *Phoenissae*." *CR* 51: 97–105.

Merwin, W. S., and Dimock, George E., Jr., trans. 1978. *Euripides' Iphigeneia at Aulis*. New York and Oxford.

Meuli, Karl. 1941. "Der Ursprung der Olympischen Spiele." *Antike* 17: 881–906. Rep. 1975 in *Gesammelte Schriften* 2: 189–208.

———. 1946. "Griechische Opferbräuche." In *Phyllobolia für Peter von der Mühll*, 185–288. Basel.

Meunier, J. 1927. "Pour une lecture candide d'*Iphigénie à Aulis*." *Musées Royaux des Beaux-Arts de Belgique* 31: 21–35.

Motte, André. 1973. *Prairies et jardins de la Grèce antique: De la religion à la philosophie*. Brussels.

Moulinier, Louis. 1952. *Le pur et l'impur dans la pensée des grecs jusqu'à la fin du IVe siècle avant J.-C.* Paris.

Mullens, H. G. 1939. "*Heracles Furens* and *Prometheus Vinctus*." *CR* 53: 165–66.

Murray, Gilbert. 1913. *Euripides and His Age*. New York and London.

———. 1927. "Excursus on the Ritual Forms Preserved in Greek Tragedy." In *Themis*, 341–63. *See* Harrison 1927.

Mylonas, George E. 1945. "A Signet-Ring in the City Art Museum of St. Louis." *AJA* 49: 557–69.

Nagy, Gregory. 1976. "Iambos: Typologies of Invective and Praise." *Arethusa* 9: 191–205.

———. 1979. *The Best of the Achaeans: Concepts of the Hero in Archaic Greek Poetry*. Baltimore and London.

Nelson, Robert J. 1976. "Ritual Reality, Tragic Imitation, Mythic Projection." *Diacritics* 6: 41–48.

Nilhard, R. 1912. "Le problème des *Bacchantes* d'Euripide." *Musées Royaux des Beaux-Arts de Belgique* 16: 91–119.

Nock, Arthur Darby, ed. and trans. 1926. *Sallustius: Concerning the Gods and the Universe*. Cambridge.

Nock, Arthur Darby. 1944. "The Cult of Heroes." *Harvard Theological Review* 37: 141–74.

———. 1972. *Essays on Religion in the Ancient World*. Cambridge.

O'Brien, M. J. 1964. "Orestes and the Gorgon: Euripides' *Electra*." *AJP* 85: 13–39.

Pachet, Pierre. 1972. "Le bâtard monstrueux." *Poétique* 12: 531–43.

Page, Denys L. 1934. *Actors' Interpolations in Greek Tragedy*. Oxford.

———. 1955. *Sappho and Alcaeus*. Oxford. Rep. 1975.

Paley, Frederick A., ed. 1880. *Euripides*. Vol. 3. 2d ed. London. First ed. 1860.

Parke, H. W. 1977. *Festivals of the Athenians*. Ithaca.

Parmentier, L. 1926. "L'*Iphigénie à Aulis* d'Euripide." *Bulletin de la classe des lettres de l'Académie royale de Belgique* 12: 262–73.

Parry, Hugh. 1965. "The Second Stasimon of Euripides' *Herakles* (637–700)." *AJP* 86: 363–74.

———. 1978. *The Lyric Poems of Greek Tragedy*. Toronto and Sarasota.

Bibliography

Pearson, A. C., ed. 1909. *Euripides, The Phoenissae*. Cambridge.

Petersen, E. 1915. *Die attische Tragödie*. Bonn.

Piccaluga, G. 1968. *Lykaon, un tema mitico*. Quaderni di *SMSR* 5. Rome.

Pickard-Cambridge, Arthur W. 1962. *Dithyramb, Tragedy, and Comedy*. 2d ed., rev. T. B. L. Webster. Oxford.

———. 1968. *Dramatic Festivals of Athens*. 2d ed., rev. John Gould and D. M. Lewis. Oxford.

Podlecki, Anthony J. 1962. "Some Themes in Euripides' *Phoenissae*." *TAPA* 93: 355–73.

Pohlenz, Max. 1954. *Die griechische Tragödie*. 2 vols. 2d ed. Göttingen.

Pottelbergh, Robert van. 1974. "Remarques sur l'*Iphigenie en Aulide*: Tragédie malmenée s'il en fût." *AC* 43: 304–8.

Powell, J. U., ed. 1911. *The Phoenissae of Euripides*. London.

Pritchett, W. Kendrick. 1971–79. *The Greek State at War*. 3 vols. Berkeley and Los Angeles.

Pucci, Pietro. 1977. "Euripides: The Monument and the Sacrifice." *Arethusa* 10: 165–95.

———. 1980. *The Violence of Pity in Euripides' Medea*. Ithaca.

Rawson, Elizabeth. 1970. "Family and Fatherland in Euripides' *Phoenissae*." *GRBS* 11: 109–27.

Rebuffat, René. 1972. "Le sacrifice du fils de Créon dans les *Phéniciennes* d'Euripide." *REA* 74: 14–31.

Redfield, James. 1982. "Notes on the Greek Wedding." *Arethusa* 15: 181–201.

Reeve, Michael D. 1972. "Interpolation in Greek Tragedy II." *GRBS* 13: 451–74.

Reimschneider, Wilhelm. 1940. *Held und Staat in Euripides' Phönissen*. Würzburg.

Ritchie, William. 1964. *The Authenticity of the Rhesus of Euripides*. Cambridge.

Robert, Carl. 1915. *Oidipus*. 2 vols. Berlin.

Rohde, Erwin. 1925. *Psyche*. Trans. W. B. Hillis. 8th ed. London.

Rohdich, Hermann. 1968. *Die Euripideische Tragödie: Untersuchungen zu ihrer Tragik*. Heidelberg.

Romilly, Jacqueline de. 1963. "Le thème du bonheur dans les *Bacchantes*." *REG* 76: 361–80.

———. 1967. "*Phoenician Women* of Euripides: Topicality in Greek Tragedy." Trans. D. H. Orrok. *Bucknell Review* 15(3): 108–32.

Rose, H. J. 1925. "The Bride of Hades." *CP* 19: 238–43.

———. 1956. "Divine Disguisings." *Harvard Theological Review* 49: 63–72.

Bibliography

Rosenmeyer, Thomas. 1955. "Gorgias, Aeschylus, and *Apatē*." *AJP* 76: 225–60.

———. 1963. *The Masks of Tragedy*. Austin.

Roussel, P. 1915. "Le rôle d'Achille dans l'*Iphigénie à Aulis*." *REG* 28: 234–50.

———. 1922. "Le thème du sacrifice volontaire dans Euripide." *Revue Belge de Philologie et d'Histoire* 1: 225–40.

Roux, Jeanne. 1961. "A propos du décor dans les tragédies d'Euripide." *REG* 74: 25–60.

———, ed. 1970 and 1972. *Euripide, Les Bacchantes*. 2. vols. Paris.

Rubino, Carl. 1972. Review of Girard 1972. *MLN* 87: 996–97.

Rudhardt, Jean. 1958. *Notions fondamentales de la pensée religieuse et actes constitutifs du culte dans la Grèce classique*. Geneva.

Sabbatucci, Dario. 1965. *Saggio sul misticismo greco*. Rome.

Sale, William. 1972. "The Psychoanalysis of Pentheus in the *Bacchae* of Euripides." *YCS* 22: 63–82.

Salingar, Leo. 1974. *Shakespeare and the Traditions of Comedy*. Cambridge.

Sandys, J. E., ed. 1900. *The Bacchae of Euripides*. Cambridge.

Sansone, David. 1975. "The Sacrifice Motif in Euripides' *IT*." *TAPA* 105: 283–95.

———. 1978. "The *Bacchae* as Satyr Play?" *ICS* 3: 40–46.

Schadewaldt, Wolfgang. 1961. "Die Wappnung des Eteocles." In *Eranion. Festschrift für H. Hommel*, 105–16. Tübingen.

Schmid, Wilhelm, and Stählin, Otto. 1940. *Geschichte der griechischen Literatur*. Part I, 3. Munich.

Schmidt, Wieland. 1963. *Der Deus ex machina bei Euripides*. Diss. Tübingen.

Schmitt, Johanna. 1921. *Freiwilliger Opfertod bei Euripides. Ein Beitrag zu seiner dramatischen Technik*, Giessen.

Schreiber, Hans-Martin. 1963. *Iphigenies Opfertod: ein Beitrag zum Verständnis des Tragikers Euripides*. Diss. Frankfurt am Main.

Schroeder, Otto. 1906. "De teichoscopia *Phoenissis* inserta." Leipzig.

Schwinge, Ernst-Richard, ed. 1968. *Euripides*. Wege der Forschung, 89. Darmstadt.

Schwinge, Monika. 1972. *Die Funktion der zweiteiligen Komposition im Herakles des Euripides*. Diss. Tübingen.

Seaford, Richard. 1981. "Dionysiac Drama and the Dionysiac Mysteries." *CQ*, n.s. 31: 252–75.

Segal, Charles P. 1962. "The Phaeacians and the Symbolism of Odysseus' Return." *Arion* 1(4): 17–64.

Bibliography

———. 1971. "The Two Worlds of Euripides' *Helen*." *TAPA* 102: 553–614.

———. 1975. "Mariage et sacrifice dans les *Trachiniennes* de Sophocle." *AC* 44: 30–53.

———. 1978a. "The Menace of Dionysus: Sex Roles and Reversals in Euripides' *Bacchae*." *Arethusa* 11: 185–202.

———. 1978b. "Pentheus and Hippolytus on the Couch and on the Grid: Psychoanalytic and Structuralist Readings of Greek Tragedy." *CW* 72: 129–48.

———. 1981. *Tragedy and Civilization: An Interpretation of Sophocles*. Cambridge, Mass.

———. 1982. *Dionysiac Poetics and Euripides' Bacchae*. Princeton.

Seidensticker, Bernd. 1978. "Comic Elements in Euripides' *Bacchae*." *AJP* 99: 303–20.

———. 1979. "Sacrificial Ritual in the *Bacchae*." In *Arktouros: Hellenic Studies Presented to B. M. W. Knox*, 181–90. Berlin and New York.

Sheppard, John T. 1916. "The Formal Beauty of the *Hercules Furens*." *CQ* 10: 72–79.

Simon, Bennett. 1978. *Mind and Madness in Ancient Greece*. Ithaca and London.

Smith, W. D. 1979. "Iphigeneia in Love." In *Arktouros: Hellenic Studies Presented to B. M. W. Knox*, 173–80. Berlin and New York.

Smith, W. Robertson. 1894. *Lectures on the Religion of the Semites*. 2d. ed. London.

Snell, Bruno. 1968. "Euripides aulische Iphigenie." In *Euripides*, 493–506. *See* Schwinge 1968.

Stengel, Paul. 1910. *Die Opferbräuche der Griechen*. Leipzig.

———. 1920. *Die griechischen Kultusaltertümer*. Munich.

Stinton, T. C. W. 1976. "'Si credere dignum est': Some Expressions of Disbelief in Euripides and Others." *PCPhS* 202: 80–89.

Strachan, J. C. G. 1976. "Iphigeneia and Human Sacrifice in Euripides' *IT*." *CP* 71: 131–40.

Strohm, Hans. 1957. *Euripides. Interpretationen zur dramatischen Form*. Zetemata 15. Munich 1957.

Sutton, Robert. 1981. "The Interaction between Men and Women Portrayed on Attic Red-figure Pottery." Diss. University of North Carolina.

Taplin, Oliver. 1977. *The Stagecraft of Aeschylus*. Oxford.

Tarkow, T. A. 1977. "The Glorification of Athens in Euripides' *Heracles*." *Helios* 5: 27–35.

Thomson, George. 1946. *Aeschylus and Athens*. 2d ed. London.

Traube, Elizabeth. 1979. "Incest and Mythology: Anthropological and Girardian Perspectives." *Berkshire Review* 14: 37–53.

Treves, P. 1930. "Le 'Fenicie' di Euripide." *Atene e Roma* 11: 171–95.

Turner, Victor. 1969. *The Ritual Process: Structure and Anti-structure.* Ithaca and London. Rep. 1977.

Valgiglio, Ernesto. 1956 and 1957. "L'*Ifigenia in Aulide* di Euripide." *RSC* 4: 179–202 and *RSC* 5: 47–52.

———. 1961. "L'esodo delle 'Fenicie' de Euripide." Univ. di Torino Pubbl. Fac. di Lett. e Filos. 13,2. Turin.

van der Valk, M. 1982. "Euripides' *Phoenissae* 1–2 and Sophocles' *Electra* 1 Again." *GRBS* 23: 235–40.

Vasquez, Penelope. 1972. "Literary Convention in Scenes of Madness and Suffering in Greek Tragedy." Diss. Columbia University.

Vellacott, Philip. 1975. *Ironic Drama: A Study of Euripides' Method and Meaning.* Cambridge.

Vernant, Jean-Pierre, ed. 1968. *Problèmes de la guerre en Grèce ancienne.* Paris and The Hague.

Vernant, Jean-Pierre. 1970. "Greek Tragedy: Problems in Interpretation." In *The Structuralist Controversy,* ed. Richard Macksey and E. Donato, 273–95. Baltimore.

———. 1976. *Religion grecque, religions antiques.* Paris.

———. 1979. "A la table des hommes. Mythe de fondation des sacrifice chez Hésiode." In *La cuisine du sacrifice,* 37–132. *See* Detienne and Vernant 1979.

———. 1980. *Myth and Society in Ancient Greece.* Trans. Janet Lloyd. Sussex, N.J. First published as *Mythe et société en Grèce antique,* Paris 1974.

———. 1981. "Théorie generale du sacrifice et mise à mort dans la *thysia* grecque." In *Le sacrifice dans l'antiquité, Entretiens sur l'antiquité classique* 27, ed. Jean Rudhardt and Olivier Reverdin, 1–21. Geneva.

Vernant, Jean-Pierre, and Vidal-Naquet, Pierre. 1981. *Tragedy and Myth in Ancient Greece.* Trans. Janet Lloyd. Sussex, N.J. First published as *Mythe et tragédie en Grèce ancienne,* Paris 1972.

Verrall, A. W. 1895. *Euripides the Rationalist.* Cambridge.

Versnel, H. S. 1981. "Self-sacrifice, Compensation, and the Anonymous Gods," In *Le sacrifice dans l'antiquité, Entretiens sur l'antiquité classique* 27, ed. Jean Rudhardt and Olivier Reverdin, 135–85. Geneva.

Vian, Francis. 1963. *Les origines de Thèbes: Cadmos et les Spartes.* Paris.

Vickers, Brian. 1973. *Towards Greek Tragedy. Drama, Myth, Society.* London.

Bibliography

Vidal-Naquet, Pierre. 1968a. "The Black Hunter and the Origin of the Athenian Ephebia." *PCPhS* 14: 49–64.

———. 1968b. "Le tradition de l'hoplite athénien." In *Problèmes de la guerre*, 161–81. *See* Vernant 1968.

———. 1981a. "Hunting and Sacrifice in Aeschylus' *Oresteia.*" In *Tragedy and Myth in Ancient Greece*, 150–74. *See* Vernant and Vidal-Naquet 1981.

———. 1981b. *Le chasseur noir: Formes de pensée et formes de société dans le monde grec.* Paris.

Voigt, P. 1896. "Die Phoinissai des Euripides." *NJbb* 153: 817–43.

Vretska, Helmuth. 1961. "Agamemnon in Euripides Iphigenie in Aulis." *WS* 74: 18–39.

Walsh, George B. 1971. "*Iphigenia in Aulis:* Third Stasimon." *CP* 69: 241–48.

Ward, Donald. 1973. "On the Poets and Poetry of the Indo-Europeans." *Journal of Indo-European Studies* 1: 127–44.

Wasserman, Felix M. 1929. "Die Bakchantinnen des Euripides." *NJbb* 5: 272–86.

———. 1949. "Agamemnon in the *Iphigenia at Aulis:* A Man in an Age of Crisis." *TAPA* 80: 174–86.

Webster, T. B. L. 1965. "The Poet and the Mask." In *Classical Drama and Its Influence: Essays Presented to H. D. F. Kitto*, 5–13. New York.

West, Martin L. 1974. *Studies in Greek Elegy and Iambus.* Berlin and New York.

Whitman, Cedric. 1964. *Aristophanes and the Comic Hero.* Cambridge, Mass.

———. 1974. *Euripides and the Full Circle of Myth.* Cambridge, Mass.

Wilamowitz-Moellendorf, U. von, ed. 1895. *Euripides Herakles.* 2d ed. 2 vols. Berlin. Rep. 3 vols., Darmstadt 1959.

———. 1903. "Der Schluss den Phönissen." Sitzungsberichte Akademie Berlin. 587–600.

Willink, C. W. 1966. "Some Problems of Text and Interpretation in the *Bacchae.*" Parts 1 and 2. *CR*, n.s. 16: 27–50 and 220–42.

———. 1971. "The Prologue of *Iphigenia at Aulis.*" *CQ* 21: 343–64.

Winnington-Ingram, R. P. 1948. *Euripides and Dionysus: An Interpretation of the Bacchae.* Cambridge.

———. 1969. "Euripides, *Poiētēs Sophos.*" *Arethusa* 2: 129–42.

Wolff, Christian. 1963. "Aspects of the Later Plays of Euripides." Diss. Harvard University.

———. 1965. "The Design and Myth in Euripides' *Ion.*" *HSCP* 69: 169–94.

Bibliography

Woodford, Susan. 1971. "Cults of Heracles in Attica." In *Studies Presented to G. M. A. Hanfmann,* ed. David Mitten, 211–225. Fogg Monograph. Cambridge, Mass.

Zeitlin, Froma I. 1965. "The Motif of the Corrupted Sacrifice in Aeschylus' *Oresteia.*" *TAPA* 96: 463–508.

——. 1966. "Postscript to the Sacrificial Imagery in the *Oresteia* (*Ag.* 1235–37)." *TAPA* 97: 645–53.

——. 1970a. "The Ritual World of Greek Tragedy." Diss. Columbia University.

——. 1970b. "The Argive Festival of Hera and Euripides' *Electra.*" *TAPA* 101: 645–69.

——. 1980. "The Closet of Masks: Role-Playing and Myth-Making in the *Orestes* of Euripides." *Ramus* 9: 62–77.

——. 1982. *Under the Sign of the Shield: Semiotics and Aeschylus' Seven against Thebes.* Rome.

Zielinski, Thomas. 1924. "De Euripidis Thebaide Posteriore." *Mnemosyne,* n.s. 52: 189–205.

Index

Note: Line and stanza numbers and other textual citations are given in italics in parentheses following the page reference.

Index

anēr aristos, 193
Année Sociologique, 25
Anthesteria, 214
Antigone: in *Phoenissae,* 73, 106–46
    passim; in Sophocles' *Antigone,* 88
Apatouria, 174
Aphrodite, 81, 86, 87
Apollo, 44–45, 56, 90, 106, 137, 142,
    144, 184, 186
Apollodorus, 133 *(3.6.7)*
Ares, 106, 136–38, 140, 142
aretē, 80, 97, 102, 150, 178, 183–85,
    193, 201–3
Argus, 128
Aristodamus: in Herodotus, 174
Aristodemus: in Pausanias, 73
Aristophanes, 17, 182, 226–28, 232–
    33, 240–41
    Acharnians, 215 *(schol. on line 243),*
        216, 252
    Birds, 37, 216 *(1764)*
    Frogs, 206, 216 *(785, 867),* 226, 229,
        233, 250 *(46)*
    Knights, 216 *(1254)*
    Lysistrata, 91
    Peace, 27 *(924–34, 1019–25),* 212
    Thesmophoriazusae, 226–27, 227
        (136)
    Wasps, 227
Aristophanes (grammarian), 113
aristos, 203
Aristotle, 17
    Nichomachean Ethics, 198 *(1101b1–
        1102a4, 1114a23–29)*
    Poetics, 126 *(1451b),* 150 *(1448b–
        1449b),* 219 *(1450b28)*
    Politics, 20 *(1252b)*
arkteia, 86
Arrowsmith, W., 202–4
Artemidorus: *Oneirokritika,* 86 *(2.65)*
Artemis, 21, 39, 58, 65–105 passim,
    86, 90, 100, 135
Arthur, M., 137, 239
Atalanta, 128
Athena, 107, 136, 155, 165
Atreus, house of, 56, 75, 135;
    Atreidae, 93
aulos, 29, 52
authadia, 201

Bacchylides, 177, 181 *(3.85),* 182
    (3.67–68), 185 *(13.17),* 188 *(5 and
    16)*
Bain, D., 103
Bataille, G., 25, 48–50, 52
Bdelycleon: in *Wasps,* 227
Beidelman, T. O., 23
belos, 173
Bergson, H., 227–32
bia, 86, 201
Bia: in Aeschylus, 157
Bond, G., 201–2
Bouphonia, 31–33, 42, 168
Bow: in *Heracles,* 167–75, 189
Bromios, 140, 223. *See also* Dionysus
Burkert, W., 25, 46–50, 52, 57, 61,
    89

Cadmus, 57, 107, 119, 136, 137–38,
    205–58 passim
Cain and Abel, 47
Calchas: in *IA,* 66, 97, 104
Calypso: in *Odyssey,* 88
Cambridge School, 52
Capaneus, 127
Casabona, J., 30
Cassandra: in Aeschylus' *Agamemnon,*
    56, 70, 105, 225; in Euripides'
    Trojan Women, 85, 88
Catullus, 82 *(64)*
Cavander, K., 69
Cerberus, 200
characterization, inconsistency of in
    Euripides, 17, 67–68, 113, 125–
    26, 149, 175–77, 190–93, 195.
    See also Heracles, tradition of
charis, 26, 27, 140
Cheiron, 191
chernibes, 47, 107
choral odes in Euripides, 17, 19, 62–
    63, 67–68, 78–84, 89, 91, 97–99,
    107–8, 111–12, 119, 128, 133,
    136–39, 140, 143, 145, 149, 175–
    88, 200–201, 221–22, 238–40,
    244–45
chorodidaskalos, 219
chreia tōn agathōn, 26, 27
Christus Patiens, 211
Cleon, 156

Index

Index

Index

Kamerbeek, J. C., 160
katharsia, 152
katharsis, 54, 60
Kirk, G., 51
klēdonomanteia, 122
kleos, 76, 80, 141, 145, 150–51, 172, 174, 178, 181, 190
Knox, B. M. W., 102–4
koina, 124
koinōniai, 167
kōmōidia, 212
kōmos, 208–17, 230–31
Kore myth, 87
Kratos: in Aeschylus' *Prometheus Bound*, 157
krokōtos, 250
kurios, 73

Labdacids, 138
Laius, 116, 143; house of, 108, 113, 114
language, in Euripides, 122–23, 126, 128, 132, 143, 245–46
laudandi, 182; *laudandus*: 184
laudatores, 184
lebēs, 41
Leda, 81
Lenaia, 216
Lesches: *Little Iliad*, 170
Lichas: in Sophocles' *Trachiniae*, 85
Linus, 191
logos, 123, 132, 179, 200, 203–4
Lorenz, K., 25, 47
Ludwig, W., 108, 133
luk-, 181 (Lycambes, Lycurgus, Lycaeon, Zeus Lykeios), 192 (Lyssa)
lussonta, 174
Lycurgus: 228. *See also* Luk-
Lycus, 17, 59, 147–204 passim
Lyssa, 154–55, 157, 161, 165, 174, 191, 192, 197, 200, 201

Macaria: in *Heracleidae*, 65, 76
madness in Euripides, 160–62, 164, 174, 190–91, 200–2, 245, 258
Margites, 150
marriage, 35, 42, 62, 64, 65–102 passim, 142, 144–45, 235, 256

and death, 85–86, 88–90
as rite of transition and incorporation, 71, 85–87, 89, 100, 102
and sacrifice, 65–102
and war, 89–90
masking in the *Bacchae*, 219, 231, 241, 246–53. *See also* Costume in the *Bacchae*
mēchanē, 133. *See also Deus ex machina*
Medea, 22, 52, 60, 87, 105,220
mēden agan, 239
Megara: in *Heracles*, 147–204 passim
Meleager, 188
Menelaus: in *Helen:* 88, 225; in *IA:* 67–68, 80, 95–98, 104
Menoeceus, 19, 65, 106–46 passim, 256
metagraphō, 94
metatheater in Euripides: in *Bacchae*, 205–58 passim; in *IA*, 94
Meuli, K., 25, 46, 47, 51, 148
miasma, 151, 162, 168, 173. *See also* Pollution
mimetic rivalry, 49, 53, 55, 59, 99, 100, 133, 138, 207. *See also* Girard, R.
mind change in Euripides, 94–99. *See also* Characterization
mitra, 250
molpē, 147, 149
morphē, 246
Murray, G., 52
Muses, 162, 184, 195–97, 207. *See also* Sacrifice, to the Muses
muthos, 113, 179
Myrmidons, 78
Myrsilus, 185
myth in Euripides, 18–19, 21, 42–43, 45–46, 59, 62–64, 73, 79, 81, 83–84, 90, 94–95, 97–99, 103, 110–12, 115, 119, 123, 126, 135–36, 139, 144–46, 150, 179, 190, 192, 198–200, 203–4, 208, 221–22, 229, 238–40, 256–58

Nessus: in Sophocles' *Trachiniae*, 85
Nestor: in *Odyssey*, 27
New Testament, 101
Nietzsche, F., 17

[281]

Index

Index

Index

Index

Thyestes, 41, 144
timē, 26, 157
Tiresias: in Sophocles' *OR*, 54; in *Phoenissae*, 106–46 passim; in *Bacchae*, 205–58 passim
tragedy, origins of, 52–59 passim
tragōidia, 52
tuchē, 20, 92, 93, 97, 99, 111, 163–68, 170, 190, 193, 197, 200, 203
Turner, V., 91, 234–35, 237, 255
Tydeus, 118, 127, 144
Tyndareus, 73, 75
Typho, 128

Unschuldskomödie, 47

Vernant, J.-P., 24, 38, 84, 89, 195
voluntary sacrifice in Euripides, 19–21, 40, 62, 65–146 passim

Wilamowitz, U. von, 160, 184
Winnington-Ingram, R.-P., 212
women in Euripides, 32–33, 42–43, 56, 62, 80, 84, 86, 88, 91, 98, 112, 114–21, 126, 132, 138–40, 142, 144–45, 206, 213, 236, 242

xenia, 27
Xenophanes, 20, 37

Zeitlin, F., 41, 43, 112, 125, 158
Zeus, 41, 46, 56, 81, 109, 127–29, 136, 138, 152, 156, 158, 163, 164, 166, 180, 183–85, 187; Zeus Lykeios, 181; Zeus Poleius, 32; Zeus Soter, 41, 152

[285]

Library of Congress Cataloging in Publication Data

Foley, Helene P., 1942–
    Ritual irony.

    Bibliography: p.
    Includes index.
    1. Euripides—Criticism and interpretation.   2. Ritual in
literature.   3. Sacrifice in literature.   4. Irony in literature.   I. Title.
PA3978.F6   1985   882'.01   84–17470
ISBN   0–8014–1692-2 (alk. paper)